Authors in Court

Authors in Court

Scenes from the Theater of Copyright

Mark Rose

Harvard University Press

CAMBRIDGE, MASSACHUSETTS · LONDON, ENGLAND

First Harvard University Press paperback edition, 2018
First printing

Library of Congress Cataloging-in-Publication Data
Names: Rose, Mark, 1939– author.
Title: Authors in court : scenes from the theater of copyright / Mark Rose.
Description: Cambridge, Massachusetts : Harvard University Press, 2016. |
Includes bibliographical references and index.
Identifiers: LCCN 2015042565 | ISBN 9780674048041 (hard cover : alk. paper) |
ISBN 9780674984134 (pbk.)
Subjects: LCSH: Copyright—United States—Cases. | Copyright—England—
Cases. | Copyright—United States—History. | Copyright—England—History. |
Authorship—History.
Classification: LCC K1420.5 .R67 2016 | DDC 346.4204/82—dc23
LC record available at http://lccn.loc.gov/2015042565

For Ann

Contents

Preface

THIS is a book about copyright and authorship. It is organized as a series of historical studies, focusing on six English and American copyright cases. Each involves an "author," a term that in copyright law can refer to an artist or a photographer or for that matter a computer programmer or recording artist as well as a writer. As a matter of statute, copyright begins in Great Britain with the Statute of Anne in 1710. I start, however, with a prologue, the trial and pillorying of Daniel Defoe in 1703 for seditious libel in connection with the publication of his satirical pamphlet, *The Shortest Way with the Dissenters.* This was an event that occurred in the old regime in which an author like Defoe might be punished for publishing something found offensive but possessed no affirmative right to appear in court on his own behalf as a plaintiff. I conclude nearly three centuries later with a discussion of a famous fair-use case involving the postmodern artist Jeff Koons.

The body of the book begins with *Pope v. Curll* (1741), a seminal case that determined private letters might be protected by copyright. Next is *Stowe v. Thomas* (1853), in which Harriet Beecher Stowe sought to establish that she had the right to prevent *Uncle Tom's Cabin* from being translated into German without her permission. In *Burrow-Giles v. Sarony* (1884) the celebrity photographer Napoleon Sarony established his right to protect his portraits of Oscar Wilde. Then in *Nichols v. Universal* (1930) Ann Nichols unsuccessfully sought to prevent Universal Pictures from making a moving picture that in her opinion closely resembled her hit play, *Abie's Irish Rose. Salinger v. Random House* (1987) concerned J. D. Salinger's successful suit to prevent the use of quotations from his unpublished letters in a forthcoming biography. Finally, in *Rogers v. Koons* (1992), Art Rogers famously sued Jeff Koons over the artist's use of his photograph in a sculpture called *String of Puppies.*

I conclude by putting these case studies in context by invoking, among other things, modern work-for-hire doctrine, which raises questions about the degree to which the author really is the central figure in copyright.

These studies do not provide a complete or even a continuous history of copyright. I am aware for example of the gap of more than a century between my discussion of *Pope* and my chapter on *Stowe* and also of course of the geographical and juridical leap from Great Britain to the United States. My purpose, however, is not to provide a survey of copyright history, but rather a series of exemplary narratives, each of which can be read as an exploration of the drama of a particular moment in the development of authorship and the law. The cases that I have chosen do, however, speak to each other across the centuries. Thus both *Pope v. Curll* and *Salinger v. Random House* involve the publication of personal letters and raise questions about the way copyright adjudicates the boundary between privacy and publicity. Likewise both *Burrow-Giles v. Sarony* and *Rogers v. Koons* involve the rights of photographers and raise questions about the nature of authorship in the context of celebrity as a commodity. The chapters in this book do not provide a coherent history; nonetheless, read in series, they do provide something of a historical narrative, a sketch of two evolving and mutually interacting institutions, authorship and the law.

I think of each chapter as an exploration of the drama of authorship as it has played out on the stage of the law. It is of course when the author becomes a public figure, sometime in the early modern period, that the role of author becomes potentially dramatic. The cases I discuss have been chosen in part for the issues they raise and in part, too, for the interesting characters they involve. I think for example of the playwright Ann Nichols, once a liberal voice for ethnic tolerance, transformed into an angry reactionary who believed that communist conspiracies were seeking to suppress *Abie's Irish Rose*. Some authors strut their roles on the public stage—I picture Napoleon Sarony dressed in his red fez and high-top campaign boots strutting along Broadway in the 1880s—and some, like the recluse J. D. Salinger, enact their dramas by conspicuously shrinking from attention. But in each of these cases the author, launched onto the public stage, becomes a character in a drama. Inevitably it is a drama only partially of his or her devising.

Individual dramas of authorship have inflected the course of the law. One theme of this book is that the law is not entirely blind to the characteristics of the authors who have appeared in court. Would Harriet Beecher Stowe have prevailed in her suit against a Philadelphia publisher if the judge in the matter had not been a committed defender of the Fugitive Slave Act? To what degree did Salinger's fame and undoubtedly genuine dread of public display inflect the outcome in his case? Still, the development of copyright law has not been merely arbitrary. Another theme is the expansive logic, the process of dematerialization and extension of the protected object that the history of copyright reveals. Originally conceived as a license granted by an author to a bookseller to print and publish a specific book, copyright was first anchored in tangible paper and ink. Soon, however, it became apparent that some distinction needed to be made between the words that authors write and the books that printers make. Literary property then was understood to inhere in a specific piece of language—"the same conceptions, cloathed in the same words," as William Blackstone put it in his *Commentaries* (1766)—an intangible object perhaps, but one that could at least metaphorically be cast as concrete and bounded. Later, when copyright was extended to protect translations and other kinds of derivative works, the nature of the object protected became more diffuse. Moreover, with the incorporation of photographs, sound recordings, and films—these media are similar to books insofar as, like print, they can be transmitters of ideas—the objects protected became even more ghostly. Today the digital revolution, which at least in principle renders all tangible forms of media obsolete, may perhaps make every aspect of copyright seem metaphysical.

Judges and lawyers like to avoid both metaphysics and aesthetic judgments. As Justice Oliver Wendell Holmes Jr. famously remarked in *Bleistein v. Donaldson* (1903), "It would be a dangerous undertaking for persons trained only to the law to constitute themselves final judges of the worth of pictorial illustrations, outside of the narrowest and most obvious limits." More recently in *New Era v. Holt* (1988), Judge Pierre N. Leval acknowledged the discomfort courts experience when compelled to serve as literary critics. Unlike many current studies, which rightly maintain that overlong and overprotective copyright laws have become a barrier to creation, my book is not explicitly argumentative. If it does approach the polemical, it is in insisting that the resolution of issues involving allegations of infringement depends upon informed literary and critical analysis and that this in turn depends upon grappling with difficulties inherent in the very notion of intellectual property. When are two works "substantially similar" to the degree that one may be said to infringe on the other? When does the doctrine of "fair use"—the principle that portions of copyrighted material may sometimes be taken without permission—allow one author or artist to use the work of another? Such questions inevitably involve critical discriminations. Willingly or unwillingly, judges in copyright cases often find themselves compelled to make judgments that reveal assumptions about literature, art, and language as well as about law.

I am an English professor, a Shakespearean by trade, not a lawyer. Nonetheless, I have some experience in legal matters, having served as an expert witness in copyright infringement cases for thirty-five years. I have found this engagement with the law fascinating and illuminating. My experiences as a literary expert led me some years ago to explore the early history of copyright in *Authors and Owners: The Invention of Copyright*, and I have subsequently lectured and written frequently on topics related to copyright and copyright history. Necessarily some of the matters raised in this study touch upon subjects on which I have written previously.

I have included a number of images that illustrate or otherwise relate to the substance of my discussions. Such images are particularly important in discussions that involve litigation over works of visual art. For reasons beyond my control, I am unable to print images of the Jeff Koons works at issue in *Rogers v. Koons* and *Blanch v. Koons*. I have, however, indicated in notes the websites where images of the two Koons works, the sculpture *String of Puppies* and the painting *Niagara*, can be found. In my discussions I have frequently cited affidavits, declarations, depositions, and testimony from original court documents on file with the U.S. National Archives and Records Administration. These were examined at the National Archives at New York City.

I think these matters are not to be decided by accountants based on percentages.

—JUDGE PIERRE N. LEVAL

CHAPTER ONE

Defoe in the Pillory

ON Thursday, July 29, 1703, Daniel Defoe was publicly humiliated by being carted from Newgate Prison to the Royal Exchange in the heart of London. There at noon he was locked into an awkward standing position with his head and arms thrust forward in a pillory erected on a raised platform in front of a crowd of citizens, probably in the middle of a heavy rain. This exposure, which lasted for one hour, was repeated on Friday at Cheapside Conduit and again on Saturday at Temple Bar. Defoe's crime was seditious libel. His offense was writing and publishing a satirical pamphlet, *The Shortest Way with the Dissenters*, which called for dissenters—those who refused to conform to the established church—to be banished or killed. Defoe was a dissenter himself, and *The Shortest Way* was conceived as a satire on those preaching violence against nonconformers. But Defoe had caught the tone and style of a repressive high churchman so exactly that it was not at all clear that his call for savage treatment of dissenters was ironic.[1]

Like the public hangings of the period, exposure in the pillory was a punishment that was essentially theatrical. The goal was to shame the criminal and reaffirm the community norm. But it was not unknown for people to be seriously injured or even killed in the pillory. For example, William Fuller, a scoundrel and imposter pilloried for seditious libel about a month before Defoe, was treated very roughly by the mob. In a pamphlet written shortly after the event, Fuller described how he was no sooner raised onto the pillory and "my head thro' the Hole" but "Dirt and rotten Eggs came about my Head, Body and Leggs, as thick and fast as Hail" and "amongst them came several Stones." The following day when Fuller was pilloried for the second time, the rain of stones, eggs, and "all manner of Dirt, Filth and Rubbish" was so heavy that he could hardly stand. Indeed, at one point Fuller fell from the stool on which he was balanced "so that I hung by the Neck, and had been choak'd but for the care of a Person standing by, who put my Feet again upon the Stool."[2]

Fuller, who was unpopular, was probably treated with unusual malice. Defoe, however, turned his three-day ordeal into something of a triumph. Defoe had arranged for friends to protect him while he stood exposed and instead of stones and offal he was, according to report, pelted with flowers. Meanwhile supporters sold copies of his works and distributed a new satire, *A Hymn to the Pillory*, written and published for the occasion. In it Defoe mocks the pillory as a machine for punishing "fancy" rather than crime and insists that a man subjected to pillorying "Bears less Reproach than they who plac'd him there." Rather than being used against a "Poor Author" whose only offense was not being understood, the pillory should be used to punish judges who "break the Laws they should defend."[3] According to one conservative journal that saw Defoe's punishment as appropriate for a "Publick Incendiary," Defoe's friends not only protected him from physical danger but at the end of his exposure "Hallow'd him down from his Wooden Punishment, as if he had been a Cicero that had made an Excellent Oration in it."[4]

Pillorying of the kind that Defoe suffered was a punishment of choice for authors who wrote seditious, blasphemous, or obscene libels. Thus in 1634 the puritan William Prynne was pilloried and had his ears partly cut off when his antitheatrical diatribe, *Histriomastix*, was interpreted as a libel against Queen Henrietta Maria. Several years later Prynne was again pilloried and lost the rest of his ears in connection with a short pamphlet, *News from Ipswich* (1636), which attacked Matthew Wren, the antipuritan bishop of Norwich.[5] And William Fuller's pillorying, the month before Defoe, was also related to his publications, specifically two books in which he alleged, among other things, that English officials had taken French bribes.[6] These examples of authors publicly disciplined for literary offenses remind us that, even as late as the first decade of the eighteenth century, the only legal identity that an author had as an author was as someone to be punished for a transgression. Authors might earn money by working for hire or by selling their manuscripts to booksellers, but writing in this period was conceived as an action rather than as a commodity, a thing, and as such it could be punished if found offensive.[7]

Defoe in the pillory. From *Jure Divino* (1706). Courtesy of the General Collection, Beinecke Rare Book and Manuscript Library, Yale University.

Defoe was sentenced not only to exposure in the pillory but also to a substantial fine of 200 marks. He was made to pledge good behavior for seven years, and, more concretely, compelled to remain in prison until he could give evidence that he would keep his pledge. After the pillory, then, Defoe was returned to Newgate for three months until Robert Harley, the Speaker of the House, decided that Defoe could be useful to him as a writer and an agent and arranged for his release.

Despite his show of contempt for the pillory, Defoe's experience of public humiliation was traumatic. Before his conviction, Defoe had been a businessman, the owner of a substantial brick and tile factory in Essex. As a writer he had been known primarily for one vastly popular poem, *The True-Born Englishman*, in which he ridiculed the idea of a true English race and defended King William from attacks based on being a foreigner. In prison, however, Defoe was unable to attend to business, and his brick and tile factory failed. After his release, Defoe became of necessity a professional writer of pamphlets and commentary as well as an agent for Harley. His principal endeavor in the years immediately after 1703 was his very successful journal the *Review*, which contained his commentary and reflections on a vast range of subjects ranging from reports of scandal to serious opinion on economic and political matters. The *Review*, which appeared three times weekly, continued until 1713 and it established Defoe, "Mr. Review," as an important public voice. All this was long before Defoe conceived the series of fictional memoirs, including *Robinson Crusoe* (1719), *Moll Flanders* (1722), and *Roxana* (1724), which are still read today.

Defoe always insisted that *The Shortest Way with the Dissenters* had been misunderstood. Thus in a subsequent essay, "A Brief Explanation of a Late Pamphlet," he maintained that *The Shortest Way* was an ironical answer to various books that had tried to present dissenters as government enemies who were not fit to be members of society. Speaking of his satirical intent, Defoe insisted, "If any Man take the Pains seriously to reflect upon the Contents, the Nature of the Thing, and the Manner of the Stile, it seems Impossible to imagine it should pass for anything but a Banter upon the High-flying Church-Men."[8] Defoe's judges, however, missed the irony. Defoe stood in the pillory because of the way his judges chose to interpret *The Shortest Way*, taking it as a provocative libel. The issue was one of literary interpretation.

THE
SHORTEST-WAY
WITH THE
DISSENTERS:
OR
PROPOSALS
FOR THE
ESTABLISHMENT
OF THE
CHURCH.

LONDON:
Printed in the Year MDCCII.

The Shortest Way with the Dissenters (1702). Courtesy of the General Collection, Beinecke Rare Book and Manuscript Library, Yale University.

Part of the reason *The Shortest Way* was subject to misunderstanding was that Defoe had captured the voice of his "high flier" so well and had done so without providing signals about his satiric intent. This becomes clear when Defoe's satire is compared to Jonathan Swift's *Modest Proposal,* which is similar to *The Shortest Way* in many respects. Like Defoe, Swift adopts a voice that is not his own, and, like Defoe, his purpose is to expose cruelty and callousness by presenting an outrageous position with mock seriousness, the idea of resolving the problem of poor children in Ireland by selling them to the wealthy for food. "I have been assured by a very knowing American of my acquaintance in London," Swift's "projector" says, "that a young healthy Child well Nursed is at a year Old a most delicious, nourishing, and wholesome Food, whether Stewed, roasted, Baked, or Boyled, and I make no doubt that it will equally serve in a Fricasie or a Ragoust."[9] Given the bizarre nature of the speaker's proposal, and the sure control with which Swift distances himself from his "projector," Swift's own position is never in doubt. But Defoe's attitude toward his "high flier" is less clear. Defoe was more a ventriloquist, an impersonator, than an ironist, and it can be argued that the voice of the "high flier," the power of the character he was impersonating, escaped his control. There is, we can note, continuity between Defoe's impersonation of the "high flier" in *The Shortest Way* and his later impersonation of such figures as Robinson Crusoe, Moll Flanders, and Roxana. This was the kind of thing that Defoe did instinctively and well.

Defoe's was the period in which a widespread interest in "character" emerged in a new and emphatic way. Not only Defoe's fictional memoirs but also novels such as *Pamela, Clarissa, Joseph Andrews, Tom Jones*, and *Tristram Shandy* advertise in their titles this new interest. It is of course an interest closely related to the large cultural and economic changes of the time, the transformation of the society from a traditional hierarchical body, a culture of deference, to a body of nominally equal individuals bound by agreements. In such a social formation, the emotions of a serving girl like Pamela or the adventures of a foundling like Tom Jones acquired new currency. Eventually, in the late eighteenth and early nineteenth centuries a similar interest in "character," but now focused on the character of the writer, would contribute to the birth of the romantic conception of authorship. I mention this because it allows us to locate Defoe, a rhetorician and impersonator rather than a prophet, as a figure perhaps closer to Shakespeare than to Wordsworth.

* * *

I take the image of Defoe in the pillory as one that captures a pivotal moment in social and legal history and in the history of authorship. As I have noted, the goal of pillorying was to shame the criminal and

reaffirm the community norm. In the case of Defoe, however, the community did not come together to heap abuse upon the criminal, as it did, for example, in the case of William Fuller. Instead, Defoe was excoriated by conservatives but pelted with flowers by others. This in itself suggests the social tension of the moment and the fact that there was no consensus that Defoe had truly committed a crime.

But Defoe was not merely an iconic figure standing on the verge of modernity; he was also an active agent who helped to create the new legal and social world that was forming at the start of the eighteenth century. In 1703 Defoe's only legal role as an author was as a potential criminal and object of punishment. But seven years later, the Statute of Anne (8 Anne c. 19), the world's first copyright act, legally empowered authors as the first owners of their writings. After 1710, then, authors might appear in court in a new and more positive role, as plaintiffs seeking redress for wrongs. In his *Essay on the Regulation of the Press*, published some six months after he was freed from Newgate Prison and drawing upon his still vivid sense of humiliation, Defoe became a crucial figure in the articulation of this innovation.

Still smarting from his experience at the hands of the judges, in this pamphlet Defoe complained about allowing judges to determine what was or was not a seditious libel. Under such circumstances it was impossible for an author to know in advance what would be found offensive. As a remedy, Defoe proposed an act that would specify precisely which topics writers would be forbidden to touch and what the punishments for transgressions should be. By this act authors would no longer be at the mercy of arbitrary judges but would "know when they Transgress, which at present, they do not."[10] A further issue was the difficulty of identifying the author of an anonymous publication. To remedy this Defoe proposed that when neither an author nor a printer's name was affixed to a publication, then, if the contents were found offensive, the last seller of the book should be held responsible. Under these circumstances, he claimed, no bookseller would risk selling an anonymous publication. But such a law would have a further consequence: mandating that an author's name be affixed to a book would also serve as a confirmation of the author's property right in his writing. Despite his satire having been misunderstood, Defoe did not doubt that some writings were libelous and should be made the cause of punishment. Still, if an author could be punished for a libelous writing, should he not also be rewarded for a beneficial writing? " 'Twould be unaccountably severe," he said, "to make a Man answerable for the Miscarriages of a thing which he shall not reap the benefit of if well perform'd."[11]

Defoe's *Essay on the Regulation of the Press* was published in the context of the lapse of the Licensing Act eight years earlier. Licensing laws had in one form or another been in effect in England since Henry VIII and the introduction of printing. Through the operation of the licensing laws the Stationers' Company, the ancient guild of printers and booksellers, enjoyed a near monopoly over printing and publishing in a comprehensive system of press regulation operated with the goal of preserving propriety and good order both in the realm and in the bookselling trade. But over the course of the tremendous social and political changes of the seventeenth century, which included the phenomenon that Jürgen Habermas has called the emergence of the "public sphere" as well as the emergence of clearly defined party divisions, the licensing laws became increasingly difficult to maintain.[12] Neither the Whigs nor the Tories were willing to grant the power of press censorship to the opposition and thus the act was allowed to lapse.

The collapse of licensing was in Defoe's eyes also a threat to authors for it meant that printers and booksellers were free to print works to which they had no right at all. "This is really a most injurious piece of Violence, and a Grievance to all Mankind" for it not only robs booksellers of their rights, "but it robs Men of the due Reward of Industry, the Prize of Learning, and the Benefit of their Studies."[13] The law that he proposed in his *Essay* would confirm the author's right. The property right of authors was a subject to which Defoe repeatedly returned in his new periodical the *Review* calling for an act specifically to secure authors' rights. "Every Man who writes what is no Breach of the Laws or God or Man to publish," Defoe declared, "His Work is his Property, and he cannot be divested of that Property at the Will and Pleasure of any Man; no, not his Prince; to suppress his Labour, is to divest him of his Property."[14]

Defoe's agitation for a law to confirm the author's property right contributed to the passage of the world's first copyright act, the Statute of Anne. The statute was a printing act and thus the successor to the old licensing laws and the Stationers' Company practices. But the statute was different from the old act and the guild regime in ways that marked the emergence of a new social and legal model, one based on equality and property rather than deference and regulation. The statute preserved some of the traditional guild practices such as the securing of rights through entry in the company registry book. But whereas under the old regime literary property was wholly a guild matter, the statute gave private persons status by vesting literary property first in the author. It did not provide the absolute property Defoe espoused— recall Defoe's claim that the author cannot be divested of his literary property by anyone, including the prince—but a limited grant adapted from the formula of the old Jacobean Statute of Monopolies: twenty-one years for books already in print, fourteen years for new books with the possibility of a second fourteen-year term if the author were still living at the end of the first. At the end of the term of protection a book would become open to all. Thus the act sought to balance the interests of authors, booksellers, and the public at large. Authors were granted limited property rights; booksellers were granted the right to purchase and protect literary properties; and the public at large was assured that after a limited term the protection of books would cease. In this way the statute in effect created the "public domain," a realm that did not exist under the guild system of perpetual monopolies.

The most fundamental transformation brought about by the statute, however, related to what it did not legislate; it made no provision whatsoever for state regulation of what could or could not be published or for the direct regulation of the printing trade. It is instructive in this respect to compare the title of the Statute of Anne with that of the Licensing Act of 1662 (14 Car. II. c. 33). The licensing act was titled "An Act for preventing the frequent Abuses in printing seditious, treasonable, and unlicensed Books and Pamphlets and for regulating of Printing and Printing Presses." The Statute of Anne, on the other hand, was titled "An Act for the Encouragement of Learning, by vesting the Copies of printed Books in the Authors or Purchasers of such Copies, during the Times therein mentioned." Rather than defining its purpose as the need to maintain good order in religion and government, as the licensing act had done, the Statute of Anne presents itself as affirmative legislation designed for "the encouragement of learning."

The purpose of licensing was to limit what might be said in print, to restrain the press in the interests of good order. The stated purpose of the Statute of Anne was to stimulate study and speech, to encourage the proliferation of discourse in the public sphere. Moreover, by vesting the copyright of a printed book initially in the author rather than the printer or bookseller, the statute presented the author as the person ultimately responsible for a book; that is, both as the authority underlying the book and, as Defoe had suggested, as the party to be held liable if a book were found to offend. Under the old regime of licensing, the printing of a book was still a kind of privilege that could be extended or not as the state decided. The statute, however, redefined copyright as a matter of right rather than privilege, an automatic grant to the author by virtue of his literary endeavor. Thus the statute gave legal reality to the author as an empowered figure, not merely a defendant but a protagonist in the theater of the law.

Genteel Wrath

Pope v. Curll (1741)

MOST of the early cases that arose under the Statute of Anne involved booksellers suing booksellers. An exception is the episode in which Alexander Pope successfully sued his ancient enemy Edmund Curll who had published, without Pope's permission, an exchange of letters between Pope and Jonathan Swift. *Pope v. Curll* was one of the first matters in which a major English author went to court in his own name to defend his literary interests.[1] This case, which established the rule that copyright in a letter belongs to the author, remains foundational in English and American law. What *Pope* records, I shall suggest, is an important transitional moment in the concept of authorship and of authors' rights, and a transitional moment, too, in the concept of literary property.

Alexander Pope, who entered upon his public career as an author at the same time as the bill that was to become the Statute of Anne was under consideration, was a sophisticated and aggressive exploiter of his literary properties. He understood the particulars of contracts and copyright assignments as well as any bookseller, and he also understood how to maximize sales by issuing and reissuing the same works in different contexts and different formats. Indeed, he made a fortune from his writing. But writing for profit was still not quite respectable in Pope's day, and Pope, who was zealous about what we would today call image management, was anxious to establish that he had nothing in common with mere "scribblers" such as Defoe whose pillorying he mocked in the *Dunciad*. Despite his industriousness, his business acumen, his financial success, and his interest in the finest details of his publishing ventures, Pope always represented himself as a gentleman, never as a professional. Thus in the *Epistle to Dr. Arbuthnot* (1735), perhaps his most characteristic self-portrait in verse, Pope presents himself as besieged in his villa at Twickenham by would-be authors who flatter and pester him. "Why did I write?" he asks:

> I lisp'd in Numbers, for the Numbers came.
> I left no Calling for this idle trade,
> No Duty broke, no Father dis-obey'd.
> The Muse but serv'd to ease some Friend, not Wife,
> To help me thro' this long Disease, my Life.[2]

Pope's suit against Curll in 1741, the first legal action in which he appeared in his own name as plaintiff, was the culmination of a long, colorful, and very public quarrel with Edmund Curll. This began in 1716 in a famous episode in which Pope secretly administered an emetic to Curll in retaliation for the publication of a small book titled *Court Poems.* At the heart of the quarrel was the difference between the two men in class. Curll was flagrantly disreputable. He was well-known as a publisher of scandal and pornography and at various times was charged with seditious, blasphemous, and obscene libel. Curll was in fact the first person in English history to be successfully prosecuted for obscenity. Moreover, when he was convicted of seditious libel in connection with the publication of the memoirs of a spy and adventurer whom he met in prison, he also, like Defoe, was sentenced to the humiliation of standing in the pillory. Pope, on the other hand, was as conspicuously genteel as Curll was scurrilous. Nonetheless, each found the other useful and each in his own way profited from keeping the contention running. In order to understand Pope's purposes in bringing suit against Curll in 1741, it is necessary to trace the history of their quarrel.[3]

* * *

The contention between Pope and Curll started in 1716 with the publication of Curll's *Court Poems,* which consisted of three slightly scandalous pieces, including two by Lady Mary Wortley Montagu.[4] The introduction suggested that the poems had been written either by Pope or John Gay or "a lady of quality." Whether Pope was chivalrously defending Lady Mary or loyally protecting his friend Gay is unclear, but shortly after the book appeared, Pope contrived to encounter Curll at a tavern in Fleet Street. There, under pretense of sharing a glass of wine as a sign of reconciliation, Pope dosed Curll's drink.

A few days later, adding insult to injury, Pope published a comic pamphlet couched in the sensationalist style of a Grub Street production, a style not entirely different from that of, say, a modern supermarket tabloid. Titled *A Full and True Account of a Horrid and Barbarous Revenge by Poison on the Body of Mr. Edmund Curll, Bookseller*, Pope's undated pamphlet, identified only as "by an Eye Witness," reports on the tavern episode and then veers off into malicious fantasy as the stricken Curll, convinced that he is dying, makes his last will and testament. In it Curll begs pardon for his many publishing offenses but insists in his own defense that his purposes were merely to make money. Leaving instructions as to how various disreputable publishing projects are to be handled, Curll prepares for death but is rescued from dissolution by "a plentiful foetid Stool."[5] Several months later Pope published *A Further Account of the most Deplorable Condition of Mr. Edmund Curll, Bookseller*, elaborating his fantasy.[6] Here, having gone mad as a result of swallowing the "poison," Curll calls a council of hireling authors. Described in mock heroic style, this council of hacks concludes with plans to libel and defame Pope. Still later—probably about four years after the meeting in the tavern—Pope published *A Strange but True Relation How Edmund Curll, of Fleetstreet, Stationer . . . was converted from the Christian Religion by certain Eminent Jews.*[7] In this pamphlet he imagines Curll, motivated by the desire to become "as rich as a Jew," bargaining over the details of his conversion.[8] Curll haggles over his fee for giving up, in turn, the apostle's creed, the thirty-nine articles, and the four evangelists, after which, to be initiated, he must undergo circumcision. At the crucial moment, however, Curll jerks upward, whereby, as Pope puts it, "he lost five times as much as ever Jew did before."[9] The pamphlet concludes with a portrait of the miserable Curll in his bookshop at the sign of "the Old Testament and Dial"—Curll's actual shop sign at this time was the Dial and Bible—where his wife is said to wring her hands and tear her hair in despondency over her loss and her husband's indignity.[10]

Pope's comic pamphlets are perhaps silly imaginative exercises, but it is worth observing that in their scatological fantasies they look forward to the mock heroic *Dunciad* (1728), Pope's great satire on the world of cheap books and hack writers in which Curll figures prominently. There in the heroic games held by the booksellers to celebrate the coronation of a new king of the dunces, Curll is portrayed as falling in a puddle of urine in pursuit of an empty-headed poet. And later in the famous episode of the pissing contest, Curll triumphs over a rival bookseller. The rival's stream is feeble and flies back in his face.

> Not so from shameless Curl: Impetuous spread
> The stream, and smoaking, flourish'd o'er his head.[11]

In the *Dunciad*, scatological humor and grotesque fantasy are transformed into something more resonant because now the subject becomes not merely the folly of a single disreputable bookseller but the tawdriness of the entire commercial print culture of the early eighteenth century. The *Dunciad*, which centers on the coronation of a new king of the dunces, portrays a kind of creation in reverse, the devolution of order and meaning into chaos, climaxing in an apocalypse of cultural decline as the reign of the goddess Dullness commences and "universal Darkness covers all."[12]

Whereas Pope turned the quarrel with Curll to imaginative account, Curll had concrete business reasons for making as much of the quarrel as he could. A fiercely energetic entrepreneur, Curll had mastered the new media world created after the lapse of licensing in 1695 by the explosion of newspapers. He used the newspapers to advertise his publications and also to build media events. As Paul Baines and Pat Rogers put it, Curll "made authorship into news, and literature a locus of scandal, a temple of infamy, a whispering gallery of rumour."[13] Curll turned Pope's attacks to account with a flurry of activity designed to publicize the quarrel and promote his business. Thus within days of the appearance of Pope's first pamphlet, Curll was advertising the second part of his antagonist's "Popish" translation of Homer and using the notice to remind the public that he still had the controversial *Court Poems* for sale. He also advertised a new ballad, *The Catholick Poet*, and put out a call for contributions to a publication to be titled *Homer Defended*, which would expose Pope's errors in his translations.[14] Curll continued this kind of activity for decades, stoking Pope's animosity with provocative advertisements and publications, and thereby keeping himself and his business in the public eye.

Pope, too, found a practical use for the quarrel. In 1726, as part of his continuing exploitation of his antagonist, Curll published several volumes of letters that Pope had written in his late teens and early twenties to an older friend, the London man-about-town Henry Cromwell. Curll had purchased these letters from Cromwell's former mistress, Elizabeth Thomas. Pope's youthful letters to Cromwell were now embarrassing to him because, among other immature affectations, they showed him trying on the pose of a rakish, sexually provocative young wag. Shortly after the Cromwell letters appeared, Pope began writing to friends to ask for the return of his correspondence. It may have been at this point that Pope began to conceive the project of publishing an authorized edition of his letters in order to fashion his own public image and, as Maynard Mack puts it, to "erect a monument to himself and the gifted writers he had known."[15] But for a gentleman to publish his own letters would have seemed inexcusably vain, and Pope had to arrange matters to legitimate an authorized edition of his correspondence.

The story of how Pope lured Curll into publishing his letters is the stuff of a drama of intrigue.[16] Evidently it was Pope himself who had his letters printed up and stored in unbound sheets. In 1733 when Curll advertised for materials to assist in preparing Pope's biography—one of Curll's specialties was patched-together literary biography—Pope surreptitiously contacted Curll, representing himself as a mysterious figure identified only by the initials "P.T." who had possession of a large collection of Pope's letters. There followed a number of teasing exchanges over several years conducted in part through newspaper advertisements, which resulted in Pope's employing a disguised actor, James Worsdale, identified as "R.S.", to sell Curll the printed sheets of letters and trick him into advertising the book as containing letters to peers.

Pope's purposes in this latest prank in his long quarrel with Curll appear to have been multiple and complex. Publication of his letters would allow Pope to protest against the indignity of being exposed in print and thereby would open the way for an authorized edition. In addition, since the works of peers were protected by privilege, luring Curll into advertising the correspondence as containing letters to and from peers could be grounds for having him hauled before the House of Lords for examination. Furthermore, in the spring of 1735, the London booksellers were campaigning for a bill that would change the statutory term of copyright in such a way as to extend the term of copyright on profitable classics such as Shakespeare and Milton. Pope does not appear to have been particularly concerned with this provision, but he was intent that no bill for the benefit of the trade should be passed without including a clause to protect authors from predatory booksellers like Curll. As James McLaverty has reconstructed this episode, Pope was using Curll as an example of an irresponsible bookseller in order to dramatize the bill's limitations and defeat it.[17] Curll was summoned to testify before the House of Lords—Pope was present for the occasion—but no letters from peers were found in the printed materials. Curll was released and proceeded with the publication. At the same time, the booksellers' bill was defeated, although not necessarily because of the affair of the letters as Pope claimed.

Pope responded to Curll's edition of his letters with a pamphlet presenting an artfully fashioned narrative that recounts Curll's dealings with "P.T." and his agent "R.S." without of course acknowledging that "P.T." was Pope himself. The pamphlet—*A Narrative of the Method by which the Private Letters of Mr. Pope Have been procur'd and publish'd by Edmund Curll, Bookseller*—stresses the issue of privacy in its title and in its text. It starts with the hope that Curll's publishing of Pope's private letters will prove "flagrant enough as an Example, to induce the LEGISLATURE to prevent for the future, an Enormity"—the unauthorized publishing of private letters—"so prejudicial to every private Subject, and so destructive of Society it self." It closes on the same note with the hope "that the next Sessions, when the BOOKSELLERS BILL shall be again brought in, the Legislature will be pleas'd not to extend the Privileges, without at the same Time restraining the Licence, of Booksellers. Since in a Case so notorious as the printing a Gentleman's PRIVATE LETTERS, most Eminent, both Printers and Booksellers, conspired to assist the Pyracy both in printing and in vending the same."[18]

Pope's desire for an act to protect authors was no doubt genuine; nonetheless, the protests in screaming capitals about private letters are difficult to reconcile with the knowledge that part of Pope's purpose had been to get his letters surreptitiously published. Curll soon realized that he had fallen for a ruse. When he issued a second volume of Pope's *Literary Correspondence*, Curll told his own version of the story,

challenging some of Pope's allegations in the *Narrative of the Method*, and declaring with respect to the two anonymous intermediaries with whom he had dealt that "P.T." stood by transposition for "Trickster Pope" and "R.S." for "Silly Rascal." Moreover, Curll bragged that he was about to expose Pope further because he had commissioned a detailed "prospect"—that is, a picture—of Pope's villa at Twickenham by a celebrated artist. This would shortly be placed on exhibit and, presumably, offered for sale. Curll declared that he had triumphed over "all the Attacks" he had suffered at the hands of "this petulant little Gentleman" and concluded with his own screaming capitals in the form of Caesar's famous brag, "VENI VIDI VICI."[19]

Shortly after this latest exchange between Pope and Curll, William Hogarth published an engraving of his painting *The Distressed Poet* in which details of the original were altered to take account of the quarrel between Pope and Curll. In its first version, *The Distressed Poet*, probably inspired by Pope's *Dunciad*, was a painting of a hack poet writing in a garret under a print of a derogatory cartoon of Pope portrayed as a triple-crowned monkey on a pedestal next to a jackass. In the engraved version of *The Distressed Poet*, Hogarth altered the print to a picture of one man cudgeling another. The figures are not identified and it is not entirely clear at first which is meant to be Pope and which Curll. But the dominant figure cries "VENI VIDI VICI," which echoes Curll's brag, and the stick with which he beats his antagonist is, as Ronald Paulson notes, "the sort used to handle the wet pages from a printing press, and it carries a page from Curll's piracy of 'Pope's Letters.'"[20]

An aggressively commercial Whig partisan, Hogarth may well have seen the exchange between Pope and Curll as Curll's triumph. Nonetheless, by enticing Curll into publishing his letters, Pope had created the circumstances that would allow him to publish his own authorized texts. This he did in 1737, printing them in multiple folio, quarto, and octavo editions, targeted at various levels of purchasers, and also issuing them as volumes V and VI of his collected *Works*. Pope's published *Correspondence* was an extraordinary commercial success, achieving sales far beyond what we today might suppose any collection of literary letters would enjoy. Maynard Mack estimates that, counting piracies and unauthorized editions as well as the various authorized

William Hogarth, *The Distressed Poet*, 1736 (detail). © The Trustees of the British Museum. Licensed under Creative Commons Attribution—Noncommercial ShareAlike 4.0 International (CC BY-NC-SA 4.0).

editions, in the first four years alone Pope's letters went through some thirty printings and issues.[21] By eighteenth-century standards they were runaway best sellers, and they clearly made a lot of money for both Pope and Curll.

The complexity of the ways in which social and commercial interests interact in the matter of the letters leaves its trace in Pope's preface to the authorized edition. Here, after explaining how and why he has allowed his private correspondence to be published, Pope expresses the wish that "no honest man may be reduc'd to the same." He goes on to complain again about a gentleman's vulnerability to a rascally bookseller. "A Bookseller advertises his intention to publish your Letters" and indicates that he will pay for copies. "Any domestick or servant, who can snatch a letter from your pocket or cabinet, is encouraged to that vile practice." Moreover, if the quantity of material falls short, the bookseller will fill out the volume with anything he pleases, so that the poor author has "not only Theft to fear, but Forgery." And the greater the writer's reputation, the greater the demand for his books and so the greater the injury to the author: "your Fame and your Property suffer alike; you are at once expos'd and plunder'd." As an author, "you are depriv'd of that Power which above all others constitutes a good one, the power of rejecting, and the right of judging for your self, what pieces it may be most useful, entertaining, or reputable to publish, at the time and in the manner you think best." Furthermore, as a man you are deprived of the right to keep your sentiments private, and as a member of society you are further injured because your conduct, concerns, secrets, passions, "tendernesses," and weaknesses are exposed to the "Impertinence of the whole world." The unauthorized printing of private letters is, he says, a form of "betraying Conversation."

> To open Letters is esteem'd the greatest breach of honour; even to look into them already open'd or accidentally dropt, is held ungenerous, if not an immoral act. What then can be thought of the procuring them merely by Fraud, and printing them merely for Lucre? We cannot but conclude every honest man will wish, that if the Laws have as yet provided no adequate remedy, one at least may be found, to prevent so great and growing an evil.[22]

Pope is asking for polite etiquette to be ratified by law. But along with the genteel discourse in which Pope represents his outrage as a man of honor, another order of discourse makes itself felt as well, one related to property. This becomes apparent when, for example, Pope complains about booksellers enticing servants to petty thievery. Such unscrupulousness means that an author must fear theft and forgery as well as exposure. The blending of the dominant discourse of gentility (marked by terms such as "honor," "generosity," and "fame") with that of property (marked by terms such as "theft," "snatch," and "plunder") produces a certain rhetorical instability. Naturally, it is the honest author who is represented in genteel terms and the unscrupulous bookseller who is associated with fraud and lucre. Nonetheless, the author's "property" suffers along with his honor and the author is not only defamed by the bookseller's practices but "plundered." Thus the discourse of property mingles with the discourse of honor. My point is that Pope's long quarrel with Curll was equally a mingled affair, one that took place at a transitional moment between the traditional position of the author as a gentleman and scholar and the emergent position of the author as a professional.

Pope the gentleman and Curll the scoundrel were polar opposites, and yet they were also in a sense strangely paired. Curll knew how to manipulate the media for his own benefit, but so did Pope. Curll profited from publishing Pope's letters, but so did Pope. Whether Pope ever realized the degree to which he and Curll were bound together is unclear, but Curll seems to have understood the symbiotic aspect of their relationship quite well. Thus in 1735, in an epistle prefixed to the second volume of his edition of Pope's *Literary Correspondence*, after recounting the long history of their quarrel, Curll concluded with a couplet addressed to his antagonist:

> A fitter Couple, sure, were never hatch'd,
> Some marry'd are, indeed, but we are match'd.[23]

Moreover, in the same year Curll changed his shop board from the "Dial and Bible" to "Pope's Head" thus doing business literally under the sign of his enemy.

* * *

The success of the collected letters whetted Pope's appetite for a new project, the publication of his collected correspondence with Jonathan Swift. But Swift, who retained most of the letters, was reluctant—or at least played reluctant—to cooperate. Thus when Pope disingenuously complained about Curll's publication of his correspondence, Swift replied that Pope need not be concerned about any letters he held because he had given orders that they were to be destroyed upon his death. According to Maynard Mack, Swift, who understood Pope's ambition for epistolary fame perfectly well, was probably teasing his friend.[24] Nonetheless, it was several years before Pope, through the assistance of an intermediary, Lord Orrery, secured the letters. But after selecting and editing them, Pope was again faced with the problem, as in 1735, of finding a pretext for publication. He accomplished this by having printed sheets of the correspondence surreptitiously transmitted to Swift who, understanding the game, passed the bundle to George Faulkner, his Dublin publisher. The Dublin printing of *Letters to and From Dr. J. Swift* in 1741 thus became the excuse that allowed Pope to publish his own edition of the correspondence in London as the second volume of his *Works in Prose,* prefaced with an explanation that publication of the letters never had Pope's consent.[25]

Six weeks later, Curll released his own edition titled *Dean Swift's Literary Correspondence,* and Pope, who probably anticipated that Curll would reprint the letters, immediately brought suit.[26] Undoubtedly Pope derived vindictive pleasure from once again making Curll his target. Clearly, too, he realized and acknowledged his financial interest in the matter.[27] Nonetheless, it seems likely that Pope thought of his purposes as primarily high-minded and genteel. In the previous decade he had failed in his attempt to get parliament to protect authors from predatory booksellers. Now, in his suit against Curll, it appears that he was trying to answer his own call for an "adequate remedy" against booksellers' invasion of authors' privacy by establishing that letters fell under the Statute of Anne. In *Pope v. Curll,* then, the statute, which was essentially a commercial regulatory act, was being used to pursue a matter that had as much to do with authors' personal rights as with economic interests. In the context of the developing marketplace culture of early eighteenth-century England, questions of authorial honor and reputation were becoming entwined with questions of commercial law.

Pope's attorney in the suit was the brilliant and still comparatively young lawyer William Murray, who had known the poet since the late 1720s before he was called to the bar. Murray later became famous as Lord Mansfield, the chief justice of the Court of King's Bench, in which role he was a key figure in the modernization of English law to adapt it to the needs of a commercial nation. More specifically, Murray was one of the major figures in the early elaboration of copyright law and his attitude toward copyright was directly influenced by his friendship with the famous poet, whom he greatly admired.[28]

Drafted by Murray, Pope's complaint begins by invoking the statute and its provision for authors. He specifies by date twenty-nine of his letters addressed to Swift and printed in Curll's edition and declares himself their sole author and proprietor. He also specifies by date twenty-nine letters addressed to him by Swift, saying that he had hoped that neither his letters to Swift nor Swift's letters to him would ever have been published without his consent. In a legal maneuver devised by Murray, he waives the penalties allowed by the statute—the act had provided, among other things, a fine of a penny a sheet for every offending copy printed—but asks for an accounting of profits, which are to be paid to himself. Any unsold copies are to be delivered to the court and disposed of as the court directs. Meanwhile, Curll is to be restrained by an injunction from any further sales.[29]

The requested injunction was issued a few days after the complaint, but Curll quickly moved to dissolve the order by filing an answer in which he makes three principal points. He argues first that since all the letters in question were actually sent and delivered, Pope cannot claim to be the proprietor of any of them. Second, he raises the question of whether, in any case, familiar letters fall under the terms of the statute, which was after all an act for the encouragement of learning. Third, he says that he has reprinted the letters from Faulkner's Dublin edition and it is his understanding that any book first published in Ireland may be lawfully reprinted in England.[30] In addition, he points out that the letters specified by Pope amount to only about one-fifth of the published book.

It is worth noting that Lord Chancellor Hardwicke, who heard Pope's case, was the same man—Philip Yorke—who thirteen years earlier as attorney general had prosecuted Curll for libel.[31] Hardwicke's decision, handed down a few days after the bookseller's filing, addresses each of Curll's principal points. He rejects outright the argument that any book printed in Ireland, where the statute did not reach, could be reprinted in England, pointing out that to affirm this proposition would have "pernicious consequences" because it would establish an easy way for booksellers to evade the statute by sending books over to Ireland to be printed first. Ironically, this was precisely what Pope had done in arranging for his correspondence with Swift to be published in Dublin so that he would have an excuse for publishing them in London as part of his *Works*. But Pope's contrivance was designed to preserve his sense of genteel propriety, not to evade the statute.

More interesting than the jurisdictional argument was Curll's claim that familiar letters consisting of matters such as "inquiries after the health of friends" cannot "properly be called a learned work." Hardwicke disagrees.

> It is certain that no works have done more service to mankind, than those which have appeared in this shape, upon familiar subjects, and which perhaps were never intended to be published; and it is this makes them so valuable; for I must confess for my own part, that letters which are very elaborately written, and originally intended for the press, are generally the most insignificant, and very little worth any person's reading.[32]

Like Defoe's judges in the matter of *The Shortest Way*, Hardwicke found himself in a position in which he was required to make a literary critical proclamation from the bench. What was the "value" of letters on familiar subjects? In declaring that spontaneous letters that were simply written and never intended to be published were of greater value than elaborate letters written for the press, Hardwicke was in fact merely repeating the received critical wisdom of the day with respect to familiar letters. Letters, like other forms of literature, were understood to be valuable because of their ability to please and instruct by, among other things, portraying acts of friendship and demonstrations of character. Their value, then, was understood to be related to the qualities of sincerity and spontaneity.[33]

Hardwicke was not making a novel critical assessment. He was, however, turning critical opinion into legal judgment. If there was to be a statute protecting certain kinds of writings—those that contributed to the advancement of learning—judges would perforce find themselves making such pronouncements. Under the aegis of the statute, literary and legal issues were converging in such a way that significant sums of money might depend upon whether a particular text or class of texts was deemed worth protecting and admitted to the privileged category.

Two senses of "value," the literary and the commercial, were becoming entangled.

Perhaps the most interesting of all Curll's arguments was the claim that letters that were sent and delivered were a gift to the receiver and therefore no longer the author's property. Hardwicke responds by making a distinction, novel at the time, between a letter as a physical object and the right to publish. He says that at most the receiver has a "special property" in the letter, a "joint property with the writer." Possibly "the property of the paper may belong" to the receiver, but this does not give him a license to publish.[34] The effect of this analysis is to draw a line between the tangible and intangible aspects of the letter. The receiver owns the tangible object; the author retains the right of publication.

Precisely what kind of property, tangible or intangible, parliament supposed it was protecting in the Statute of Anne is unclear. In all likelihood metaphysical distinctions such as those between the tangible object and the right of publication never occurred to the legislators. The Statute of Anne prescribed specific and concrete penalties for the invasion of literary property. As I have noted, it provided a fine of one penny for every offending sheet. In addition it provided that all offending books and sheets be surrendered to the rightful owner "who shall forthwith damask, and make wast[e] paper of them."[35] This meant that the printed sheets were to be defaced by overprinting them with meaningless lines, a physical act that, like the burning of a book deemed to be a libel such as Defoe's *The Shortest Way*, retained a sense of retribution being visited upon the offending object itself. Benjamin Kaplan has remarked that the draftsman of the statute was "thinking as a printer would—of a book as a physical entity; of rights in it and offenses against it as related to 'printing and reprinting' the thing itself."[36] So, too, Curll's defense depended on the conception of a letter as a thing that once sent and delivered passed wholly to the recipient. Hardwicke's judgment, however, involved an abstraction of literary property from its material basis in ink and paper.

Terminology can be an index to legal and cultural development. Significantly, the Statute of Anne never mentioned "copyright" but employed the old term "copy"—a term related to the still current notion of "printer's copy"—in the sense that it had long been used by printers and booksellers as denoting the right to print a particular title. The stationers' term retained some feeling for "copy" as a material object, the manuscript on which a printed edition was based. It is interesting to note, then, that the new term "copyright" was just coming into general use in the early eighteenth century. Thus in 1732 Pope wrote a letter to Gay in which he mentioned that he understood that several mercenary booksellers had been soliciting "some Copyright" assignments from Swift.[37] The new term suggests an attenuation of the sense of the property as materially based in ink and paper. It emerges, significantly, at about the same time as Hardwicke's distinction between the receiver's physical property and the writer's intangible property. In Hardwicke's decision the author's words have, in effect, flown free from the page on which they are written. Not ink and paper, but pure signs, separated from any material support, have become the protected property.

* * *

I have suggested that one of Pope's purposes in pursuing his complaint against Curll was to achieve in the courtroom what he had been unable to accomplish through parliament, to establish an author's right to protect his letters from a predatory bookseller. It is worth emphasizing the historical specificity of Pope's distress about the unauthorized printing of private letters. The early eighteenth century witnessed a surge of letter writing. This depended on the development of the post office, an institution that was originally designed by Henry VIII to serve the crown but by the end of the seventeenth century had begun to provide general service to anyone who could afford the penny post.[38] The expansion of the postal service is a phenomenon related to the development of the public sphere in the late seventeenth century and the appearance of the new dialectic of public and private. In this context the familiar letter, modeled in part on classical precedents such as the letters of Cicero, became established as a significant literary form.

The publishing of a familiar letter involved the exposure of something personal and intimate to the world at large. In a letter to his friend the painter Charles Jervas, Pope represented his letters as windows into his bosom, saying that what such a window achieved was "to render the Soul of Man visible."[39] Likewise, in the preface to his authorized

1737 edition of his correspondence, Pope declared that his letters displayed his "real Sentiments, as they flow'd warm from the heart." Furthermore, he emphasized that he was not a public figure but a "private man" who was concerned with his own circle of friends rather than great matters such as religion or government.[40]

The appeal of letters in the early eighteenth century was a manifestation of a new interest in private life. The reader of a published set of correspondence was admitted as an observer to an intimate social circle to which he or she would not otherwise have had access. Moreover, this voyeuristic pleasure could be justified by the assurance that reading letters was useful insofar as they provided examples of virtue and vice. The interest in letters resulted not only in the printing of collections of actual correspondence such as Pope's but also in fictional collections. The most notable of these was of course Samuel Richardson's *Pamela*. Published in 1740, the year before Pope initiated his suit against Curll, *Pamela* consisted, in the words of the original title, of a "Series of Familiar Letters from a Beautiful Young Damsel to her Parents." This collection, which like Pope's published correspondences included letters both from and to the principal figure, told the story of the young serving girl's resistance to her master's amorous approaches and her ultimate triumph in becoming his wife and a gentlewoman. It was one of the greatest publishing successes of the eighteenth century, and its appeal was clearly related, like that of Pope's correspondence, to the effect of intimacy that it conveyed combined with the assurance of edification. In the case of *Pamela*, of course, there was also an erotic dimension that contributed to the book's allure.

Pope's image of letters as a window in his bosom implied that his letters revealed his true self. In securing the ruling that familiar letters came under the statute, Pope was thus in effect establishing that his "self" was protected by law. But such a proposition cut two ways. To establish that Curll could not print Pope's letters without permission was also to establish that Pope could print them and could do so for profit. The tension implicit in this aspect of *Pope v. Curll* thus reflected the tension that characterized all of Pope's complex and devious dealings with respect to his correspondence. On the one hand Pope insisted on the inviolability of his privacy, but on the other he labored to create situations in which he would be constrained to publish his let-

George Vertue, frontispiece, *The Works of Mr. Alexander Pope* (1717). Courtesy of
The Beinecke Rare Book and Manuscript Library, Yale University.

ters. Embedded in the question of whether the letters came under the
statute was thus the presumed conflict between gentility and professional authorship that bedeviled Pope's entire career. Moreover, in
Pope's case, the conflict was unusually intense because his career as
an author was in large part based on his persona as a gentleman.

The *Epistle to Dr. Arbuthnot* with its representation of the gentle-man poet besieged by self-seeking suitors is perhaps the most obvious example of Pope dramatizing his gentility. But Pope's self-dramatization went back at least to 1717 when, not yet thirty years old, he issued a handsome edition of his collected *Works* adorned with a huge foldout engraved portrait of himself designed to be sold separately as well as part of the book. "From 1717 onwards," McLaverty aptly remarks, "Pope was printing versions of himself."[41] The verse epistles, the sa-tirical works such as the *Dunciad,* the various collected editions of his poems, and of course the collected letters were all in effect portraits of Pope's integrity, generosity, and wit in contrast to the madness of a world of scribblers and charlatans. As the foldout engraving of 1717 suggests, Pope was also concerned with his visual representation and was diligent about assuring that appropriate images of him were avail-able, especially in the light of some of the unflattering cartoons that were circulated. The engraving of 1717 was just one of the many au-thorized portraits and engravings of the poet. Indeed, according to William Wimsatt, "Pope was probably the most frequently portrayed English person of his generation, perhaps of the whole eighteenth century."[42] Considering that "celebrity" in the modern sense is a product of media and mass circulation, it is not perhaps inaccurate to think of Pope as the first author-celebrity of the print era. Oversimplifying and putting it perhaps too baldly, one might say that Pope made himself into his own best commodity. Edmund Curll conducted business under the sign of Pope's Head. So, in effect, did Pope.

* * *

Pope's published letters were not quite the spontaneous writings that Hardwicke may have supposed. Nor were they the unpremeditated sentiments flowing "warm from the heart" that Pope claimed in his preface to the 1737 edition. As nineteenth-century scholars discovered, Pope carefully revised his letters for publication cutting trivialities and indecorous remarks and elevating the style and tone. He also trans-ferred letters from one addressee to another in order to refine the image of himself that he wanted to project.[43] Charles Dilke, who discovered these revisions, was dismayed by Pope's "want of sincerity, honesty and truthfulness."[44] Whitwell Elwin, who provided the introduction to a new edition of the letters in 1871, was outraged. He complained that the letters that Pope "feigned to be all ease and nature" were in fact "doubly artificial" since "they were elaborately composed at the outset, and industriously edited at an interval of years." Pope's dishonesty in his manipulation of Curll and later of Swift was scandalous. "He feared that the representation he had prepared of his extemporaneous talents, and native goodness, would lose its effect if he was known to have selected and published the letters, and he plunged from infamy to infamy that he might invest his counterfeited virtue with a specious appearance of truth."[45]

Such strong reactions to Pope's manipulation of his image in his letters reveal cultural changes between Pope's time and the revolution in sensibility in the late eighteenth century. Among other things, the nineteenth-century reactions point to a change in the moral and psychological conception of the individual in relation to society. Some years ago in a landmark series of lectures at Harvard published under the title *Sincerity and Authenticity*, Lionel Trilling suggested that a reorientation in the sense of selfhood came about at the end of the eighteenth century. Trilling warned that any attempt to trace the "history of the self" is like writing about "shadows in a dark land."[46] Nonetheless, he proposed a distinction between the moral ideal of "sincerity," which appeared in the early modern period, and the later ideal of "authenticity," which emerged at the end of the eighteenth century. Sincerity was social in orientation; its imperative was to be honest in one's dealings with the world at large. Authenticity, on the other hand, involved being true to an essential self such as that implicit in Rousseau's *Confessions* that was conceived as more fundamental than any social role.

Two decades after Trilling's lectures, the philosopher Charles Taylor published his magisterial *Sources of the Self: The Making of the Modern Identity*. Employing intellectual history and philosophical analysis to illuminate the specifically modern notion of the interiorized, independent self, Taylor traced the history of conceptions of the self from the ancients through the transformations of the late eighteenth and nineteenth centuries.[47] More recently, Dror Wahrman has reframed the subject by taking an anthropological and cultural-historical approach to the notion of the self. In *The Making of the Modern Self*, Wahrman distinguishes between what he calls the "*ancien régime* of identity" and the modern regime of "selfhood." The older formation, which was characteristic of the early modern period, understood identity as social and dramatic. Identity was performative; one man could, literally, play many parts as he matured or rose or fell in social status. The later formation, the "modern self," which according to Wahrman becomes dominant in England at the end of the eighteenth century, conceives personal identity as "an innate, fixed, determinate core," a psychic substance derived from a "deep inner core of selfhood."[48]

Trilling, Taylor, and Wahrman all point to the same historical change from a more social to a more inward and psychological sense of self. Brook Thomas appropriately warns against "accounts based on simple oppositions between two types of subjectivity."[49] Private and public, self and other, are after all dialectical, entangled terms. Thus, as Thomas has suggested, Pope's social self, his concern for reputation, implies a private self that needs protection from scoundrels like Curll.[50] But recognizing that Trilling's opposition between sincerity and authenticity involves a certain rhetorical simplification, we can observe that, insofar as his orientation was social and public, Pope falls into the category of the "sincere" rather than the "authentic" man. Yet "sincerity" was precisely what Dilke and Elwin accused Pope of lacking. Was Pope in fact sincere—that is, "honest"—in his dealings with the world at large? According to his own lights and the ethos of the early modern period, I think he was. When Pope edited his correspondence to remove trivialities and indecorous remarks, he did so not to deceive his readers but rather, as I understand it, to excise what he regarded as distracting and inessential blemishes. Likewise, when Pope reassigned letters from one correspondent to another, he did so, as Maynard Mack suggests, to present a more complete picture of certain relationships—especially those with Congreve and Addison—than the actual documents that he had at hand could supply.[51] In his reworking of his correspondence Pope was not attempting to portray a complex inner self in the manner of Rousseau; he was attempting to sketch a picture of his eminent social circle and to show his own honest dealings in it. He was demonstrating his gentility.

As the inclusion of his correspondence in his collected *Works* implies, Pope conceived of his familiar letters as literary artifacts comparable to his verse epistles and satires. When Pope represents his let-

ters as windows in his bosom, he does not mean that his letters reveal an authentic inner self. Rather, he is asserting his honesty and he is doing so in a characteristically learned and witty way that involves an allusion to Lucian's *Hermotimus*, a philosophical dialogue that plays with the idea of a window to show a man's heart so that the world might discern his truth or falsehood. James Winn, who points out the classical allusion, remarks, "Pope obviously did not show 'his Heart to all the world'; the window he made in his bosom in his published letters was carefully constructed to reveal only a few aspects of his mind, selected and polished for public display."[52] Pope's letters, then, should be seen not as expressions of his "self"—spontaneous emanations of an inner core of selfhood—so much as crafted representations of himself as a gentleman.

Along with the trope of the window in the bosom, which he used at least twice, Pope often referred to his correspondence as conversation or "talking on paper," a metaphor that also had classical antecedents. Thus in an early letter to Henry Cromwell, Pope claimed that the freedom and familiarity of style with which he and Cromwell corresponded was more like "Talking upon Paper, than Writing," and Pope later employed the trope, as we have seen, in the preface to his edition of his correspondence when he protested against unauthorized printing of letters as a form of "betraying Conversation."[53] Significantly, Pope's published correspondences were collections involving letters from multiple writers. As I have noted, they were monuments not to Pope alone but to Pope in the context of his circle of distinguished friends. Thus the full title of the official quarto edition of the 1737 collection was *Letters of Mr. Alexander Pope and Several of His Friends*, and it contained letters from Wycherley, Addison, Arbuthnot, Gay, and Swift as well as other notables. Since Pope's conception of his identity was social rather than psychological, an adequate representation of him required that he be seen in his social context. In a sense the social context *was* his identity.

In an excellent discussion of Pope's letters to which I am indebted, Sören Hammerschmidt emphasizes the variety of epistolary styles that Pope developed to address various correspondents. Drawing on recent scholarship about the history of the self, he argues that rather than presenting an authorial unveiling of an integrated and interiorized self,

Pope's letters present him in multiple roles and guises, among them the young rake and wit, the mature poet, the companion, the dutiful son, and the friend.[54] Hammerschmidt's point about the dispersed and distinctly premodern form of identity that the letters reveal is well taken. Nonetheless, a constant that persists through all Pope's published letters, one that is also emphasized in the preface to the authorized 1737 collection, is Pope's status as a gentleman. It was as a gentleman not a mere scribbler that Pope represented himself in his *Epistle to Dr. Arbuthnot* and other poems and it was as a gentleman—the trusted friend of Swift, Gay, Arbuthnot, and Bolingbroke, among others—that he consistently represented himself in his letters. Defoe, too, inhabited the early modern, socially oriented regime of identity. But whereas Defoe was an impersonator who enacted various figures such as Crusoe, Moll, and Roxana, Pope repeatedly enacted a single figure, the poet as gentleman.

Recognizing the importance of social status to every aspect of Pope's self-representation helps to explain how he could conceive of himself as sincere and honest and yet have no compunctions about tricking Curll with the emetic in 1716, mocking him in pamphlets such as *The Full and True Account*, and finally deceiving him with the elaborate scheme involving "P.T." and "R.S." Edmund Curll was no gentleman. Therefore, Pope, according to his understanding of the obligations of a gentleman, owed Curll neither deference nor respect. Indeed, it was precisely by mocking, tricking, exposing, and humiliating Curll as a greedy and unprincipled scoundrel that Pope asserted his social superiority.

* * *

In the Chancery case against Curll, Pope was seeking to establish that his status and privacy as embodied in his letters were protected by law. In the next few years, Pope returned to court at least three times in matters that more simply involved literary property in the economic sense. Two of these concerned unauthorized printings of the *Dunciad*, and the third concerned the *Essay on Man*.[55] Perhaps having gone to court on genteel grounds in the matter of the Swift letters, Pope was now comfortable appearing as plaintiff in more mundane matters. These cases remind us that although Pope always presented himself as a gentleman, he was also in practice an aggressive professional who was directly concerned with the exploitation of his literary properties.

The *Dunciad* and the *Essay on Man* litigations were similar to other essentially commercial cases of the period. *Pope v. Curll*, however, was different insofar as it involved a new subject, letters. This led Hardwicke to his distinction between the physical letter and the literary property, an analytical novelty that foreshadowed the doctrinal future of copyright. Even though it granted property rights to authors, the Statute of Anne was still, in many respects, a booksellers' rather than an authors' law. Thus the draftsman, as I have noted, was thinking of books rather than texts as the subject of the act. Printers are concerned with books; authors are concerned with texts. In Hardwicke's distinction between the tangible property in the physical letter—the ink and paper—and the intangible property in the words, the legal concept of the author's right of property in the text might be said to have been born.

Hardwicke's decision that familiar letters fell under the statute also looked forward to later developments. By establishing that his correspondence was protected, Pope was seeking to confirm a personal rather than a specifically economic right—that is, as I put it earlier, he was seeking to establish that his privacy and even, in a sense, his "self" was protected. In the preface to the authorized edition of his letters, Pope protested against the injury that a predatory bookseller did to an unwillingly published writer: "As an Author, you are depriv'd of that Power which above all others constitutes a good one, the power of rejecting, and the right of judging for your self, what pieces it may be most useful, entertaining, or reputable to publish, at the time and in the manner you think best."[56] Three decades later, Pope's friend and attorney William Murray—now Lord Mansfield—seems to have been thinking back to *Pope v. Curll* when he declared in the great case of *Millar v. Taylor* (1769) that authors have a common-law right in their unpublished writings. Indeed, Mansfield may not only have been thinking back to the Pope case in general but specifically echoing Pope's words about the author's right of publishing "at the time and in the manner" he thinks best. From what sources, Mansfield asked, is the common-law right drawn?

> From this Argument,—Because it is just, that an Author should reap the pecuniary Profits of his own Ingenuity and Labour. It is just, that He should judge when to publish, or whether he ever will publish. It is fit he should not only choose the Time, but the Manner of Publication; how many; what Volume; what Print. It is fit, he should choose to Whose Care he will Trust the Accuracy and Correctness of the Impression; in Whose Honesty he will confide, not to foist in Additions: With other Reasonings of the same Effect.[57]

In this often-cited passage, Mansfield continued the process begun in *Pope v. Curll* of blending personal and property rights.

The Statute of Anne may have begun as legislation about books, and the thrust of the enactment may have been essentially commercial, but under the pressures brought by the preeminent author of the first half of the eighteenth century and the preeminent jurist of the second, copyright law began to acquire some of the features of a law of personal rights as well and thus to move toward being more nearly an author's as well as a bookseller's law, one that specifically addressed authors' concerns. A hundred and twenty years later, Samuel D. Warren and Louis D. Brandeis, arguing for the recognition of the right to privacy, invoked the common-law right of an individual to determine "to what extent his thoughts, sentiments, and emotions shall be communicated to others" and cited *Millar v. Taylor* as a precedent and authority.[58] Warren and Brandeis did not specifically cite *Pope v. Curll*, a case they probably did not know; nonetheless, the effect of Pope's case, like the radiation from some distant astronomical event, can still be detected in their famous essay.

The "self" that Pope acted to protect in *Pope v. Curll* was, as I have suggested, not the modern determinate core of unique identity but an older, more explicitly social formation. As the new conception of selfhood emerged, however, it too became a part of copyright discourse. The earliest instance I know in which the new conception enters legal writing is a pamphlet published by the attorney Francis Hargrave in 1774. In this pamphlet Hargrave, considering the immaterial nature of literary property, attempted to establish the basis on which one property might be distinguished from another. He located this in style. One man's style might resemble another; nonetheless, every "man has a mode of combining and expressing his ideas peculiar to himself." Thus any original literary work will always, like an individual human face, "have some singularities, some lines, some features, to characterize it, and to fix and establish its identity."[59] In this argument, I believe we can see an early instance of the modern conception of a determinate inner core of selfhood that is prior to social identity—every man has a personal style—and also an early instance of the notion that literary property is ultimately founded on and justified by the author's unique personality. Such a theory of literary property will of course become commonplace in the nineteenth century, and it will mark a further stage in the transformation of copyright from a booksellers' into an authors' law.

[CHAPTER THREE]

Emancipation and Translation

Stowe v. Thomas (1853)

In 1853 Harriet Beecher Stowe sued F. W. Thomas, a Philadelphia publisher who had brought out a translation of *Uncle Tom's Cabin* for the German-language trade. In a controversial decision, Justice Robert Grier, a supporter of the 1850 Fugitive Slave Law that was Stowe's immediate target, ruled that the German translation did not infringe her copyright. "By the publication of her book," Grier wrote, "the creations of the genius and imagination of the author have become as much public property as those of Homer or Cervantes. Uncle Tom and Topsy are as much *publici juris*"—that is, public possessions—"as Don Quixote and Sancho Panza." Did Mrs. Stowe suppose that her characters were her slaves? On the contrary, Grier implied, publication amounted to emancipation. "Her absolute dominion and property in the creations of her genius and imagination have been voluntarily relinquished." Stowe's copyright, he ruled, protected only the literal reprinting of her novel.[1]

Justice Grier's ruling was consistent with the narrow tenor of American copyright law in the early nineteenth century, a legal regime epitomized in the foundational U.S. case of *Wheaton v. Peters* (1834) in which the Supreme Court held, among other things, that failure to fulfill every one of the formalities specified in the copyright statute, including registration, deposit, and formal notice, invalidated a copyright claim. Put in positive terms, one might say that American copyright doctrine in this period still reflected the classical republican values of the revolutionary period. A broad concept of the public good implied the ready circulation of books to ensure a well-read and educated citizenry. And this emphasis on a civil, literate society inflected the notorious American resistance to an international copyright agreement, one that would secure the rights of popular British authors such as Walter Scott or Charles Dickens.[2] But America was changing in the decades before the Civil War as a small-scale agrarian society based on land was becoming an expanding capitalist society based on commerce, and, naturally, American copyright doctrine was evolving as well.[3] By 1853 Grier's constricted vision of copyright was old-fashioned, and within two decades it would be rejected when Congress in 1870 explicitly granted authors the right to translations of their works.

The work at issue in *Stowe v. Thomas* was a phenomenon. Nothing like the startling success of *Uncle Tom's Cabin* had been seen before on either side of the Atlantic. Published first as a weekly serial from June 1851 to April 1852 in an abolitionist weekly, the *National Era*, Stowe's tale painted a vivid picture of the horrors of slavery just as the tensions between Northern and Southern states were becoming increasingly intolerable. In one of the great misjudgments in publishing history, the prominent Boston house of Phillips, Sampson and Company passed up the opportunity to publish the novel in book form because they were doubtful about the appeal of an antislavery story and concerned about offending customers in the South. John P. Jewett, however, a comparatively small Boston publisher, saw the book's potential and invested heavily in advertising beginning with announcements of the forthcoming novel that promoted it as the "story of the age" starting several weeks before the March 20 publication date.[4]

From the beginning, sales were extraordinary. Three thousand copies of the two-volume edition were sold on the day of publication, and by the following day the entire printing of five thousand copies was gone. Two weeks later the second printing, another five thousand copies, was gone as well. We know these numbers in part because Jewett used sales figures to create a calculated air of frenzy, for example, as in a notice that appeared in the *National Era* on April 15: "The fact that *ten thousand copies have been sold in two weeks* is evidence sufficient of its unbounded popularity. Three paper mills are constantly at work, manufacturing the paper, and three power presses are working twenty-four hours per day, in printing it, and more than one hundred bookbinders are incessantly plying their trade, to bind them, and still it has been impossible as yet to supply the demand."[5] In early June he advertised: "Uncle Tom's Cabin. 50,000 Copies in Eight Weeks! A Sale Unprecedented in the History of Bookselling in America."[6] By December, just nine months after publication, some two hundred thousand copies were in print with one hundred thousand more to follow in 1853.[7]

Like a modern movie blockbuster, the success of the novel led to a flood of *Uncle Tom* spinoffs. Jewett commissioned John Greenleaf Whittier to write a poem about Little Eva and hired a composer to set Whittier's poem to music. Many other poems, songs, diorama and panorama displays, and dramatizations appeared. At one point three separate *Uncle Tom* plays, including one staged by P. T. Barnum, competed in New York City. Manufacturers produced china plates with scenes from the novel, commemorative figurines of Uncle Tom and Little Eva, spoons, engravings, hats, and scarves, and there was even an *Uncle Tom* card game, advertised for Christmas 1852. This turned on the theme of the separation and reunification of families. By Christmas 1853, the abolitionist paper the *Liberator* was able to announce as one of the favorable signs of the times that "artists, of all grades, now find it not only congenial, but a remunerative work, to represent the creations of Mrs. Stowe's genius in pictures and statues."[8]

Naturally, British publishers took notice of the *Uncle Tom* phenomenon. In the absence of a copyright agreement, foreign publishers were free to reprint Stowe's novel just as American publishers had been freely reprinting popular foreign authors such as Dickens. The first English printing appeared less than two months after Jewett's edition, and within a year some forty different printings had been issued by eighteen separate British houses, including an "Author's Edition" published by Thomas Bosworth. This announced that it was published by agreement and that Stowe would receive some money in connection with sales. Perhaps more than a million and a half copies were sold in Britain and the colonies.[9] These numbers were remarkable by any standards; for an American author, they were astonishing. Several years later, Gamaliel Bailey, the editor of the *National Era*, recalling his serial publication of Stowe's novel, noted that no production of an American writer, so far as he knew, had "excited more profound and general interest." But it was not completely surprising, Bailey remarked, that "a work of such power upon such a subject, eagerly looked for every week, for nearly a year" in its serial form, "read on the car, in the steamboat, at the hotel, in parts, just enough to stimulate, without satisfying desire, should, the moment it appeared in book form, have run like fire on the prairie."[10] Bailey's metaphor captured two distinctive aspects of Stowe's novel, its incendiary quality—this was, after all, a book that helped ignite the Civil War—and its peculiarly American subject.[11]

Provocative and timely as Stowe's novel was, the *Uncle Tom* phenomenon could not have occurred before the social and industrial changes of the nineteenth century. The first fifty years of the century saw, along with the expansion westward, improvements in the American postal and railroad systems that led to the creation of a great national market. Thus Jewett distributed and sold *Uncle Tom* both from his Boston firm and from his Cleveland affiliate, Jewett, Proctor and Worthington, which handled sales west of the Alleghenies.[12] Equally important were technical developments. From the late fifteenth through the eighteenth centuries, printing had remained an essentially unchanged craft process. But the introduction of industrial technology such as the rotary press and stereotyping made it possible to produce books on an entirely new scale. "Never since books were first printed has the success of Uncle Tom been equaled," wrote the editor Charles Briggs in *Putnam's Monthly Magazine* in 1853. Briggs declared that the novel marked the start of a new era in literature. "Such a phenomenon as its present popularity could have happened only in the present wondrous age. It required all the aid of our new machinery to produce the phenomenon; our steam-presses, steam-ships, steam-carriages, iron roads, electric telegraphs, and universal peace among the reading nations of the earth. But beyond all, it required the readers to consume the books, and these have never before been so numerous."[13] Briggs was correct. Literacy in the United States was high—perhaps 90 percent of white citizens could read—and by 1850 the population, less than four and a half million in 1800, had grown to more than twenty-two million, a population roughly comparable to that of Britain at the time.[14]

For writing *Uncle Tom's Cabin* as a serial, Harriet Beecher Stowe was paid $400. For the first three months' sales in book form, she received from Jewett a check for the enormous sum of $10,300. "We believe that this is the largest sum of money ever received by any author, either American or European, from the actual sales of a single work in so short a period of time," commented the *New York Times*.[15] In all, Jewett probably paid Stowe a total of about $30,000 for *Uncle Tom* plus perhaps another $10,000 for *A Key to Uncle Tom's Cabin*, a rapidly prepared follow-up volume documenting the validity of the novel's portrayal of slavery. Stowe probably received some payments from at least three of the British publishers; furthermore, British readers took up a "penny offering" to express gratitude to Stowe—each purchaser was asked to donate a penny to the fund—and this amounted to more than $20,000. Over an eighteen-month period, then, Stowe probably earned an extraordinary total of some $60,000.[16] It is of course difficult to translate such a sum into present-day terms, but certainly $60,000 in 1853, a time in which less than 1 percent of Americans earned more than $5,000 a year, would be worth some millions of dollars today.[17]

* * *

The abolitionist movement emerged from the culture of sentiment, the new insistence upon the humane value of sympathy and fellow feeling that developed in the late eighteenth century. "Am I not a Man and a Brother?" read the banner on the seal of the British Society for the Abolition of the Slave Trade, founded in 1787. Stowe's nineteenth-century treatment of slavery partakes of the general valorization of fellow feeling characteristic of the culture of sentiment, but, more specifically, it dwells on the evil of families broken up, mothers separated from children, husbands separated from wives. *Uncle Tom's Cabin* begins with just such a moment of domestic destruction when the kindly slave owner, Shelby, is compelled to sell Uncle Tom and Eliza's son Harry. This double event, the novel's version of the fall from Eden, initiates the two narratives, the story of Uncle Tom's journey downriver, wrenched from his wife and children, and the complementary story of Eliza's flight northward to avoid losing her child. The negative climax of the novel is the martyrdom of Uncle Tom at the hands of Simon Legree; the more positive is the reunion of Eliza and her child with her husband George.

At the emotional and polemical core of *Uncle Tom's Cabin* is the opposition between commerce and the home. Slavery is seen as malign because it represents the intrusion of the market into the domestic sphere, the place of family, love, and the nurturing of children. As many have noted, Stowe sees blacks as naturally domestic. "In order to appreciate the sufferings of the Negroes sold south," she writes, "it must

be remembered that all the instinctive affections of that race are peculiarly strong. Their local attachments are very abiding. They are not
naturally daring and enterprising but home-loving and affectionate."[18]
Moreover, her treatment of blacks depends in part upon thinking of
them as childlike. Thus, describing Uncle Tom's life under the benevolent master Augustine St. Clare, Stowe launches into a reverie about
Africans' natural "gentleness" and "childlike simplicity of affection."

> If ever Africa shall show an elevated and cultivated race,—and come it
> must, some time, her turn to figure in the great drama of human
> improvement,—life will awaken there with a gorgeousness and
> splendor of which our cold western tribes faintly have conceived. In
> that far-off mystic land of gold, and gems, and spices, and waving
> palms, and wondrous flowers, and miraculous fertility, will awake
> new forms of art, new styles of splendor; and the Negro race, no longer
> despised and trodden down, will, perhaps, show forth some of the
> latest and most magnificent revelations of human life. Certainly they
> will, in their gentleness, their lowly docility of heart, their aptitude
> to repose on a superior mind, and rest on a higher power, their child-
> like simplicity of affection, and facility of forgiveness. In all these
> they will exhibit the highest form of the peculiarly *Christian life*,
> and, perhaps, as God chasteneth whom he loveth, he hath chosen
> poor Africa in the furnace of affliction, to make her the highest and
> noblest in that kingdom which he will set up, when every other
> kingdom has been tried, and failed; for the first shall be last, and the
> last first.[19]

Precisely because Stowe thinks of blacks as naturally domestic and
childlike, it becomes unbearable for her to observe these gentle souls,
the epitome of Christian humility, reduced to commodities by the slave
system.

Against the destructiveness of commerce and slavery, Stowe holds
up the positive domestic image of the loving, well-ordered home, and at
the heart of Stowe's image of domesticity is the nurturing relationship
of mother and child, a benevolent form of possession that she portrays
as beyond the taint of trade. As figured in, for example, Eliza's desperate
flight to keep possession of her son Harry, motherly love becomes for
Stowe the touchstone of ethical principle.[20] It is interesting, then, to

Harriet Beecher Stowe. Photograph by Napoleon Sarony (ca. 1875). Courtesy of The Stephan Loewentheil Photograph Collection, no. 8043. Division of Rare and Manuscript Collections, Cornell University Library.

note that Stowe characterized her own relationship to writing in maternal terms. Thus she was reported as saying that, for her, writing a story was "like bearing a child." Creating a story, she supposedly remarked, "leaves me in as weak and helpless a state as when my baby was born."[21] At the time she began *Uncle Tom's Cabin*, Stowe had in fact borne seven children, the most recent about eight months earlier. She was at this time newly settled in Brunswick, Maine, and she was, for the first time in some while, not pregnant. Perhaps then the idea of her developing book as the latest in her brood of children was on her mind.

Stowe consistently spoke about *Uncle Tom's Cabin* as if the story had been thrust upon her by a higher power. In 1852 she wrote to the Scottish clergyman Ralph Wardlaw insisting that she could take no personal credit for the book. "It was an instinctive, irresistible outburst and had no more merit in it than a mother's wailing for her first born."[22] Some years later, writing an introduction to a new edition of the novel, Stowe reported that the germ of the book came to her, significantly, at church, where it manifested itself as a "tangible vision" of the climactic scene of Uncle Tom's death. Stowe described how, overcome with tears, she hurried home, wrote out the scene, and read it to her two young sons. "From that time," Stowe wrote, speaking of herself in the third person, "the story can less be said to have been composed by her than imposed upon her. Scenes, incidents, conversations rushed upon her with a vividness and importunity that would not be denied. The book insisted upon getting itself into being, and would take no denial."[23] Likewise, late in life, Stowe was visited by a neighbor, a retired sea captain, who wished to shake the hand that wrote *Uncle Tom's Cabin*. " 'I did not write it,' answered the white-haired old lady gently, as she shook the captain's hand. 'You didn't?' he ejaculated in amazement. 'Why, who did, then?' 'God wrote it,' she replied simply. 'I merely did his dictation.' "[24]

Stowe's description of her novel as a gift from God that "insisted upon getting itself into being" sounds very much like what one would say of a baby. Of course the trope of writing as childbearing was a commonplace going back at least to Plato, one that perhaps first became current in the sixteenth century. Typically the notion of the "brainchild" depicts the relationship between the author and the work, often emphasizing the way in which the work resembles its begetter. Thus, in the prologue to *Don Quixote* (1604) Miguel de Cervantes apologizes to his readers that his knight is not, as he says, "the handsomest, the liveliest, and the wisest that could be conceived." But, he explains, "I could not violate Nature's ordinance whereby like engenders like. And so, what could my sterile and uncouth genius beget but the tale of a dry, shriveled, whimsical offspring, full of odd fancies such as never entered another's brain."[25] In Stowe's case, the emphasis in thinking about her relationship to her novel seems to be less one of identity—the book as her baby because it is somehow like her—than responsibility. *Uncle Tom's Cabin* is both a gift and a charge given to Stowe.

The familiar metaphor of writing as childbearing of course becomes problematic when the author is an active figure in a literary market-place. One does not ordinarily sell one's children. And yet, if an author bargains for the sale of a book, is that not exactly what he or she is doing? Daniel Defoe used the trope in a particularly colorful passage in a piece that he published in his journal the *Review* in 1710 as part of his agitation for the literary property bill that eventually became the Statute of Anne. "A Book is the Author's Property," Defoe wrote, " 'tis the Child of his inventions, the Brat of his Brain." He went on to explain that if the author "sells his Property, it then becomes the Right of the Purchaser," but if he does not sell, " 'tis as much his own, as his Wife and Children are his own." But "behold," Defoe exclaimed, "in this Christian Nation, these Children of our Heads are seiz'd, capti-vated, spirited away, and carry'd into Captivity"—that is, pirated by unscrupulous printers—"and there is none to redeem them."[26] The degree to which Defoe is aware of the tension to which the "brat of his brain" metaphor led is entirely opaque. Stowe would never have spoken flippantly about her book as a "brat." Nonetheless, she was, I think, caught in a parallel difficulty because of the specific way in which her novel framed its ethical system as an opposition between domesticity and commerce. The domestic values that *Uncle Tom's Cabin* espoused were plainly in tension with its commercial success.

Stowe's domestic ethos was no doubt genuine. Still, by 1851 she was something more than an amateur. Stowe had first begun writing—as did Jane Austen among others—by producing "parlor literature," ama-teur sketches and stories, as an integral part of family life and polite society. By the late 1830s and early 1840s she had begun publishing in magazines and receiving payment for her productions. These payments were important; her husband Calvin's meager earnings as a scholar meant that keeping a steady flow of money coming into the household from her writings was a necessity. By 1842 Stowe was consulting her brother-in-law, an attorney, for advice about what she should be paid for her writing, and she was also on a business trip negotiating with Harper Brothers on the terms for a collection of her short stories.[27] By the time of *Uncle Tom's Cabin*, she was sophisticated enough to take what Melissa Homestead calls "the prescient and somewhat unusual step" of registering copyright before allowing serial publication to begin.[28] Once the extent of her novel's success became evident, she was also concerned with whether she was being adequately remunerated. Thus when it had become apparent that Jewett was making much more than she was, Stowe wrote him a cool letter asking for assurances that he had treated her fairly, and, after the publication of the follow-up, *A Key to Uncle Tom's Cabin*, she switched publishers to Phillips, Samson and Company, ironically the same firm that originally passed on *Uncle Tom's Cabin*. In fact it was Calvin rather than Harriet who had conducted the negotiations with Jewett over *Uncle Tom's Cabin*. Calvin had proposed a 20 percent royalty agreement, but Jewett had insisted on 10 percent, arguing that this would allow him to promote the book aggressively—as indeed he did—and the result would be to their mutual advantage. Nevertheless, the aftermath of the negotiations left Stowe herself uneasy.[29]

When she began writing *Uncle Tom's Cabin* neither Stowe nor anyone else could have predicted the phenomenon that the novel would become. Something of the frame of mind in which she began the project is evident, however, in the letter that she wrote Bailey, proposing a story that would deal with the "patriarchal institution." This was in March 1851, six months after the passage of the Fugitive Slave Law had made it a crime punishable by a $1,000 fine and up to six months' imprisonment for anyone in the United States to assist a runaway slave. Like many others in the North, Stowe regarded the Fugitive Slave Law as abhorrent because it made every citizen, no matter his or her sentiments, complicit in the support of slavery. "Dear Sir," she wrote to Bailey:

> I am at present occupied upon a story which will be a much longer one than any I have ever written, embracing a series of sketches which give the lights and shadows of the "patriarchal institution," written either from observation, incidents which have occurred in the sphere of my personal knowledge, or in the knowledge of my friends. I shall show the *best side* of the thing, and something *faintly approaching the worst*.
>
> Up to this year I have always felt that I had no particular call to meddle with this subject, and I dreaded to expose even my own mind

to the full force of its exciting power. But I feel now that the time is come when even a woman or a child who can speak a word for freedom and humanity is bound to speak. The Carthagenian women in the last peril of their state cut off their hair for bow-strings to give to the defenders of their country; and such peril and shame as now hangs over this country is worse than Roman slavery, and I hope every woman who can write will not be silent.[30]

She went on to explain that she regarded herself as a kind of painter and that, since there is "no arguing with *pictures*," her purpose would be to hold up a portrait of slavery. Thus Stowe presented her project as descriptive and polemical, but above all as an act of conscience. She presented herself as a female patriot, a woman who, like the ancient Carthagenian women cutting their hair to defend their country from Rome, was compelled to give up an element of her femininity to speak out against the shame hanging over her country. For a woman to address such a subject, the allusion implies, was both a duty and a sacrifice.

Later, in December 1852, nine months after the publication of the novel, she wrote another letter that reveals, I think, something of the complexity that she had begun to feel in the light of the book's success. At this time Stowe was compiling the *Key to Uncle Tom's Cabin* and planning a trip to England to meet with admirers. She had received a letter from Eliza Cabot Follen, a well-known New England abolitionist and author of children's books—Follen popularized, if she did not write, the children's rhyme about the three little kittens and their mittens—who asked for information about Stowe's life. In her long reply, which soon was circulating in newspapers and magazines, Stowe presented a carefully calculated image of herself as a modest, domestic lady and above all as a wife and mother.

"So you want to know something about what sort of a woman I am," she began, "well, if this is any object, you should have statistics free of charge." She went on to describe herself as "a little bit of a woman— somewhat more than 40—about as thin & dry as a pinch of snuff— never very much to look at in my best days—& looking like a used up article now." She then spoke about her marriage, her household, and her children. Her husband Calvin she described as "a man rich in Greek & Hebrew, Latin & Arabic, & alas! rich in nothing else." When she "went to housekeeping," she said, her "entire stock of china for parlour & kitchen was bought for 11 dollars." This lasted for several years until her married brother came to visit when she "thought it best to reinforce the establishment by getting me a tea-set which cost 10 dollars more, & this, I believe, formed my whole stock in trade for some years." But then, she continued, turning to the subject of her seven children, she "was abundantly enriched with wealth of another kind." After discussing the anguish of losing her favorite child to cholera, she described the financial stress that she and Calvin suffered after the bank panic of 1837 and how this led, through the efforts of friends, to her first efforts to write for money:

> Some of my friends pitying my toils, copied & sent some of my little sketches to certain liberally paying annuals, with my name. With the first money that I earned in this way, I bought a feather bed! for as I had married into poverty & without a dowry, & as my husband had only a large library of books, & a great deal of learning, this bed & pillows was thought on the whole, the most profitable investment. After this, I thought I had discovered the philosopher's stone, & when a new carpet or a mattress was going to be needed, or when at the close of the year, it began to be evident that my family accounts, like poor Dora's, *"wouldn't add up"*, then I used to say to my faithful friend & factotum Anna, who shared all my joys & sorrows, "now if you'll keep the babies & attend to all the things in the house for one day, I'll write a piece, & then we shall be out of the scrape", & so I became an authoress.

She then described, as context for her antislavery novel, her experiences with black people in Cincinnati—servants and escaped slaves—and finally turned to the matter of the book's success.

Follen, who was in England at the time, had evidently read about the extraordinary $10,300 payment Stowe received from Jewett for the first three months' sales. "You ask," she said, "with regard to the remuneration which I have received for my work, here in America." Stowe denied that money was a motive in writing the novel. "Having been poor all my life, & expecting to be poor to the end of it, the idea of making anything by a book which I wrote just because I could not help it, never occurred to me. It was therefore, an agreeable surprise to receive ten thousand dollars as the first fruits of 3 months sale." She continued, "I presume as much more is now due." Moreover, she noted that several English publishers were offering her an interest in their editions. "I am very glad of it," she said, "both on account of the value of what they offer, & the value of the example they set in a matter, wherein, I think, justice has been too little regarded." She then quickly explained that she intended to use the money, or much of it, for charitable purposes. "I have very much wished that some permanent memorial of good to the coloured race, might be erected out of the proceeds of a work, which had so unprecedented a sale." She added that her own "share of the profits will be less than that of the publishers either English or American."[31]

The mixture of pride and embarrassment that one can hear in Stowe's response to Follen's query about "remuneration" suggests the awkwardness she felt about her remarkable position as probably the most highly paid author of the day. It was one thing for a genteel domestic lady, the daughter and wife of prominent clergymen, to publish polite sketches or essays or to take up a cause of conscience, but to profit from the activity on such a large scale was quite another matter. Nonetheless, along with denying that money was her motive, Stowe went out of her way to note that another $10,000 was probably due her and then quickly to add that her profits would be less than those of the publishers. This was an issue that bothered her as did the fact that she had no legal claim to copyright in Britain.

The letter to Follen is notable, then, both for the domestic image that Stowe seeks to project and for her pride in her earnings. It is interesting, too, that in the letter much that is private and domestic is couched in commercial diction. This pattern begins when Stowe offers to provide "statistics" about herself "free of charge" and refers to her husband as a man "rich in Greek & Hebrew, Latin & Arabic." It continues with her reference to her household "stock in trade" and to her children as "wealth of another kind." This bleeding of commercial language into domesticity recalls similar patterns in, for example, *Moll Flanders* (1722). There Defoe's protagonist, taking account of her resources as she struggles to thrive, repeatedly reckons her "stock."[32] In Defoe's case the commercial language reflects Moll's entrepreneurial spirit and at times her precarious circumstances. In Stowe's case, where a certain irony is evident, the allusions to trade become a device to portray herself as a modest wife and mother and at the same time suggest her awareness of the ubiquity of commerce. The commercial diction in the letter can thus be understood in relation to her deployment of domesticity in opposition to marketplace values in *Uncle Tom's Cabin*. But the commercial diction, along with the mixture of pride and embarrassment that Stowe evidently felt about her novel's commercial success, also suggests the tension between the ideals espoused in the novel and her career. As well as recalling Defoe, then, the rhetorical instability in Stowe's letter to Follen perhaps also recalls Pope's preface to the authorized edition of his letters in which, as we have seen, the discourse of property mingles uneasily with the discourse of honor. Both Pope and Stowe are of course uncomfortably trying to balance their roles as authors with the proprieties of their social positions. Moreover, in both cases the values that Pope and Stowe promulgated as authors—gentility in his case, domesticity in hers—might seem to ring hollow if the commercial context in which they were being promulgated were considered too closely.

Stowe's commercial success exposed her to charges of hypocrisy both from angry southerners and from northerners who feared that abolitionism would destroy the Union. Thus William J. Grayson, a South Carolina politician, defended slavery in a long poem, *The Hireling and the Slave* (1854)—a title that suggests an equivalence between wage labor and slavery—in which he ridiculed Stowe whom he accused of prostituting her pen and slandering her country. Anxious only about how her "libel" sold, Stowe was, for Grayson, a "moral scavenger," collecting trash about the South and trading "for gold the garbage of her toils."[33] A year earlier the anti-abolitionist Philadelphian, George R. Graham, editor of *Graham's Magazine*, devoted a review essay, called "Black Letters; or Uncle Tom-Foolery in Literature," principally to attacking Stowe. Graham found the book clumsily constructed and poorly written. He objected not only to what he considered Stowe's inaccurate portrait of slavery but also to her damaging indictment of her country, and to the Barnum-like publicity machinery that he saw as having procured the book's extraordinary sales. Finally, he said, "the whole business" should be seen as a commercial, not a literary or political, affair, "for it is a *business*, and nothing more."[34]

Stowe's aggressiveness in seeking to suppress the German-language publisher F. W. Thomas's translation of *Uncle Tom's Cabin* provoked similar attacks from German speakers. "What light," asked one writer, does her insistence on her lawsuit "shed on the character of the 'pious' and 'Christian' Mrs. Stowe?"[35] Another, a staunch abolitionist himself, saw the whole project of American abolitionism rendered suspect by Stowe. "Thus does an American abolitionist propagate her teachings. Will we in Europe finally realize that this abolitionism, at least the whining pietistical abolition of Mrs. Stowe is a humbug and a money business, like Barnum's Sea Tiger or Tom Thumb?"[36] Moreover, the ambiguity in Stowe's position also opened her to Justice Robert Grier's contemptuous dismissal in *Stowe v. Thomas*. Did Mrs. Stowe suppose that her brainchildren, Uncle Tom and Topsy, were her slaves?

* * *

A flood of German immigrants came to the United States in the mid-nineteenth century, and there was a small but significant domestic market for German translations of American literature. It was to take advantage of this market that Stowe authorized a German translation of her novel. Like the original, this was published by John P. Jewett. Meanwhile, F. W. Thomas, a German immigrant and Philadelphia publisher, began issuing a superior translation in his German-language newspaper, *Die Freie Presse*. Evidently Thomas, seeking to avoid the threatened legal action, offered the copyright of his version as a gift to Stowe, but Stowe refused and proceeded with her suit.[37] Probably Stowe's purpose was not just to suppress Thomas's publication but to establish in principle that her copyright extended to translations. She was applauded for doing so by a sympathetic article in the *New York Weekly Tribune*. The *Tribune* expressed doubts as to whether, given the current state of the law, Stowe would prevail. But if she did not, her suit would demonstrate that "a revision of the statute on copyright" was "more than ever necessary."[38]

Mid-nineteenth-century American copyright law in many respects still resembled that of the original English Statute of Anne of 1710 and its American successor, the Copyright Act of 1790. Essentially this law forbade piracy—that is, the literal reprinting of a work or a substantial portion of a work. A key term in the Copyright Act of 1831 was "copy," which descended from the old printers' and stationers' term for the right to print a particular title, but which now had come to mean, in the more familiar modern sense, a "reproduction." Thus the 1831 act forbade the printing or publishing of any copy of a book without the consent of the copyright holder. But was a translation a "copy"?

Traditionally, adaptations such as abridgments were regarded as noninfringing unless they were merely "colorable" products designed to evade the law. An abridgment, after all, required labor and judgment and might be seen as performing a useful service beyond that of the original.[39] There was one very early case, *Burnet v. Chetwood* (1720), in which an English lord chancellor had opined that a translation could perhaps be considered a new work "on account that the translator has bestowed his care and pains upon it," but this hedged statement was never taken as definitive.[40] Translations from the classics and foreign authors had long been treated as protected, but would the author of a novel written in English retain the right to a translation into a foreign language? George Ticknor Curtis, the author of the leading American copyright treatise of the antebellum period, had recently expressed the opinion that an author did retain the translation right, but he had acknowledged that in both England and America the question had never been directly addressed and therefore was unresolved.[41]

The issue of the translation right went to the heart of the conception of copyright. What did a literary work consist of and what did the law protect? What was the subject of copyright? The classical understanding was framed by William Blackstone in his authoritative *Commentaries on the Laws of England* (1765–1769), where he defined the subject of copyright, the author's "original literary compositions," as a fusion of "sentiment" and "language." The "same conceptions, cloathed in the same words, must necessarily be the same composition," Blackstone wrote. Over this object of property, the author exercised dominion.[42] Blackstone's use of the common eighteenth-century metaphor of the "dress" of language, an ancient trope going back to the Roman rhetorician Quintillian, was the hinge on which his formulation turned. This formula was designed to meet the objections that ideas should be allowed to circulate and that in any case they were too amorphous to be reserved. Not ideas alone but ideas realized in language—ideas made, in a sense, concrete—were what the law protected. There might of course be cases in which questions of whether two works really were the "same" arose—for example, cases in which a publisher seeking to evade charges of infringement changed the text somewhat—but the principle, as Blackstone framed it, seemed clear. This principle underlay the traditional application of copyright doctrine. When Alexander Pope sued Edmund Curll in 1741, for example, it was for the literal reprinting of his letters.

But in the early nineteenth century, as Oren Bracha has shown, in the context of technological developments and the emergence of a national market in the United States—the same developments that made the phenomenal sales of *Uncle Tom's Cabin* possible—the traditional doctrine of copyright had begun to come under pressure.[43] Traditionally, copyright had been founded on the concept of the author's labor and genius—it was what an author put into a work that gave it value—but in the early 1840s, the emphasis was shifting from the author to the work and its market value. Thus Justice Joseph Story, one of the most influential figures in antebellum American law, pressed an expansive reconception of copyright in the landmark case of *Folsom v. Marsh* (1841). This case, which pitted the publishers of a popular biography of George Washington against the original publisher of Washington's letters, turned on the question of what would be a "fair use" of such letters. In his decision, Story found that the distinction between piracy and fair use could be understood as a matter of market value. A piracy occurred, he said, when "so much is taken, that the value of the original is sensibly diminished."[44]

Piracy had always been understood as illegal reprinting. *Folsom*—along with a number of other cases—suggested that the emphasis was shifting from "identity" to "value." Naturally, such a reconception of infringement analysis in terms of market value put pressure on the notion of the work as well, the "subject" of copyright, for now the discussion had to be refocused to consider not just the words of which a protected work was composed but what of value was transmitted by the words. Thus in his treatise Curtis offered an understanding of the subject of copyright quite different from Blackstone's. Using Blackstone's own metaphor, Curtis asked whether "the mere act of giving to a literary composition the new dress of another language" meant that reproduction was permitted?

The property of the original author embraces something more than the words in which his sentiments are conveyed. It includes the ideas and sentiments themselves, the plan of the work, and the mode of treating and exhibiting the subject. In such cases, his right may be invaded, in whatever form his own property may be reproduced. The new language in which his composition is clothed by translation affords only a different medium of communicating that in which he has an exclusive property; and to attribute to such a new medium the effect of entire originality, is to declare that a change of dress alone annihilates the most important subject of his right of property. It reduces his right to the narrow limits of an exclusive privilege of publishing in that idiom alone in which he first publishes. But we do not find that his privilege is thus circumscribed; because a mere change of phraseology is not held to justify the adoption of matter that is under the protection of the law.[45]

As this passage from Curtis suggests, the concept of the "work" was now becoming more problematic. Once again questions related to the protection of ideas or sentiments were being raised.

The case presented on behalf of Stowe by her Philadelphia lawyers, Samuel H. Perkins and Samuel C. Perkins, followed Curtis in arguing that the author's rights went beyond the protection of the literal words of a work. An author was not just a writer of words but the creator of "the ideas—the thought—the plan—the arrangement—the style of expression" incorporated in a book. "The exclusive right to sell these is what is secured by copyright." A translation attempted to convey the original work—ideas and thoughts, shadings, manner and form of expression—as exactly as possible. "All changes, all variations in any of these particulars, are failures, and are studiously guarded against." Language, they argued, was merely accidental, a window onto the author's thoughts, a sign of the author's ideas. "A perfect translation will present the identical creation and mental production in a way that the sign is never thought of." A translation was an attempt to capture the entire work and thus was an infringement. After developing this line of thought with examples and providing a discussion of precedents, the argument climaxed with the citation of Curtis's treatise.[46] In effect, then, Stowe's lawsuit was a test case to see if a new doctrine of copyright as articulated by Curtis, the notion that copyright extended to more than the particular language in which the author's ideas were conveyed, would be ratified in court.

The defendant's response was argued by Benjamin H. Brewster, a future attorney general, and Charles Goepp. Brewster and Goepp reminded the court that the key term of the Copyright Act was "copy," used in the sense of a reprint and that "thought, independent of its language, cannot be protected." The issue was not how much of Stowe's book Thomas had taken. "We have confessedly taken not a part, but the whole. We concede and we boast that we have taken every syllable, comma and i-dot of the original." The only question was what they had done with the book. They had translated it, not copied it. A translation was not a "servile and mechanical imitation" but a new work in itself, one that "depends entirely for its success upon its individuality, and for that reason, is original with the translator." A translation could not be understood as a "copy" in the sense used by the statute. As for George Ticknor Curtis's opinion on translations, the defendant cited the 1823 English treatise of Richard Godson, who reported that translations had been held to be new works. Curtis's treatise, though valuable, the response claimed, "goes to lengths quite untenable on the subject of protection to authors."[47]

The Plaintiff's argument was couched in terms of "property." Stowe alleged that it was a property right that Thomas had infringed. The Defendant's argument, on the other hand, spoke of copyright as a "monopoly." Implicit in this difference in language was the long-standing debate reaching back to the earliest days of copyright over whether copyright was a natural right, a property like any other, or a limited grant created by the state. Both the landmark British case of *Donaldson v. Becket* (1774) and the landmark U.S. case of *Wheaton v. Peters* (1834) had determined that copyright was positive law, a limited monopoly. Nonetheless, the more expansive natural-right position continued to color discussions of copyright theory, and in fact the language of "monopoly" was, in the middle of the nineteenth century, becoming more rare. Godson, the authority cited by the defendant, began his 1823 treatise with a general treatment of monopolies that served as the foundation for his discussion of patents and copyrights. These were limited monopolies that he regarded as beneficial rather than irksome.[48]

On the other hand, Curtis, who represented the new and more expansive doctrine, began his treatise with a general treatment of the rights of authors as founded in natural law and then proceeded to a discussion of legislation limiting the term of copyright as a compromise with the underlying right.[49] If copyright was a right founded in natural law, then it was the limitation of the right that had to be justified. If it was a monopoly grant, however, it was the grant, not the limitation that required justification.

Stowe v. Thomas was heard in Circuit Court for the Eastern District of Pennsylvania with Justice Robert C. Grier presiding in his capacity as a Circuit Court judge.[50] At this time justices of the U.S. Supreme Court also served as Circuit Court judges and Grier, a Pennsylvanian, had been appointed to the Supreme Court in 1846 in part on the basis of his knowledge of Pennsylvania land law so that he could serve effectively in the Third District. He was also appointed because of his support of the slave laws. President James J. Polk, himself a Southerner and slave owner, had been assured that Grier was "hostile to the mad spirit of abolitionism" and that he would uphold the "constitutional guarantees of the right of the master to his slave."[51] In fact Grier turned out to be a particularly vigorous and committed enforcer of the Fugitive Slave Law, who, as Homestead observes, used his charges to juries in cases involving fugitive slaves "to pontificate on the importance of enforcement of the law to the preservation of the union."[52] Thus in an 1850 case that concerned two families of slaves who had escaped while being transported through Pennsylvania to Maryland, Grier told the jury that the Constitution and the law demanded that fugitive slaves who had escaped from one state to another be returned to their masters. Those unwilling to acknowledge their obligations, he added sarcastically, "should migrate to Canada" or some other country "whose institutions do not infringe upon their tender consciences." There were "unhappy agitators" who with "mad zeal" were plotting the ruin of the Union, but the "time has not yet come," he said, "when the jury box will be contaminated by men whose moral perceptions are so perverted by a strange hallucination that they will not render a true verdict according to their oaths and the law of the land."[53] A few years after the *Uncle Tom's Cabin* case, Grier provided the crucial fifth vote in the notorious *Dred Scott* decision striking down Congress's authority to

Justice Robert C. Grier. Photograph by Mathew Brady. Courtesy of the Brady-Handy Photograph Collection Prints and Photographs Division, Library of Congress. LC-BH82-4590.

ban slavery in the territories.[54] It was certainly not a good omen for Harriet Beecher Stowe that her case was to be decided in Justice Grier's court.

For the most part Grier's decision in favor of Thomas was couched in traditional terms. An author might be said to be the creator of ideas as well as the particular combination of words in which they were represented, but once published all the author's conceptions became the common property of readers. Employing the conventional metaphor of language as the dress of thought, Grier affirmed that, after publication, the author's right no longer lay in creations as abstractions "but only in the concrete form which he has given them, and the language in which he has clothed them." Citing Blackstone, Grier repeated the traditional formula for the nature of the work protected. "Its identity does not consist merely in the ideas, knowledge or information communicated, but in the same conceptions clothed in the same words, which make it the same composition." From this it followed that the same conceptions "clothed in another language"—a translation—could not be considered a "copy" of the protected work.[55]

After citing authorities on the matter of translation from the judges' decisions in the classic English case of *Millar v. Taylor* (1769), Grier went on to the remarkable concluding section in which he turned the subject matter of Stowe's novel against her copyright claim.

> By the publication of Mrs. Stowe's book, the creations of the genius and imagination of the author have become as much public property as those of Homer and Cervantes. Uncle Tom and Topsy are as much publici juris as Don Quixote and Sancho Panza. All her conceptions and inventions may be used and abused by imitators, play-rights, and poetasters. They are no longer her own—those who have purchased her book, may clothe them in English doggerel, in German or Chinese prose. Her absolute dominion and property in the creations of her genius and imagination have been voluntarily relinquished. All that now remains is the copyright of her book; the exclusive right to print, reprint and vend it, and those only can be called infringers of her rights, or pirates of her property, who are guilty of printing, publishing, importing or vending without her license, "copies of her book." A translation may, in loose phraseology, be called a transcript or copy of her thoughts and conceptions, but in no correct sense can it be called a copy of her book.[56]

In this passage Stowe's characters Uncle Tom and Topsy are made to stand for her novel as the creations of her "genius and imagination," just as Cervantes's knight and squire are made to stand for *Don Quixote*. Don Quixote and Sancho Panza may perhaps metonymically represent Cervantes's novel, but Uncle Tom and Topsy—particularly Topsy—do not represent *Uncle Tom's Cabin*, a book that also includes Eliza, Harry, and George and prominent white characters such as Little Eva and Simon Legree, in quite the same way. Grier has perhaps chosen Tom and Topsy for alliteration but even more because they are black slaves. Does Stowe suppose that Tom and Topsy remain her property even after she has published and thus voluntarily relinquished her rights in them for public use? On the contrary, Tom and Topsy have now become "public property" and may be "used and abused"—Grier's choice of terms is savagely pointed—by anyone who chooses. Moreover, reverting to the trope of language as the dress of thought, Grier asserts that Stowe's characters may now be clothed in any language a purchaser chose, including English doggerel or Chinese as well as German prose.

Grier was perhaps hurling back at Stowe the question that was implicit in her novel. Who owns Uncle Tom? The various masters who buy or sell him in the course of the story? God? Or Tom himself? So far as the law of copyright was concerned, Grier responded, no one "owned" Uncle Tom. He belonged to the public at large. In casting his decision in the provocative language of slavery and ownership, Grier may well have been influenced by the essay on "Black Letters; or Uncle Tom-Foolery in Literature" that his fellow Philadelphian, George R. Graham, had published in *Graham's Magazine* less than a year earlier. In that essay the anti-abolitionist Graham had sneered that those who would not have a slave to till their ground nevertheless "use him pretty severely in the press-room."[57] But Grier hardly needed to go to Graham for the idea of turning Stowe's abolitionist position against her copyright claim. The slavery association had a long history in relation to writing, publishing, and the book trade. The Roman poet Martial had equated the writer's act of lifting his hand from the page to "manumission," the formal act whereby the master lifted his hand from a slave's shoulder to signify liberation.[58] Likewise, since the late seventeenth century, writers for money had been portrayed as "slaves to the quill."[59] In his famous speech in the House of Lords in *Donaldson v. Becket* (1774), Lord Camden extended this trope when he sneered at the avarice of the booksellers who were seeking to establish that copyright was perpetual. If they succeeded, he declared, all "learning" would be locked up in the booksellers' hands "till the public become as much their slaves, as their own hackney compilers."[60] Moreover, in the first half of the nineteenth century, when American publishers could freely reprint British books, the slavery association was a favorite of copyright reformers who often spoke of American reprinters as "slave traders."[61] Thus when Stowe was celebrated at a public meeting in Scotland on the occasion of her triumphal visit to Britain in 1853, one of the speakers recalled that, before *Uncle Tom's Cabin*, the British had been accustomed to despise Americans and American literature, alleging that Americans "lived entirely on plunder—the plunder of poor slaves, and of poor British authors." But now, "Let us hear no more of the poverty of American brains, or the barrenness of American literature."[62] Of course Grier's opinion in *Stowe v. Thomas* was essentially complete without his play on the idea of Stowe as a slave owner. Grier's deployment of Stowe's abolitionist politics against her copyright claim was mere gratuitous insult.[63]

In addition to drawing on the metaphor of slavery, Grier was also of course drawing on the trope of writing as childbearing and the associated idea that the work itself might, like a child come of age, acquire a life independent of its author. Thus we can note that the original terms of copyright protection set by the Statute of Anne in 1710 and copied by the U.S. copyright statute of 1790—fourteen years for new works with the possibility of renewal for another fourteen, twenty-one years for works already in print—probably relate to ancient formulas having to do with emancipation. Seven years is the traditional term of an apprenticeship, a formula that is as old as the Book of Genesis. Fourteen is twice seven. Twenty-one, the traditional age of majority, is three times seven. Implicit in the original copyright term was the notion that, like a child, a protected work would eventually be emancipated.[64] Grier, however, was focusing on the subject of copyright rather than the term. Unlike Curtis who had insisted that the author's property included the substance of the work as well as the form, Grier insisted that the author's rights did not extend to the substance. By the act of publication "the creations of her genius and imagination" had been emancipated, the author's "absolute dominion" had been "voluntarily relinquished." What remained was merely a right of printing and reprinting located in the specific text she had written. How, in any case, could an author protect her ideas? Once released to the world, ideas were mobile and fleeting. Grier, the enforcer of the Fugitive Slave

Law, did not make explicit the somewhat problematic implications of his own indulgence in metaphor. Metaphors inevitably cut two ways. If Stowe's dominion over her characters was problematic, so was dominion over men. "Fugitive properties" were finally impossible to shackle and restrain.[65]

Grier's opinion in the *Uncle Tom's Cabin* case proved to be, as Oren Bracha puts it, "the swan song of copyright's traditional paradigm," the doctrine that what copyright protected was merely the right to print a specified text.[66] While Stowe's case was pending, the *New York Weekly Tribune*, as we have seen, remarked that if she did not prevail, her suit would demonstrate the need for a revision of the copyright statute. Seventeen years later Congress did indeed pass a revision of the copyright act in which authors were granted, among other things, the right to reserve translations of their works.[67] With this legislation Congress in effect overturned Grier's decision. Nine years later in 1879 when Eaton S. Drone published what became for many years the new authoritative treatise on U.S. copyright, he included a long discussion refuting Grier. "Of the reported copyright decisions of England and America, there is none which is more clearly wrong, unjust, and absurd than that in *Stowe v. Thomas*," Drone wrote.[68] An author's right, he said, articulating the new doctrine that had emerged in the previous forty years, "can be secured only by protecting not merely the form of his production, but also its substance. Hence the principle has been judicially recognized, and may be regarded as established, that the unauthorized appropriation of the substance, in whole or in part, of a copyrighted literary composition, to the injury of its owner, is piracy."[69] Drone, too, employed the old dress of thought metaphor but in a way that followed Curtis rather than Blackstone or Grier. Curtis had dismissed the idea that "a change of dress alone" annihilates the author's property in a work. Likewise, Drone asserted that other than the new language in which the original is rendered, the translator creates nothing. "He takes the entire creation of another, and simply clothes it in a new dress."[70]

* * *

The protected literary work, Curtis and Drone's use of the old metaphor implied, was no longer a specific text—"the same conceptions, cloathed in the same words," as Blackstone put it—but now the body beneath the dress. Justice Grier's position had been that Stowe did not own ideas or conceptions. Once she had published, the "creations of her genius and imagination" were free for anyone to use or abuse as he or she saw fit. Following the traditional copyright paradigm, Grier had no difficulty in specifying the limited nature of Stowe's right. But when copyright was understood as extending beyond the right to print and reprint to the "substance" of the work the question of the subject of copyright immediately became more problematic. What was the "body" beneath the dress of language? The metaphor of the body conveyed a reassuring sense of solidity but how was the protected substance to be defined? Justice Joseph Story, who was instrumental in establishing the changed conception of copyright, had some sense of the difficulties that were emerging. In *Folsom v. Marsh* he remarked that patents and copyrights—what we now call, in something of an oxymoron, "intellectual property"—"approach, nearer than any other class of cases belonging to forensic discussions, to what may be called the metaphysics of the law, where the distinctions are, or at least may be, very subtle and refined, and, sometimes, almost evanescent."[71]

In *Pope v. Curll*, Lord Chancellor Hardwicke had made a distinction between the physical property in a letter—the ink and paper—and the author's intangible property, the copyright. Pure signs, separated from any material support, became the author's protected property. In the 1870 Copyright Act, with its tacit reversal of Justice Grier's decision in *Stowe v. Thomas*, copyright doctrine moved another step toward abstraction, toward "metaphysics," for now not even the particular signs in which the author "clothed" his thought were the delimiters of the author's property. It was at this time, as Bracha has indicated, that the modern version of the idea/expression dichotomy—the doctrine that copyright protects only the expression of ideas, not ideas themselves—became important. It developed, Bracha suggests, exactly in the period when the scope of copyright protection was expanding beyond the old right to reprint a particular text. "The more abstract and broad copyright protection became, the stronger was the insistence that it was limited to concrete expressions. The more copyright came to resemble general control of an abstract and elusive object that could cover a manifold of forms, the more fundamental became the assertion that all ideas were left absolutely free for public use."[72]

The notion of "concrete" expression as distinguished from "abstract" ideas is of course a metaphor. "Expression" may be particular and singular, but it is not a physical object. Likewise, the notion of a writing as a kind of "child" is a metaphor, and so is the notion of language as the "dress of thought." Stowe's characters were not of course her slaves, and publication was not equivalent to emancipation. Indeed, the very concept of literary "property," which depends on the notion that works have boundaries that may, like the concrete boundaries marking off a house or a field, be transgressed, is itself a metaphor. Like many other cultural constructions, copyright doctrine is framed in metaphors. Moreover, as copyright has expanded and become more abstract—as it has become, in Justice Story's term, increasingly "metaphysical"—so the underlying metaphors have become more fluid and amorphous. What indeed is the "body"—slave or free—beneath the dress of language? How in considering the "substance" of a work does one distinguish between abstract idea and concrete expression?

The development of copyright has also been entangled with the development of the author as a professional. Alexander Pope made a career through marketable performances of his status as a gentleman who stood aloof from the marketplace. Harriet Beecher Stowe's public presentation of herself as a lady involved a similar suppression of her status as a professional. Stowe was of course more self-effacing than Pope. Her authority, as she presented it, came from the substance of her message rather than from her wit and learning. *Uncle Tom's Cabin* mattered because it was true, not because it was artful. Thus in *A Key to Uncle Tom's Cabin* she declared that her novel, "more, perhaps, than any other work of fiction that ever was written, has been a collection and arrangement of real incidents,—of actions really performed, of words and expressions really uttered,—grouped together with reference to a general result, in the same manner that the mosaic artist groups his fragments of various stones into one general picture. His is a mosaic of gems,—this is a mosaic of facts."[73] It was as a portrait of slavery that *Uncle Tom's Cabin* was to be judged. Moreover, as we have seen, Stowe repeatedly insisted that *Uncle Tom's Cabin* was a gift and a responsibility bestowed upon her by a divine power. But, as we have also seen, Stowe was at the same time, like Pope, a canny professional who was concerned with her rights and her profits. Moreover, like Pope she employed the law in an attempt to assert and expand her rights. Stowe was accused of hypocrisy because she made money from her novel. Likewise, Pope was accused of dishonesty because he manipulated the image of himself in his letters. But in both cases, I think, what the accusations reveal is less an indication of some kind of moral failing than a sign of the essentially performative nature of authorship in the modern era. Clearly Pope was selling himself. But Stowe, too, was in a sense selling herself, not as a wit but as the modest instrument through which a great truth about the evil of slavery was revealed. The authorial roles that Pope and Stowe embraced obviously differed in multiple respects—as their genders, nationalities, and historical moments differed as well—but both Pope and Stowe, as authors, found themselves playing out sometimes convoluted dramas of identity.

CHAPTER FOUR

Creating Oscar Wilde

Burrow-Giles v. Sarony (1884)

CONGRESS extended copyright protection to include photographs in 1865. Some twenty years later, however, the protection of photographs was challenged when the Burrow-Giles Lithographic Company published copies of the photographer Napoleon Sarony's portrait of Oscar Wilde, and Sarony sued. Burrow-Giles contended that the legislation was invalid, arguing that a photograph was merely a mechanical production and therefore Sarony was not an author entitled to copyright protection. The Supreme Court, however, ruled in Sarony's favor, declaring that he was indeed entitled to protection. This was the first case in which the Supreme Court addressed the legal definition of authorship, and it has influenced American copyright law to the present day. Interestingly, Wilde himself played no part in the case. He was never deposed, he did not testify, and, so far as is known, he never even commented on the matter. The case was concerned solely with Wilde's image and Sarony's claim to have the exclusive right to publish and sell it. But Wilde's celebrity and its commercial value were crucial elements of the matter and *Burrow-Giles* is interesting, too, for the way it refracts the emergence of the commodified self and the problematic notion of personality dissociated from person.[1]

Although largely forgotten today, in 1882 when he photographed Wilde in New York, Napoleon Sarony was no less a celebrity than his English subject. Radically different from Wilde in appearance, Sarony shared Wilde's taste for dramatic self-presentation. Wilde was a large and fleshy man, six feet three inches tall with shoulder-length hair, who delighted in wearing outlandish but elegant costumes. The tiny photographer, on the other hand, was bald and bandy-legged. Almost a dwarf at five feet one inch, Sarony enjoyed making a display of his oddity by entering a room in a crouch and walking about in that position with his wig pulled down to his eyebrows. Perhaps playing on his name's martial associations, he sported a prominent beard and long, military-style mustaches together with high-top campaign boots that reached halfway to the hip and a calfskin waistcoat worn hairy side out. His trademark was an exotic red fez that he wore indoors and out. Parading the avenues with his wife, Louie, who was much taller than him and who also wore striking costumes, Sarony was regarded as one of the sights of New York, and his regular walks were accompanied by excited signs of recognition like those accorded a celebrated actor. One newspaper essay of the period described him as a Broadway landmark.[2]

Born in Quebec in 1821, the year Napoleon died on St. Helena, Sarony was named in Bonaparte's honor by his English father, a lithographer who had fought against Napoleon with the Austrian army. Sarony came to New York as a young man in the 1830s where he founded a lithography firm and was successful enough to withdraw from business to study art in Paris in 1858. In the 1860s when the Civil War radically reduced the income he was receiving from his American investments, Sarony moved to England, where he established himself in the new trade of commercial wet plate photography. This was a technology developed in the 1850s that employed glass negatives. It was relatively inexpensive compared to the traditional daguerreotype. Equally important, the glass negative allowed for an unlimited number of positive prints to be made from a single negative and thus lent itself to the mass production of popular images such as portraits of celebrities. In 1866, at the end of the Civil War, Sarony returned to New York where he set up, first on Broadway and later at Union Square, as a specialist in theatrical and celebrity portraits. The core of his trade was the production of "cabinet cards," 3¾-by-5½-inch images mounted on 4¼-by-6½-inch cards. Generally selling at retail for 35 cents each, these were popular as collectibles that could be displayed in albums or on stands. They were printed in quantity—sometimes Sarony produced multiple negatives in order to be able to meet the demand for particularly popular subjects such as Sarah Bernhardt and Lillie Langtry—and then marketed from his studio and through dealers who sold them at theaters and hotels and by mail. Each card was typically branded with Sarony's large and distinctive signature below the image.

Napoleon Sarony, self-portrait. Courtesy of The Harry Ransom Center, The University of Texas at Austin.

Sarony's trade depended on the burgeoning cult of celebrity that gathered momentum in postbellum America. During his career Sarony was said to have photographed more than thirty thousand celebrities, including presidents, statesmen, and writers, as well as actors and actresses, and perhaps two hundred thousand members of the general public. Among his best-known theatrical subjects in addition to Bernhardt and Langtry were Edwin Forrest, Ellen Terry, Helena Modjeska, and Edwin Booth. Sarony also photographed Buffalo Bill, Henry Wadsworth Longfellow, Walt Whitman, Mark Twain, and Harriet Beecher

Stowe as well as famous wrestlers and acrobats. It was said that in the latter part of the century practically every person of note who visited New York passed through his studio. Sarony himself claimed that over two hundred thousand sitters had sat in one particular carved chair.[3]

Sarony was of course not the first to achieve celebrity by portraying celebrities. More than a hundred years earlier in the mid-1700s, Joshua Reynolds anticipated this strategy by painting actors such as David Garrick, Sarah Siddons, and Fanny Abington, writers such as Samuel Johnson, Laurence Sterne, and Oliver Goldsmith, and celebrated courtesans such as Kitty Fisher and Nelly O'Brien. Subjects such as Garrick and Siddons were delighted to sit for Reynolds who then exhibited their portraits at the Royal Academy, adding to their fame and stature even as they ratified his standing as an artist. Sarony's closest antecedent, however, was Mathew Brady, today the best-remembered American photographer of the nineteenth century. Brady, too, sought to achieve fame and social standing by photographing notables, including nearly all the American presidents from John Quincy Adams to William McKinley. But whereas Brady recorded solemn images of illustrious men marketed to an elite audience, Sarony specialized in portraits of entertainers designed for a mass market. Thus, for example, in one popular photograph, Sarony showed the contemporary strongman Eugen Sandow, nude except for a fig leaf, standing on a leopard skin in the posture of the Farnese Hercules. In another he showed the acrobat Leona Dare in her skimpy circus costume grasping a trapeze. Like many of Reynolds's theatrical portraits, Sarony represented actors and actors costumed in the roles that made them famous, including James O'Neill, the father of Eugene O'Neill, in his signature role as the Count of Monte Cristo. By 1882, when Wilde came to New York, Brady was almost forgotten and Sarony dominated the photographic scene.[4]

Sarony's prominence was objectively realized in his large establishment at 37 Union Square in the heart of the contemporary entertainment district. This was a five-story building that rented for the enormous sum of $8,000 a year, and served as both a studio and a production facility. Perhaps modeled in part after the Boulevard des Capucines studio of the contemporary Parisian photographer Gaspard Félix Tournachon, known as "Nadar," the building was marked by a huge sign bearing the same flowing signature used to brand the cabinet cards. The ground floor had showcase windows displaying the latest celebrity images; the middle floors were used for manufacture and storage. Clients and celebrities rode an elevator to the top floor where they entered Sarony's famous reception room, fitted out with exotic items reminiscent of a renaissance cabinet of curiosities. Sarony's collection included an open-jawed crocodile hung from the ceiling, an Egyptian mummy protected by chicken wire, medieval arms and armor, exotic Toltec and Aztec antiquities, Japanese vases and metal castings, American Indian headdresses, scalps and other curiosities, stuffed birds and animals, and stores of carved furniture, statuary, and musical instruments. One contemporary described the room as a "sort of dumping-ground of the dealers in unsalable idols, tattered tapestry, and indigent crocodiles."[5] This collection had a utilitarian function insofar as it provided settings and properties for Sarony's portraits, but perhaps most important it functioned as an advertisement of the photographer's cosmopolitan artistic sensibility. As a contemporary article remarked, Sarony was "the first New York photographer to turn his reception room into an artist's studio."[6]

From the reception room, sitters ascended to a loft fitted with skylights and windows as well as curtains and screens that were used to control the illumination. The most conspicuous object was the large studio camera. The dominant figure, however, was Sarony who ruled the studio as an impresario, employing a repertoire of tricks to elicit the poses and expressions that he believed would bring out his sitters' distinctive characters. Sarony bragged that he knew nothing about the mechanical or chemical aspects of photography. His stock-in-trade, he said, was composition, grace of outline, and suggestive light and shade.[7] He would dress, light, and pose his subject, then turn away and gaze out the window while his assistant Benjamin Richardson exposed the plate. Eliciting personality, he insisted, was an art that belonged exclusively to him rather than to his sitters. In a famous anecdote, Sarony told the story of the American theatrical sensation Adah Isaacs Menken complaining to Richardson that all attempts to photograph her in her signature role as Mazeppa—a somewhat scandalous trouser role—had been unsuccessful. Menken demanded that Sarony take her picture in eight different poses that she would choose for herself. Sarony agreed on the condition that she would also allow him to photograph her in eight poses of his own design. Sarony first showed her the pictures of her own posing. Menken exclaimed, "They are perfectly horrible; I shall never have another photograph taken of myself as Mazeppa as long as I live." Then he presented her with the pictures that he had designed. "She threw her arms around me and exclaimed: 'Oh, you dear, delightful, little man, I am going to kiss you for that,' and she did."[8] As Sarony put it in an 1896 interview, the essential point in achieving a revealing portrait was something mystical, a "current of magnetism or of sympathy—whatever you choose to call it, between artist and subject." To produce an image that captured the sitter's spirit, confidence was essential, "the surrender of self on the part of the sitter."[9]

In addition to Richardson, his operator who remained with him throughout his career, Sarony employed a staff to manufacture and mount the portraits and to manage the practical details of his large business. He himself, the man who as one essayist put it, "took our beloved science out of the rut and placed it on the pedestal of art," was beyond such concerns.[10] But even as he basked in his carefully wrought reputation as an artist with a camera, Sarony complained that photography was keeping him from more important work. "All day long," he confessed to an interviewer, "I must pose and arrange for these eternal photographs. They *will* have me. Nobody but me will do; while I burn, I ache, I die, for something that is truly art. All my art in the photograph I value as nothing. I want to make pictures out of myself, to group a thousand shapes that crowd my imagination. This relieves me, the other oppresses me."[11]

In fact Sarony painted and sketched throughout his life and he belonged to multiple artists' clubs, among them the Kit Kat, which met in Sarony's studio, the Palette, the Salmagundi, the Arcadian, the Lotos, and the Tile, which promulgated the Victorian aesthetic movement in America. Moreover, late in his career, Sarony attempted to turn the "shapes crowding his imagination" to commercial account by publishing a series titled *Sarony's Living Pictures*. Issued monthly for about a year, these portfolios combined mildly erotic photographs with freehand charcoal work and painted backgrounds. Some were modeled after paintings by nineteenth-century artists such as William-Adolphe Bouguereau; others represented his own designs. Titles included

Cupid on Watch and *The Butterfly*, both fanciful nudes of young girls outfitted with wings, and, for those with more mature tastes in women, *The Birth of Venus* and *The Siren*. As C. M. Fairbanks, who provided commentary for the portfolios, explained, in Sarony's photographs the painter's dream is "made real, and with a fidelity to nature and a regard for the beauty of line and form such as must be both the despair and the high aim of every idealist in art."[12] Thus the portfolios sought to fuse the real and the ideal. In this they echoed the theory that informed the cabinet card portraits as well, the desire to use the world of the visible to create an image that, beautiful in itself, acquired depth and significance by capturing the essence of something unseen, the sitter's personality or soul.

* * *

Oscar Wilde arrived in New York harbor on the steamship *Arizona* on the evening of January 2, 1882. He was immediately besieged by a crowd of American reporters who had hired a launch to interview the famous aesthete about his Atlantic crossing and get him to say something quotable. The headline that emerged—"Mr. Wilde Disappointed with the Atlantic"—was probably fabricated from a remark reported by one of his fellow passengers, but it cleverly served to suggest Wilde's supposedly exquisite connoisseurship of all things beautiful or sublime. It also helped to frame him as the latest in the series of celebrity marvels—domestic celebrities such as Buffalo Bill Cody and imported notables such as Sarah Bernhardt—to present themselves to the American public. It was the next day, January 3, that Wilde disembarked and reportedly made his famous comment to a customs officer: "I have nothing to declare but genius."[13]

Wilde was brought to New York by the British impresario Richard D'Oyly Carte who, in addition to producing the great Gilbert and Sullivan collaborations, operated a New York concert and lecture agency. In the absence of a copyright agreement with the United States, D'Oyly Carte had been unable to prevent the widespread pirating of *H.M.S. Pinafore* after its London premiere in 1878. To preempt imitators, D'Oyly Carte opened *The Pirates of Penzance*, the next Gilbert and Sullivan show, in New York in December 1879 prior to its London premiere. *Patience*, however, opened in London. It may be that D'Oyly Carte thought that this show, which mocked the English aesthetic movement, was too local in appeal to open in New York. The comic protagonist is Reginald Bunthorne, a poet besieged by lovesick maidens, who is portrayed as in competition with a rival aesthete, Archibald Grosvenor. Bunthorne and Grosvenor are generalized comic figures rather than direct portraits of individuals. Nonetheless, Bunthorne particularly evoked Wilde, who was known for giving parties attended by the most beautiful women in London, including Lillie Langtry. Grosvenor evoked the recently founded Grosvenor Gallery, which featured the work of "aesthetic" artists such as Wilde's friend and rival, James McNeil Whistler.[14]

After the smashing success of *Patience* in London in April 1881, D'Oyly Carte arranged to bring the show to America the following September. Shortly after the New York opening, D'Oyly Carte contacted Wilde with a proposal that he make a series of appearances in America. D'Oyly Carte's plan was synergetic. He would use Wilde's notoriety to publicize *Patience* and establish the authenticity of the D'Oyly Carte production while at the same time *Patience* would help to create an audience for Wilde's lectures. Negotiating through his New York manager, Colonel W. F. Morse, D'Oyly Carte offered to cover Wilde's expenses and to share equally the profits from his appearances, first in New York and then in other parts of the country. Wilde, who had been living beyond his means, readily accepted. Part of the agreement was that Wilde should appear in a suitable costume. Wilde, who had always liked dressing up, immediately ordered a number of outfits for his tour. These included a velvet jacket to be worn with knee breeches and silk stockings—an aristocratic style last popular in the eighteenth century—pumps, a cape, and, for warmth in the harsh American winter, an elaborate fur-lined and fur-trimmed overcoat. According to a newspaper report published some years after the fact, the agreement between D'Oyly Carte and Wilde specified that Wilde should wear his "esthetic costume" in all public places and that he should not cut his hair until the expiration of his lecturing contract.[15]

Shortly after his arrival in New York, Morse displayed Wilde wearing his velvet coat, knee breeches, and silk stockings in a box at the theater where *Patience* was playing. In London, Bunthorne had been made up with curly hair and a monocle to resemble Whistler, a strategy perhaps designed to counter direct identification with Wilde. Now in

New York the comic lead was wigged and dressed to resemble Wilde, and the audience had the experience of being able to turn its gaze from the stage to the box to compare the character with the celebrity. Several days later Wilde, again in breeches and stockings, gave his much anticipated lecture at fashionable Chickering Hall. Titled "The English Renaissance," a reference not to the period of Shakespeare but to the renewal of poetry and painting in the English aesthetic movement, Wilde's lecture was a rather humorless manifesto, largely drawn from his Oxford mentors Ruskin and Pater, insisting upon the transcendent values of beauty and art. The world of art, Wilde proclaimed, was a realm absolutely separate from the world of fact. "Into the secure and sacred house of Beauty the true artist will admit nothing that is harsh or disturbing, nothing that gives pain, nothing that is debatable, nothing about which men argue."[16] The genuine artist was a man set apart by his distinctness, "an individuality remote from that of ordinary men."[17] For the artist there was "but one time, the artistic moment; but one law, the law of form; but one land, the land of Beauty."[18] The modern incarnation of the spirit of art, Wilde claimed, was Keats in whose "Ode on a Grecian Urn" art "found its most secure and faultless expression."[19] But, standing in his breeches and silk stockings with his long hair flowing to his shoulders, it was obvious that Wilde was presenting himself as art's latest avatar.

We do not know whether Napoleon Sarony was present at the Chickering Hall lecture, but if so he might well have reflected that Wilde's representation of art creating an ideal world would aptly describe the studied celebrity portraits that he created in his studio. In any case, Sarony had by this time met Wilde. Several days before the lecture, Morse brought Wilde to Sarony's Union Square establishment to be photographed. "A picturesque subject, indeed!" Sarony is reported to have exclaimed when the aesthete, his flowing hair parted in the middle, arrived carrying a white cane. Sarony took at least twenty-seven images of Wilde in different postures and costumes, first in his heavy fur coat, then in his velvet jacket and waistcoat, his evening jacket, his smoking jacket, and his cape, both bareheaded and wearing a high-crowned, broad-brimmed hat.[20]

One photograph in particular was to become important. Labeled *Oscar Wilde, No. 18*, this picture shows Wilde dressed in his velvet jacket, knee breeches, silk stockings, and pumps, seated at the end of a large couch in front of a vaguely suggestive painted background. A heavy dark fur piece is thrown in the corner of the couch. Wilde is seated partially on the fur and partially on an elaborately patterned piece of fabric. His left leg rests on a portion of worn oriental carpet that has been raised with a hidden box, and his head reposes on his left hand, which is supported by the elbow on his raised knee. The right leg, lower than the left, is thrust forward toward the viewer and on this knee he rests the edge of a book, which identifies him as a literary man. Staring directly into the camera, full lips slightly parted, Wilde is posed to give the impression of a writer caught in a moment of deepest thought. At the same time the angle at which he sits foregrounds the long silk-clad legs and shiny pumps and the large buttoned and piped cuff of his left arm. These effects, together with the varied textures of the throws on the couch, create an impression of luxury and elegance as well as dreaminess. The picture might well be taken as the emblem of Wilde's Chickering Hall evocation of the distinctness of the genuine artist.

To secure copyright Sarony delivered copies of his Wilde photographs to the Library of Congress shortly after processing them. But within a month after the new photographs went on sale, the Burrow-Giles Lithographing Company had produced lithographic versions of *Oscar Wilde, No. 18* and other images in quantity. Ehrich & Company, for example, a New York department store, bought thirty thousand copies of Burrow-Giles's version of *No. 18* to publicize a new line of hats trimmed in "delicate combinations" and "tasteful styles." They marketed this line as "The English Renaissance," making explicit the connection to the Chickering Hall lecture by printing their circular on the back of the Wilde image stamped "Compliments of Ehrich Bros." Meanwhile, Straiton and Storm, a tobacco company, was using a different Wilde image to promote "aesthetic" cigars.[21] Just as D'Oyly Carte had employed Oscar Wilde to publicize and authenticate his American production of *Patience,* so retailers were employing Sarony's images of Wilde to publicize and authenticate their wares.

The lawsuit began in April when Sarony's attorney, Guernsey Sackett, filed a copyright infringement claim against Burrow-Giles in Circuit Court in New York.[22] Sarony's complaint was accompanied by

Napoleon Sarony, *Oscar Wilde, No. 18*. Courtesy of The Prints and Photographs Division, Library of Congress. LC-USZ62-44773.

Ehrich Brothers Circular (1882). Courtesy of The Prints and Photographs Division, Library of Congress. LC-USZ62-138240.

an affidavit from Alexander F. Blinn—probably an attorney associated with Sackett—who testified that he had visited the Burrow-Giles offices where he saw and purchased prints of *No. 18*. Blinn reported he had been told that in addition to the thirty thousand copies of the lithograph sold to Ehrich's, another one hundred thousand copies had been printed for Mandel Brothers, a Chicago department store. Furthermore, he said he had learned that some two hundred thousand copies of a second, smaller print—most likely the image used by Straiton and Storm—had also been sold. An affidavit from Sarony emphasized that the case was urgent because the sale of celebrity pictures depended upon "the interest of the moment." A further affidavit from a dealer in prints and photographic supplies testified that the Burrow-Giles prints, if distributed, would almost entirely stop the sale of Sarony's pictures.[23] Within days the court issued an injunction. Burrow-Giles acquiesced in the restraining order and turned over to Sarony some 85,000 copies of *No. 18* along with the lithographic plates. But, having a great deal at stake for their future business, the printers decided to use the issue to test the 1865 law extending copyright to photographs. Was a photograph protectable? Was a photographer an author?

The status of photography had been debated, especially in France and England, ever since the invention of the daguerreotype in 1839. At the heart of the issue was always the role of the camera. Could an image made by a mechanical device employing the effect of sunlight on a chemically treated surface be considered art? From the beginning there were objections that photographs lacked the trace of the human hand and spirit. Some like Baudelaire regarded photography as perhaps "a very humble servant of art and science" while others such as Delacroix regarded the daguerreotype as "a wonderful invention" that would help to improve art, but neither would declare that it was an art in itself.[24] In England, John Ruskin, the preeminent art critic of the English-speaking world, first welcomed photography for its ability to record architectural details rapidly and accurately, but later when he saw the medium commercialized he rejected it as mechanical and trivial.[25] In the mid-1850s the Parisian photographer Nadar produced several cartoons that summarized the debate. One showed photography, personified as a camera with a portfolio under its arm, asking and being refused "just a little place" among the fine arts. A second showed an

Nadar, *The Ingratitude of Painting* (1857). Courtesy of Bibliotheque Nationale de France, Paris.

artist's palette kicking away a camera seeking a place in an exhibition. In personifying photography as a camera, Nadar was of course inevitably recapitulating the chief argument against the new medium. How could a machine be an artist?[26]

Burrow-Giles's arguments both at the Circuit Court level and later on appeal to the Supreme Court rested on this established position. Unlike painting, sculpture, and engraving—all protected by copyright—the practice of photography, Burrow-Giles argued, required nothing but mechanical skill. After all, a photograph was not made by a human hand like an engraving but by a machine. Moreover, the essence of photography was the production of an accurate, objective record, not the creation of something new. Burrow-Giles insisted, too, that to be protected a work must bear the imprint of personality, or as their brief put it, the "ever living stamp of individuality."[27] The concept of personality as a kind of branding imprint was employed in the English copyright debates of the eighteenth century when it was mustered to support the notion that protectable writings, like faces, were necessarily individuated.[28] But the idea acquired a new urgency in the nineteenth century as a result of the Industrial Revolution and the large-scale production of machine-made goods. Ruskin insisted on the importance of individual expression in even the most humble goods and Wilde in his Ruskinian "English Renaissance" lecture called for the American workman to be surrounded by "happy influences" and "beautiful things" so that he might have the opportunity of "expressing his own individuality."[29] Since no genius was required to produce a photograph and no stamp of originality could be imprinted on one, Burrow-Giles argued, the contested picture of Oscar Wilde could not be considered a writing, nor Sarony an author. The law extending copyright to photographs was not valid. In addition to challenging Sarony's copyright frontally, Burrow-Giles also put forward a technical argument about formalities, asserting that Sarony, who merely stamped his productions "N. Sarony," had not complied with the requirement that his full name should appear on a work for which he claimed protection.

Whereas Burrow-Giles's position dwelled on the physical process of photography, Sarony's centered on the concepts of "invention" and "design." Sarony had not merely captured a preexisting subject, he had created "a new, useful, harmonious, characteristic, and graceful picture." *Oscar Wilde, No. 18*, he argued,

> is the original invention and design of this plaintiff, for the reason that it was made by this plaintiff entirely from his own original mental conception, to which he gave visible form by posing the said Oscar Wilde in front of the camera, selecting and arranging the costume, draperies, and other various accessories in said photograph, arranging the subject so as to present graceful outlines, arranging and disposing the light and shade, suggesting and evoking the desired expression, and from such disposition, arrangement, or representation,

made entirely by this plaintiff, producing the picture which is the subject of this suit.[30]

The conception of the picture, Sarony's attorney insisted, was present in Sarony's mind prior to making the exposure and it was this "ideal invention or creation of the mind" that the law was designed to protect.[31] Of course, direct protection of a mental concept was impracticable and therefore artistic creations had to be given intelligible expression in material form. Sarony might have made his conception manifest as an oil painting, an engraving, or a sculpture, in which case his right to protection would not be questioned, but he had chosen to do so in a photograph. A photographer was subject to limitations peculiar to the art because, among other things, there was "no chance for adding artistic touches" after the exposure was made.[32] The camera merely recorded what it saw. Therefore there might well be some photographs, purely documentary images, that did not incorporate a mental conception. Each case would have to be decided on its merits.

The language in which Sackett framed Sarony's claim was calculated to echo the constitutional clause empowering Congress to enact both copyright and patent laws: "To promote the progress of science and useful arts, by securing for limited times to authors and inventors the exclusive right to their respective writings and discoveries." Most often this clause has been understood as providing separately for authors' "writings" to promote the progress of "science" broadly understood and for inventors' "discoveries" to promote the "useful arts." Sackett sought to make as powerful a claim as possible by blurring the distinction between copyrights and patents. Thus he represented the picture of Wilde as an "invention"—he was using the term in the classical rhetorical sense of "invention" as the process of selection and disposition—as well as a "design." Moreover, he claimed that not only was the picture new, graceful, and harmonious, but also that it was "useful," an odd term to use in relation to a portrait. We should note, too, that the making of the picture was framed in active terms. Sackett spoke of Sarony "selecting" the costume and accessories, "arranging" the subject, "disposing" the light, and "evoking" the desired expression, language chosen to counter Burrow-Giles's claim that the photograph was merely the product of a machine. Perhaps most evocative in Sarony's claim was the use of the word "design," a term with deep historical resonance.

Was Sarony an artist or a mechanic? Putting the question in this way suggests how the contention over photography as it came to a head in *Burrow-Giles v. Sarony* can be seen as a modern version of a dispute that reaches back to early debates over the status of painters, sculptors, and architects. Were drawing and painting—both manual activities—liberal arts? Alberti's *Della pittura* (1435), the first modern treatise on the subject, defended painting as noble, and thereafter various writers, including Castiglione, presented drawing and painting as practices worthy of gentlemen.[33] The crucial concept for the validation of artists was *disegno*—"design"—which Vasari identified as the "father" of architecture, painting, and sculpture. Design was invoked in an English context by Shakespeare's contemporary, Inigo Jones, who used it to establish that architecture was genteel.[34] Moreover, the term acquired legal significance in the early eighteenth century when William Hogarth, along with other London engravers, used it in his successful lobbying for a statute that would protect printmakers in a manner parallel to the way the Statute of Anne protected writers. It was the design that created the value of an engraved image and therefore it was the design that must be protected.[35] As Ann Bermingham points out, the notion of design was somewhat ambiguous insofar as the term was applied both to the initial mental conception and to its execution in drawings and sketches.[36] The invocation of "design" thus blurred the line between the intellectual and the physical, the conceiving "eye" and the executing "hand." The language in which Sackett framed Sarony's claim at first seemed to acknowledge this ambiguity insofar as Sackett conceded that mental conceptions had to be given intelligible expression in material form. Nonetheless, by presenting Sarony as forming the picture first in mental conception and then giving it visible form through his arrangement of the subject prior to making it permanent in the exposure of the negative, Sackett's argument wound up severing conception from execution, the mental eye from the physical hand.

Burrow-Giles's argument against protectability rested on the mid-nineteenth-century characterization of photography as purely mechanical. The photographic profession had developed a response to this dismissal based on the idea that the photographer was an artist because he looked through surfaces to the mysterious truths of soul. As the prominent Boston photographer Albert Southworth explained in 1870, the art of photographic portraiture involved capturing the inner essence of character. This required "genius," the "acquaintance with mind in its connection with matter," and rigorous "discipline of mind and vision." The true artist will feel and portray "the soul of the subject itself." Nature is not to be represented as it is but "as it ought to be, and might possibly have been."[37] Sarony's studio practices, his proclaimed concern with "character" together with grace of outline and beauty of light and shade and his insistence that he had nothing to do with the mechanical or chemical aspects of photography, partake of this move toward mystification. And so, too, does the argument that Sackett framed in Sarony's behalf in which "mental conception" was represented as occurring in an ethereal realm unsullied by material constraints.

We should observe, too, that Sackett's argument exaggerated the gap between the mental and the physical by insisting that once a photograph was taken there was "no chance for adding artistic touches." In a limited sense this was perhaps true—the camera only recorded what was before it—but to make this statement categorically ignored the fact that images, as Sarony well understood, might be manipulated in the processing and that photographs could be retouched or colored.[38] This simplification appears to have been strategic: it avoided opening Sarony's claim to the argument that only a manipulated or retouched photograph could be protected. Moreover, by locating the artistic dimension of Sarony's picture completely in what happened before the plate was exposed, dwelling on the process rather than the image itself, Sackett's claim preserved the notion of photography's objective, documentary power. Presenting Sarony's claim in this way meant that the Oscar Wilde photograph might be validated as a work of art without undermining the status of the ordinary photograph as legal evidence.[39] It also meant that the conceptual opposition between Burrow-Giles's position and Sarony's was unbridgeable. Since neither side acknowledged the possibility of complex interaction between the camera, the artist, and the subject, the court was given little room to maneuver.

The Circuit Court ruling was issued in spring 1883.[40] Judge Alfred C. Coxe dismissed as "too narrow" the technical claim that Sarony had not fully complied with the terms of the statute by merely placing "N. Sarony" on the picture rather than his full name. Coxe ratified as a finding of "fact" the language of Sarony's representation of the Wilde photograph as "a useful, new, harmonious, characteristic, and graceful picture" made "entirely from his own original mental conception" to which he gave "visible form" by posing, arranging, and lighting the subject in his studio. Based on this finding, Coxe declared that, as a matter of law, Sarony was indeed "the author, inventor, designer, and proprietor of the photograph at issue." But was the 1865 law extending copyright to photographs valid under the constitutional clause? On this question Coxe, following precedent, stated that the presumption had to be in favor of the validity of the act, otherwise endless complications would result as judges in different circuits ruled differently. In order to pronounce an act of Congress invalid a judge would have to hold a "clear and unhesitating conviction" that it was indeed unconstitutional. The question might be "involved in doubt" but he was obliged to defer to Congress. Phrased in this way, Coxe's decision implicitly invited an appeal to the Supreme Court as the one authority that could rule with finality. Burrow-Giles accepted the invitation.

The arguments submitted to the Supreme Court the following autumn followed the lines already described, with Burrow-Giles insisting on the mechanical nature of photography and Sarony responding with a representation of the photograph of Wilde as an intellectual invention. The decision came on March 17, 1884, just under two years after the legal process was begun.[41] Written by Samuel F. Miller, a distinguished justice who had been nominated by Lincoln, the court quickly dismissed the technical argument concerning formalities, noting that even the name Sarony alone would have been sufficient for purposes of notice. The court then adopted broad definitions of the key constitutional terms, defining an *author* as "he to whom anything owes its origin" and including as a *writing* any form "by which the ideas in the mind of the author are given visible expression." The only reason photographs had not been included as copyrightable materials in 1790 was that "photography as an art was then unknown." Miller's decision observed that the question of whether the "ordinary production of a photograph" would be protected by copyright was not at issue. As already noted, Sarony's claim had cleverly preserved the legally significant notion of photography's objective, documentary power. But as for the picture at issue, *Oscar Wilde, No. 18*, Miller accepted Judge Coxe's findings of fact about the nature of the photograph, repeating again the language from Sackett's Circuit Court brief that described the picture as deriving entirely from Sarony's "own original mental conception" given visible form by posing and arranging the subject for the camera. He wrote, "These findings, we think, show this photograph to be an original work of art, the product of plaintiff's intellectual invention, of which plaintiff is the author, and of a class of inventions for which the Constitution intended that Congress should secure to him the exclusive right to use, publish and sell."

The court's decision thus ratified Sarony's status as an artist not a mechanic. Ironically, at about the same time, state-level cases arose in Tennessee and Louisiana in which photographers contended they were mechanics, not artists. In the Tennessee case, decided before *Burrow-Giles*, a photographer's equipment had been seized in payment of a debt. The debtor attempted unsuccessfully to argue that the property was exempt under a statute that prevented seizure of a mechanic's tools of trade. But the court rejected his claim, holding that a photographer was an artist, not an artisan, and no more a "mechanic" than a painter.[42] In a second, later case a New Orleans photographer argued that as a "mechanic" he was exempt from paying a $25 professional license fee, but again the court rejected the argument, maintaining that photography was a scientific or artistic pursuit and the man was not an exempted laborer.[43]

One further irony may also be worth noting. On February 4, 1890, on the occasion of celebrations of the Centenary of the Federal Judiciary, the nine justices of the Supreme Court traveled to New York for the festivities. One of their engagements at this time was to pay a call, like Oscar Wilde before them, at Sarony's studio. There Sarony photographed them as a group. Executed in his top-floor loft, this portrait of the court employs typical decorative elements from Sarony's collection of "artistic" properties, including an elaborately carved column and various draperies. Annual court photographs had become the practice by the 1880s, but the 1890 occasion on which the justices repaired en

Napoleon Sarony, *The Supreme Court* (1890). Courtesy of the U.S. Supreme Court; collection of the Supreme Court of the United States.

banc to Sarony's Union Square studio appears to have been the first time such a portrait was made outside of Washington.[44]

* * *

The court's decision in *Burrow-Giles* introduced an expansive definition of *author* as the one to whom anything owes its origin, a definition that has proved significant in the subsequent extension of copyright protection to sound recordings and other kinds of productions.[45] It also confirmed the severing of conception from execution that Guernsey Sackett had developed in crafting Sarony's argument, and in the process introduced a metaphysical element into the legal discourse of authorship. Perhaps this element can be understood as a doctrine in some respects parallel to that promulgated by Wilde when he spoke in his Chickering Hall lecture of the "absolute difference between the world of art and the world of real fact." Wilde portrayed the artist as inhabiting a "separate realm" from the ordinary person, "a sacred house of Beauty."[46] Likewise, the figure of the artist, as incorporated in the *Burrow-Giles* decision, inhabits a separate sphere of "mental conception," relying upon others such as Sarony's assistant Richardson to give his ideas protectable visual form.

The confirmation of Sarony's photograph of Wilde as a work of art was not surprising. Sarony, like Wilde was theatrically "artistic" and his portrait of Wilde dressed in velvet jacket and knee breeches was no less a synecdoche for aestheticism than Gilbert's invocation of Bunthorne strolling Piccadilly with a poppy or a lily in his hand. Produced at a moment when "art" and "beauty" were tropes of mass as well as elite culture—recall Straiton and Storm's line of "aesthetic cigars"—the *Burrow-Giles* decision both concerned an aesthetic subject and was itself based on the court's aesthetic judgment. But within two decades the Supreme Court would take a quite different line in *Bleistein v. Donaldson Lithographing Co.* (1903), a case involving the question of whether circus posters were eligible for copyright.[47] In this matter, there was no attempt to elevate the producers of the lithographs to the level of fine artists. On the contrary, Justice Oliver Wendell Holmes declared that it was not the business of lawyers "to constitute themselves final judges of the worth of pictorial illustrations." Even "a very modest grade of art has in it something irreducible which is one man's alone"—again the "imprint of personality" was being invoked—and therefore eligible for copyright. Henceforth the courts would avoid making discriminations on the basis of aesthetic value.

Burrow-Giles can perhaps be seen as the legal high-water mark of nineteenth-century aestheticism, but of course more than aesthetic considerations were at play. By the 1880s, portrait photography, including the mass marketing of celebrity portraits, had become an industry. Given the vested economic interests, together with legislative recognition of those interests in the 1865 act, it was perhaps inevitable that the courts would find some way of confirming the protected status of at least some photographs.[48] But the commercial value of the photograph of Oscar Wilde depended only in part on strictly aesthetic value. Sales of celebrity photographs were directly related to the notoriety of the subject.

Celebrity, as Martin Postle has observed, can be understood as a hybrid of the classic concept of fame inflected by commerce and the cult of personality.[49] By the late nineteenth century, celebrity had become a commodity, and the celebrity photograph—especially the kind of photograph that purported to capture the celebrity's personality—emerged as one of the ways the commodity was marketed. Paying to photograph celebrities was a convention established by Dickens on his second U.S. tour in 1867–1868 when he demanded a fee for posing, and Sarony typically paid substantial sums to his celebrity sitters: $300 to Fanny Kemble, $1,500 to Sarah Bernhardt, and $5,000 to the beautiful Lillie Langtry, who was in effect famous for being famous.[50] But Sarony also possessed celebrity value and this, too, was capable of commodification. Thus it is worth noting that in some instances Sarony, rather than paying a fee, was himself paid by actors and actresses who wished to have his images of themselves circulated along with those of more established public figures.

It is not clear what the arrangement was in the case of the Oscar Wilde photograph. Sarony's complaint against Burrow-Giles claimed that he had paid "a large and valuable consideration" for "the sole and exclusive right and privilege of making and selling" portraits of Wilde in the United States, but it may be significant that the portion of the complaint that speaks about the payment appears as part of a printed form that was adapted to the immediate occasion. The name "Oscar Wilde" was entered by hand.[51] Other evidence suggests that Colonel Morse, the D'Oyly Carte agent in New York, was so eager to have Wilde photographed by Sarony that he waived the customary charge.[52] Perhaps what passed between Sarony and Wilde, then, was not money at all but a complex exchange of intangibles in which Wilde promoted his celebrity by being photographed by Sarony, and Sarony in turn acquired aesthetic capital as well as an addition to his vendible stock of portraits.

Wilde was unabashedly self-promoting and commercial. As already noted, Wilde accepted D'Oyly Carte's proposal because he needed the money and in America he worked extraordinarily hard, traveling across the entire continent and delivering some 140 lectures over the course of about nine months. After expenses, Wilde's half share in the profits from this enterprise came to about $5,600, a substantial sum in the 1880s.[53] To some Wilde's frank commercialism seemed incongruous in conjunction with aestheticism. For example, a satiric cartoon published in the *New York Daily Graphic* shortly after his Chickering Hall lecture showed Wilde holding a large coin with a dollar sign: "Conceive me if you can, / A pallid and thin young man, / A crotchety, crank'd young man, / A greenery-yallery, chickering gallery, / Dollar and a half young man." The cartoon was titled, "Aestheticism as Oscar Understands it."[54] Newspaper interviewers from papers across the country commented ironically on Wilde's interest in money. A reporter from the *Boston Globe*, for example, remarked that the famous aesthete was receptive to interviews because "he very well understood the advantage of free advertising, and didn't so much care whether he was represented or misrepresented, as long as he was as far from a failure as at present."[55]

Wilde ultimately had only one product to sell—himself—and so he produced himself as a vendible personality.[56] His aesthetic costume and his provocative quips were grounded as much in his ability to exploit the emergent mass consumer society as they were in his attempt to distinguish himself from it. Parallel observations can be made about Sarony. Sarony did have a tangible product to sell, his cabinet cards; however, the value of these products did not derive from paper and ink but from the image. Ratifying the authenticity of the image was of course Sarony's signature on the cardboard mounting. And underwriting the signature was the bohemian persona—the beard, fez, and boots—that Sarony had constructed. Like Wilde's aesthetic persona, Sarony's self-presentation served both to distinguish him from more ordinary Broadway strollers, marking him as a creator rather than a consumer, and to produce the value of his signature. The commercial value of *Oscar Wilde, No. 18* depended in part on the notoriety of the sitter. But at the same time the picture's value also depended on Sarony's authority as embodied in his stamped flowing signature. Art, celebrity, and commerce had at this moment in history become inextricably entangled.

* * *

The *Burrow-Giles* case was widely reported in American newspapers. "The Creator of Oscar Wilde"—so read the wry headline of the *New York Tribune*'s report on the arguments of counsel before the Supreme Court.[57] Wilde himself was by this time back in England lecturing on his impressions of America. What he might have thought about the dispute—or for that matter about the use of his image to sell hats and cigars—is unclear. But, given Wilde's interest in self-promotion, it is unlikely that he was offended by additional free publicity.

Neither is it evident precisely what Wilde might have thought of Sarony and his commercial portraits. It is worth noting that about a week after his Chickering Hall appearance, Wilde made a pilgrimage to Camden, New Jersey, to call on Walt Whitman. Whitman presented Wilde with two copies of a photograph of himself, possibly one taken by Sarony a few years earlier, one copy for himself and one for Wilde to give to Swinburne as a token of Whitman's esteem. In return Wilde promised to send Whitman a copy of the Sarony photograph of himself.[58] In October when Lillie Langtry arrived in New York, Wilde took her to Sarony for the sitting for which the photographer paid $5,000. Wilde appears to have directly mentioned Sarony only once. This was in "The Canterville Ghost," published in 1887. In this satiric tale an American diplomat buys an ancient English estate, Canterville Chase, haunted by a family ghost. The ghost, however, becomes increasingly frustrated by its inability to make much of an impression on the commonsensical Americans. At one point the ghost descends to the entrance hall and discovers that the Canterville family portraits have been replaced by large Sarony photographs of the diplomat and his wife. It has been suggested that this detail is meant to invoke American vulgarity.[59] Perhaps so, but it seems to me that the story's attitude toward the members of this American family and their refusal to be intimidated by ancient tradition is wry but not unsympathetic. The pride that they take in their Sarony portraits is of a piece with their brisk, unsuperstitious modernity.

Wilde's disappearance from the photography case except in the form of his image is striking. In a sense the case was all about personality. Could the imprint of personality, the "ever living stamp of individuality," be found in Sarony's picture? The subject of the photograph was indisputably Wilde, but the personality at issue was always Sarony's, never Wilde's. Of course Wilde had sold to Sarony—if indeed Sarony paid him—the exclusive right to make and sell his picture.[60] Had Wilde therefore sold Sarony some element of his personality? Was Sarony legally—as the *Tribune* headline put it—Wilde's creator or at least his proprietor? We recall Justice Grier's sneering dismissal of the notion that Harriet Beecher Stowe might claim dominion over Uncle Tom and Topsy.

The problematic notion of the commodified self, of personality dissociated from person, opens a vista that challenges concepts of authenticity.[61] Oscar Wilde, who famously spoke of life imitating art, in a sense created himself as a vendible work of art. Sarony then—himself an artful construction—captured an interpretation of that work of art in an endlessly reproducible form warranted by his printed and endlessly reproducible signature. In such a world of artifice and duplicability what constitutes authenticity? The notion of the constructed self also challenges concepts of identity. As Jane Gaines proposes, there is a suggestive parallel between Wilde's novel *The Picture of Dorian Gray* (1884) and Sarony's lawsuit, insofar as both involve the dissociation of personality and self. In Wilde's fantasy, Dorian Gray preserves his youth and beauty, his personality, while his portrait becomes monstrous, revealing the living man's corruption. The painting thus exposes Dorian's decaying soul in a manner that literalizes the notion of the true artist capturing, as the photographer Southworth put it, "the soul of the subject itself." The supernatural relationship between Dorian and his portrait perhaps also echoes photography's uncanny quality. After all, a photograph is not merely a representation like a painting or a sculpture but a literal trace recorded on the prepared plate. To gaze at the photograph of someone long dead is, in a sense, to gaze at the actual person. Thus, as Susan Sontag puts it, "Between two fantasy alternatives, that Holbein the Younger had lived long enough to have painted Shakespeare or that a prototype of the camera had been invented early enough to have photographed him, most Bardolators would choose the photograph." Faded and browned though such a photograph might be, it would provide in some sense direct access to the sacred figure. "Having a photograph of Shakespeare would be like having a nail from the True Cross."[62]

That Sarony emerges from the logic of the *Burrow-Giles* decision as Oscar Wilde's "creator" is a function of the process of abstraction that the law case involved. The actual situation in which the photograph was made was clear enough. A few days after disembarking in New York, accompanied by Colonel Morse and a servant bearing his trunk of costumes, Oscar Wilde visited Sarony's studio where he spent several hours putting on various outfits and posing in front of settings that Sarony had chosen. When a satisfactory pose was arranged, Richardson was instructed to remove the cap from the lens and make an exposure. But in the legal process through which these activities were transformed into the foundation for Sarony's assertion of rights, the

concrete events lost particularity and solidity as the essential act became "original mental conception." Like God creating the universe
from his divine idea, Sarony had manifested his authorial will and produced *Oscar Wilde, No. 18*.

Copyright originated in the Statute of Anne as the exclusive right
to print and market a particular book, conceived as a physical entity.
In *Pope v. Curll*, faced with the question of who owns a letter, Lord
Chancellor Hardwicke found it necessary to make a distinction between the material substance of the letter, the ink and paper, and the
words written on it. Thus the words were separated from material substance and a process of abstraction began. Likewise, in *Stowe v. Thomas*,
Harriet Beecher Stowe, suing to have a German translation of her
novel declared an infringement, contended that her copyright extended
beyond the precise words of *Uncle Tom's Cabin* to encompass "the
ideas—the thought—the plan—the arrangement—the style of expression" incorporated in her book. Rejected by Justice Grier, Stowe's
contention was vindicated in the 1870 Copyright Act, which established the author's translation right. Let us note that in confirming
Sarony as the author of *Oscar Wilde, No. 18*, the Supreme Court in
effect built on Stowe's claims about thought, plan, and arrangement
but carried the process of abstraction a step further by explicitly locating the essence of the property in "mental conception." With this
step, copyright doctrine moved even closer to metaphysics. Intelligible expression in material form was necessary, as Sarony acknowledged. But it was the immaterial "creation of the mind" that the law
was designed to protect.

CHAPTER FIVE

Hollywood Story

Nichols v. Universal (1930)

Abie's Irish Rose, which opened on Broadway on May 22, 1922, was a phenomenal success. Despite reviews that were at best lukewarm and at times contemptuous, Anne Nichols's feel-good comedy about an Irish–Jewish romance became in its time the most popular play ever produced in the United States. Four years later, when Universal Pictures produced *The Cohens and Kellys*, a movie with a roughly similar theme that the studio advertised as "The *Abie's Irish Rose* of the Screen," Nichols's play also became the subject of a landmark copyright infringement suit.[1]

Hollywood, as one prominent copyright attorney has observed, rarely steals; it imitates.[2] But when does imitation become infringement? This was an old question, one that had come up as early as the eighteenth-century case *Gyles v. Wilcox* in which the issue was whether an abridgment was the same book as the original.[3] Still it was a question made more urgent by the change in doctrine ratified by Congress after Harriet Beecher Stowe's unsuccessful suit to prevent a German translation of *Uncle Tom's Cabin*. By the late nineteenth century, the emphasis in copyright doctrine had shifted from the author's labor to the author's product, from the learning and effort required to create a poem or book or play to the literary work itself and its life in the marketplace. A translation was a derivative work. So of course would be a sequel or for that matter a new version of a story that was substantially similar to an author's original. But what constitutes "substantial similarity?" When does one work follow another so closely that, despite the fact that there is no literal copying, despite the fact that neither the characters, settings, nor plots are precisely the same as those of an earlier work, nonetheless a legal boundary is crossed?

Moses L. Malevinsky believed he had an answer in the form of a test that could determine infringement with the same accuracy that a fingerprint could determine identity. One of the most prominent theatrical lawyers in New York in the 1920s, Malevinsky had been Nichols's attorney for years and had written a critical study of theater in which *Abie's Irish Rose* figured prominently as a model of dramatic construction.[4] When *The Cohens and Kellys* was released, Malevinsky seized on the occasion to apply his theories about drama and win a victory for his client. Nichols lost at the District Court level, but, convinced of the strength of the case, Malevinsky pressed on with an appeal. This brought the issue before Judge Learned Hand of the Second Circuit Court of Appeals, where it was decided against Nichols in a classic decision that still influences the determination of infringement cases.

*　*　*

A kind of *Romeo and Juliet* with a happy ending, *Abie's Irish Rose* concerns a young Jewish man, Abie Levy, and his Irish bride, Rose Mary Murphy. The two have met in France during the Great War and later secretly married. But how are Abie and Rose Mary to convince their widower fathers, each determined that his child should wed only a person of the same background and religion, to accept their marriage? There is comic byplay generated by Abie's attempts to pass Rose Mary off as Rosie Murpheski, a Jewish girl, and further broad comedy when Rose Mary's father Patrick arrives from California to discover that his son-in-law is a Jew. But in the end the antagonistic fathers are reconciled when the young couple has twins, a boy named for Patrick and a girl named for Abie's late mother.

This skeletal plot is fleshed out with broad ethnic humor—the Jewish father frets about the cost of everything, the Irish father is choleric but warmhearted—and classic vaudeville material. In the first act, for example, when Abie telephones to say that he is bringing Rose Mary home for dinner, his father launches into a monologue that audiences probably recognized as a comic routine known as "Cohen on the Telephone." "Hello! Who iss it? Yes vot? Me! Yes, it's me! Who am me? Say who are you? What number? I don't know the number! I didn't get the phone to call myself! Oh, Abie wishes to speak vid his fadder? Pud him on!"[5] And later when Abie points out that the suit his father has bought for the wedding is too large and should be altered, Solomon objects, "Vot? I paid fifty-nine dollars and ninety-eight cents for this suit. Und den you vant I should have some of it out? No, sir. I vant all I paid for."[6] Nichols's comedy opened first at the Morosco Theatre in Los Angeles. "It is not a big play, nor a strong play, nor a great play," wrote Edwin Schallert, the *Los Angeles Times* reviewer, but "unless I miss my guess by a long and large margin, it is going to have a run that will make the shekels come hopping into the box office."[7] Brought to New York a few months later by Nichols herself as both producer and director, the play was savaged in the *New York World* by Heywood Broun, who called it "cheap and offensive," and in the *New York Tribune* by Percy Hammond, who called it childish, comparing it to "something in a perambulator; noisy but inarticulate."[8]

Audiences in New York were at first thin but, gradually, the play began to catch on. Within a year it was playing to full houses on Broadway and also in multiple road companies in Washington, DC, and throughout the Midwest. By May 1925, *Abie's Irish Rose* had broken all records for a Broadway play and had been celebrated in a special issue of *Variety* as the "World's Greatest Comedy."[9] The New York production continued until late 1927, when it closed after 2,327 consecutive performances, a world record for a theatrical run.[10] Anne Nichols had become not only a celebrity but a wealthy and powerful woman profiled, for example, in the *Wall Street Journal* under the punning headline "Nichols—and Dollars." The paper estimated that *Abie's Irish Rose* had grossed some $20 million in its five-year run and the *New York Times* speculated that Nichols's personal share might have been as high as $5 million.[11]

How is one to understand the play's remarkable success? Neither the plot nor the comic routines were sophisticated or novel, but the play's social argument was timely. The years after World War I were a period of swelling isolationism, racism, and nativist reaction against the great immigration waves of the late nineteenth century. In 1921, a year before the play opened, Congress had drastically limited immigration from Southern and Eastern Europe. Harkening back to an earlier Progressive idea of America as the place where all the races and peoples of Europe would be blended—the America of Israel Zangwill's *The Melting Pot* (1909)—*Abie's Irish Rose* provided a liberal response to the harsh anti-immigrant mood of the 1920s. It also reinforced contemporary assimilation narratives, suggesting that through the younger generation, even Jews, the least "white" of all Europeans, might become indistinguishable from other Americans.[12] Significantly, one of the heartiest expressions of applause regularly broke out after a second act exchange in which a priest and a rabbi, both former military chaplains, recall ministering to wounded soldiers. As the priest puts it, "Shure they all had the same God above them. And what with the shells bursting, and the shrapnel flying, with no one knowing just what moment death would come, Catholics, Hebrews and Protestants alike forgot their prejudice and came to realize that all faiths and creeds have about the same destination after all."[13] Tapping into a counterreactionary current of social energy, *Abie's Irish Rose* insisted that now, after the war, Levys and Murphys alike were, above all, Americans.

The play's success was in part due to Nichols's belief in its message. Born in rural Georgia in 1891, one of Nichols's earliest memories was of being startled when a young black boy informed her that they were cousins. Writing years later, Nichols said that although she was disturbed and confused at the time, later experiences had convinced her that "there is no such thing as Negro blood or white blood or any other sort of blood except red blood which God gives to everyone without discrimination."[14] The play's success was also due to Nichols's grit and determination. Undismayed by the sneers from New York critics such as Broun and Hammond, Nichols cut actors' salaries, mortgaged her house, and sold her jewelry to keep the play running.[15] She was after all an experienced actor and playwright who had written a number of earlier pieces including the book for a successful musical, *Linger Longer Letty* (1919) and, together with a collaborator, a successful comedy, *Just Married* (1921). She was also brash and self-assured. Once offered a minor role in a production, Nichols turned it down flat, insisting that she was only willing to play leading ladies.[16]

Nichols was tough in both her personal and professional lives. The child of an unreliable father, Nichols developed, as she put it, "a fierce determination to make my own way and be independent of any man as long as I lived."[17] The theater provided an opportunity for independence. At around the time *Abie's Irish Rose* was produced in Los Angeles, Nichols separated from her actor husband, Terry Duffy, taking custody

Anne Nichols (ca. 1920–1925). Courtesy of The Billy Rose Theatre Division, The New York Public Library for the Performing Arts, Astor, Lenox and Tilden Foundations.

of their young son. "I was blamed by everyone but a few for the breakup," she wrote. "I was the cold-hearted Hannah but me thinks he over did his heartbreak a bit."[18] She never married again. Shortly after, dissatisfied with her Los Angeles producer Oliver Morosco's delays in bringing the play to New York, Nichols took matters into her own hands, fending off Morosco's suit for an injunction to prevent the New York opening and countering with a suit of her own for $28,250 that she claimed he owed her. Morosco replied with a suit for $57,000 in damages and for the value of the scenery and other items he claimed Nichols had taken. It appears that these matters were ultimately resolved in Nichols's favor with Morosco paying her $7,000.[19] But the following year Nichols filed suit against the Columbia Amusement Company to recover scenery and other property that she claimed had been wrongly detained after the Washington run of *Abie's Irish Rose*.[20] And a month later, she was embroiled in a court fight with the Shubert theatrical organization over the right to open *Abie's Irish Rose* at the prominent Studebaker Theatre in Chicago.[21]

The movie rights to a theatrical success like *Abie's Irish Rose* would be a prize for any of the Hollywood studios. In 1925 Universal negotiated with the playwright but failed to reach an agreement. Nichols, it was said, was demanding a million dollars, an unprecedented sum. The studio then turned in a different direction and bought the rights to another New York play, Aaron Hoffman's *Two Blocks Away*, which had been produced in 1921. This was a story about a benevolent Jewish shoemaker on the Lower East Side who suddenly inherits a fortune and turns into a pretentious monster, moving his family into an elaborate mansion. The mansion is just two blocks from the shoemaker's old neighborhood—hence the title—but, socially, it is another universe. Taking on the airs of a great magnate, the shoemaker rejects his friends and tries to end his daughter's romance with a young man of modest means. But when he learns that his inheritance really belongs to one of his old pals, he has a change of heart in which he renounces his fortune and his pretentions, reconciles with his friends, and accepts his daughter's modest suitor.[22]

In the course of story development, Universal turned Hoffman's play into a comedy about ethnic conflict, centering the action on the antagonism between a Jew, Nathan Cohen, and an Irishman, Patrick

Movie advertisement (1926). Courtesy of the National Archives at New York City.

Kelly, who live with their families in neighboring apartments. More-over, in a plot change that brought the story even closer to *Abie's Irish Rose*, Universal linked the romantic subplot to the ethnic drama by giving the Irishman a son who served as the Jewish daughter's romantic interest. As in Hoffman's play, the central plot device remained the shoemaker's sudden translation to wealth followed by his change of heart and reconciliation with his Irish antagonist at the end. Filled out with conventional ethnic comedy and slapstick gags, Universal dropped the title *Two Blocks Away*, which emphasized the shoemaker's social transformation, and called the movie *The Cohens and Kellys*, which emphasized the ethnic conflict. Universal then advertised its movie as "The *Abie's Irish Rose* of the Screen." Some two months later Nichols filed suit for copyright infringement.

The Cohens and Kellys was clearly an attempt to exploit the popularity of *Abie's Irish Rose* but did it amount to either infringement or plagiarism? Infringement, a violation of copyright law, is a legal wrong. Plagiarism, an act whereby one passes off someone else's work as one's own, is an ethical transgression but not necessarily a legal wrong. Nonetheless, in the early twentieth century the two terms were not always clearly distinguished, including by Learned Hand. Given the boldness with which Universal advertised the relationship of *The Cohens and Kellys* to *Abie's Irish Rose*, Universal could hardly be accused of suppressing the similarity of its movie to Nichols's play. But was there a legal transgression?

Nichols's attorney, Moses L. Malevinsky, was like Nichols a self-made professional who had gravitated to New York from a provincial background and achieved great success. Born to struggling Russian Jewish immigrants in Austin, Texas, Malevinsky was almost completely self-taught, never having reached high school. Nonetheless, he had audited lectures at the University of Texas School of Law and passed the bar examination. After practicing in Texas, Malevinsky had moved to New York where in 1910 he formed a partnership with Dennis O'Brien, a prominent entertainment lawyer who represented, among other famous clients, George M. Cohan, Mary Pickford, and Douglas Fairbanks. Joined by O'Brien's nephew, Arthur Driscoll, the new Irish–Jewish firm of O'Brien, Malevinsky, and Driscoll became known in theatrical circles as "the kosher sandwich."[23]

Malevinsky was a passionate theatergoer who habitually diagrammed dramatic structures using a specially designed form that he had printed up in quantity. One of his goals was to use his analyses to develop a sound basis for the consideration of issues relating to infringement. As Eaton Drone had pointed out years earlier, the determination of "substantial identity" in cases involving allegations of copyright infringement was a "task of great difficulty" in which judges might reach different conclusions.[24] Even a leading authority on drama such as Brander Matthews, a professor at Columbia University, who sometimes served as an expert witness in infringement matters, when questioned as to how infringement was determined was, according to Malevinsky, unable to say more than that the process was like a Treasury official examining a banknote and declaring that it was or was not genuine.[25] Clearly something more methodical and reliable was required. It was to fill this need that Malevinsky published *The Science of Playwriting*, a book in which *Abie's Irish Rose* figured prominently as a model of dramatic construction.

A sardonic profile published in "The Talk of the Town" section of the *New Yorker* in connection with the book identifies Malevinsky as the current leading authority on "plagiarism." It presents him as an intense, humorless man prepared to hold forth for hours while expounding his formula for detecting infringement. "Authors and Judges will now understand what a play is really about," Malevinsky is quoted as saying.[26] The root of the difficulty in copyright cases, he explained, was that there was no legal or literary definition of a play on which to base comparison when allegations of infringement arose. His theory of drama, he believed, resolved the problem. Drama was fundamentally a matter of emotion. A well-made play would be dominated by a single "basic emotion"—for example, "love" in the case of *Abie's Irish Rose*—which would then be realized in the play's chief character and elaborated through other elements such as the context in which the emotion played itself out. For analytical purposes Malevinsky reduced his theory to what he called an "algebraic formula." The "basic emotion"—the underlying passion that drove and defined the play—was Part A of the formula. Part B was the central character, the figure that "personified" the emotion. Part C was a series of elements, the most important of which was the social field in which the drama occurred, which Malevinsky called the "crucible." As Malevinsky put it in his book, "A plus B plus C of the Algebraic Formula when paralleled in two plays proves infringement."[27]

Malevinsky's algebraic formula bears the marks of a quirky autodidact. Insofar as Nichols's attorney proposed a single element—emotion—as the font of drama, his theory was an essentialist scheme that echoed Aristotle who had posited plot as the "soul" of tragedy, specifying other elements such as character and spectacle as subsidiary. Centering a theory on emotion rather than plot apparently reflected the new influence of Freudian theory. Just as Freud had proposed a methodical, scientific understanding of emotional life, so Malevinsky was proposing a methodical, scientific understanding of the representation of emotional life in drama. Thus Malevinsky's title, *The Science of Playwriting,* was not a casual label but a polemical claim. Drama was as much a subject for the rigor of scientific analysis as human behavior. And this analysis, he maintained, could lead to a scientific method for determining whether one dramatic work infringed another.

Shortly before *The Science of Playwriting* was published, Malevinsky had drawn upon his theory in winning a case in which he represented the author of a novel about interracial sexual relations in West Africa against the author of a play on a similar theme.[28] Now the release of *The Cohens and Kellys* provided him with the opportunity to apply his ideas more fully and explicitly in what, given the prominence of Nichols' play, was sure to be a closely followed battle. Before proceeding, however, he retained Charles Evans Hughes to counsel him. Hughes, who had served on the U.S. Supreme Court and was later to be appointed chief justice, studied Malevinsky's theory and his argument. "Mr. Malevinsky, you are right. Absolutely right," Malevinsky reported Hughes as saying. "But you will have great difficulty getting the courts to accept your work."[29] Perhaps Hughes, to whom Malevinsky had paid a substantial fee, was merely being polite in declaring Malevinsky "absolutely right." In any case Nichols's attorney chose to take Hughes's comment as an endorsement and ignore his warning about difficulties. Convinced that his client would prevail, Malevinsky turned down Universal's offer of several hundred thousand dollars to settle and so the matter proceeded to trial.

Given Anne Nichols's prominence and the fame of *Abie's Irish Rose,* it is not surprising that the trial was closely reported in the *New York Times* and other papers with stories describing each of the thirteen days of testimony.[30] Nichols herself was the first witness. An experienced professional who exploited her work with skill and intelligence, Nichols nonetheless presented herself at trial as a completely intuitive artist, a kind of natural genius. "I do not read many plays," she said. "I did not make a study of dramatic art. I just write from the heart. It all comes naturally to me." She claimed not to have read Shakespeare and in particular not to have read *Romeo and Juliet* although she acknowledged knowing the general story. Moreover, she claimed not to be familiar with contemporary drama either. "I do not write that way. I do not think things are done that way," she said, apparently referring to the notion of a playwright studying in preparation for composition. "I think things just come to you and you put them on paper."[31] But a professional playwright was also a property owner wary of theft. A playwright might write "from the heart," Nichols noted, but she then must "get it into Washington and copyright it so it cannot be taken."[32] When pressed as to precisely what aspects of *Abie's Irish Rose* she claimed to be original, Nichols deferred to Malevinsky. "He has a theory and I have not," she said. "I always think I am original, else why waste time?"[33]

In miniature we can perhaps see here something of the way the relationship between Nichols and Malevinsky depended on a mutually acceptable differentiation of roles. He was the intellectual with the theory who could explain what Nichols's play was about and why it was a work of genius. She was the intuitive artist, the playwright who instinctively understood emotion. He was the intellectual man, she was the intuitive woman. Professional women were still uncommon in the 1920s, a period in which women had only recently secured the right to vote. Thus Nichols's performance of untutored genius helped to preserve her femininity. She deferred to Malevinsky, a man, so far as dramatic theory and details of law were concerned—these belonged to the masculine sphere—but reserved for herself the role of creator.

Like many cases involving charges of infringement, *Nichols v. Universal* turned into a battle of expert witnesses. Offering himself as an expert on the basis of his experience and his published book, Malevinsky, led through his direct testimony by an associate from his office, expounded his method of infringement analysis. With it, he claimed, "I can determine plagiarism with the same precision and accuracy that I can identify a person by the prints of his fingers."[34] The centerpiece of Malevinsky's testimony was a diagram consisting of two quadrangles that illustrated the parallels between the works. One quadrangle represented the scheme of *Abie's Irish Rose*. At the top Malevinsky placed Solomon Levy, the Jewish father, and identified both the "basic emotion" he personified—love—and a list of subsidiary emotions starting with "affectionate, anger, anguish, anxiety, arguing" and continuing in alphabetical order to "trepidation, troubled, and worry." The second quadrangle represented the scheme of *The Cohens and Kellys*. At the top Malevinsky placed Nathan Cohen, who embodied,

Malevinsky maintained, not only the same basic emotion but precisely the same set of subsidiary emotions. Likewise, the quadrangles represented the parallels between the two Irish fathers and the emotions they embodied, starting with "prejudice," and the parallels between the young Jewish and Irish lovers. At the center of each quadrangle was an open space identifying the social field in which the drama occurred, in each case labeled "family life."

Malevinsky was on the witness stand for the better part of seven days, much of which was occupied by cross-examination. Universal's attorney, Nathan L. Miller, a former governor of New York, pressed him to acknowledge differences in the concrete incidents in the two works but Malevinsky insisted on the correctness of his analysis. In opposition, Governor Miller offered the expert testimony of Harrison R. Steeves, a professor of English at Columbia University. Steeves testified that *Abie's Irish Rose* and *The Cohens and Kellys* shared only four story elements: parental opposition, secret marriage, separation of the couple from their parents, and reconciliation through the birth of grandchildren. These were merely general ideas and commonplaces, not protectable by copyright. Moreover, the principal conflict in *The Cohens and Kellys* was the feud between neighbors. The love story was a dispensable subplot. Providing a historical survey as a context for his findings, Steeves described multiple early plays to demonstrate that the general theme of parental opposition to intermarriage, besides having Shakespearean antecedents, was a commonplace of the American stage. In the 1870s and 1880s American plays typically portrayed conflicts involving Irish and German lovers, but beginning in the 1890s, he testified, the emphasis shifted to Jews in relation to Irish families, following in this way the path of immigration.[35]

By modern standards of procedure, it must seem bizarre that Malevinsky served as his client's expert witness. Even more bizarre, after Universal's expert completed his direct testimony, Malevinsky stepped up to cross-examine Professor Steeves. From Malevinsky's point of view in which a drama was the playing out of intense emotions, particulars such as setting and incident were relatively inconsequential. Indeed, to Malevinsky mere incident must have seemed dreamlike and fleeting compared to the more fundamental reality of driving passion. Thus Malevinsky attempted to get Steeves to acknowledge that if the emotional structure of *The Cohens and Kellys* was identical to that of *Abie's Irish Rose,* a conclusion of infringement would follow. But Steeves would not accept Malevinsky's assumptions. Nor would Steeves join Malevinsky in calling dramaturgy a science. A particularly telling moment came when Malevinsky, committed to the idea of the artist as intuitive genius, asked Steeves whether he really believed that plays might be constructed from rational calculation. "Of course, I do," Steeves responded. Malevinsky was incredulous. "I am talking about artistic purposes," he insisted. "Do you think any playwright ever wrote a play logically with a definite idea in his own mind in the very beginning as to where he would start or where he was going to and what he was going to develop in the dramaturgy of the play?"[36] The two men were, of course, at a complete impasse.

District Court judge Henry W. Goddard, wrote a straightforward and workmanlike opinion. He accepted that *The Cohens and Kellys* might have incorporated some general ideas taken from Nichols, and he acknowledged what he politely called Malevinsky's "deep study of the technical construction of plays and motion pictures," but he rejected the claim of copyright infringement. "Counsel for the complainant seeks to show infringement by what seems to be a new test, or at least a new method of approach," he wrote, one that consists of "the extraction and comparison of the ideas or emotions forming the collocation of the play and picture under consideration." But ideas and emotions are not protected.

> It is the incidents or elements, or grouping of them, which produce the emotions that are to be compared. Similar emotions may be caused by very different ideas. It is obvious that the underlying emotions reflected by the principal characters in a play or book may be similar, and yet that the characters and expression of the same emotions be different. While it is true that a sequence of like events will awaken in the average person like emotions, it does not follow that it may be correctly deduced that like emotions were produced by the same events, or substantially identical episodes.[37]

In other words, one had to take account of character, incident, and sequence in order to determine infringement. Accepting Professor Steeves's testimony, Goddard found that any elements that *The Cohens and Kellys* shared with *Abie's Irish Rose* were commonplace.

Nichols appealed. Judge Goddard's decision, following the testimony of Universal's expert, had cited various works to demonstrate that elements such as the secret marriage and parental opposition were not new. Among the pieces mentioned were *Joseph Lewis & Son*, a play in which the objections of an orthodox Jew to his son's Christian bride are overcome; *Krousemeyer's Alley*, which involved opposition between an Irishman and a Jew to the marriage of their children; and *The Little Brother* in which the parents of a Jewish girl and her Catholic husband are reconciled after the birth of children. But there was no evidence, Nichols argued, that Universal had in fact consulted any of these works and therefore they were irrelevant. In her appeals brief, Nichols cited Learned Hand's well-known decision in *Fisher v. Dillingham*.[38] This involved an allegation that Jerome Kern had infringed another songwriter's copyright by using a particular, distinctive element. Kern's defense showed that the musical element in question, an ostinato, had appeared in public domain works prior to the plaintiff's song. Nevertheless, Judge Hand found that since the plaintiff had not copied the ostinato from any earlier work it must be original to him. Moreover, the evidence suggested that, even if prior art existed, Kern had indeed copied the ostinato from the plaintiff, albeit unconsciously, and therefore was liable for infringement. Likewise, Nichols argued, Universal had copied dramatic elements from *Abie's Irish Rose* and therefore was guilty of infringement whether or not similar material could be found in prior works.

Universal responded that Nichols' whole claim was ultimately based on Malevinsky's testimony, which ignored the concrete details of the works in question. Universal also noted that Malevinsky's approach to the issue by way of elaborated technical analysis ignored the "ordinary observer" test set down in *Dymow v. Bolton*, a case in which it had been ruled that although technical analysis might reveal that two works had certain elements in common, the similarity must nonetheless be apparent to an ordinary observer. "The copyright, like all statutes, is made for plain people, and that copying which is infringement, must be something which ordinary observation would cause to be recognized as having been taken from the work of another."[39] Ironically, *Dymow* was one of Malevinsky's best-known triumphs as a defendant's attorney. Furthermore, Universal argued, it was grossly inappropriate for Malevinsky to present himself as a disinterested expert witness.

* * *

These were the claims when in 1930 the *Abie's Irish Rose* case came before the Circuit Court of Appeals and Judge Learned Hand, a man often regarded as the most distinguished American jurist never to be elevated to the Supreme Court. Educated at Harvard College, where he studied philosophy with William James, Josiah Royce, and George Santayana, and at the Harvard Law School, Hand became one of the youngest federal judges in history when he was appointed to the bench in 1909 at thirty-seven years old. Fifteen years later he was advanced to the Second Circuit Court of Appeals, where he continued to be active as a judge, even after retirement, until he died in 1961 at age eighty-nine.[40]

Consideration of Nichols's appeal began with preliminary memos circulating among the three judges on the panel: Learned Hand, Thomas W. Swan, and Augustus N. Hand. Swan was a former dean of Yale Law School; Augustus Hand was Learned Hand's cousin and a distinguished jurist in his own right. As a group, the three, who sat together multiple times, constituted an appeals panel still remembered today as extraordinary. The memos circulated among them indicate that the judges were convinced that the movie had in fact copied elements of *Abie's Irish Rose*. It seemed plain, Learned Hand remarked, that Universal was attempting to trade on the success of the play. Still the issue was not whether Universal had sought to piggyback on *Abie's Irish Rose* but, more narrowly, whether Universal had taken anything protected from Nichols' play. There were indeed similarities between *The Cohens and Kellys* and *Abie's Irish Rose*, but were the similarities such as to impinge upon original expression? What should be the standard for a finding of infringement? "No standard probably exists," Hand wrote in his preliminary memo, "it is like invention; we must make the standard in each instance as it arises, with no better guide than general admonition on the one hand that there are variances which will not exonerate the plagiarist and on the other that it is only the concrete expression which the law protects."[41]

Trained in the Harvard pragmatic tradition, Hand was intellectually as well as temperamentally averse to quasi-scientific claims such

Judge Learned Hand (ca. 1910). Courtesy of Historical and Special Collections, Harvard Law School Library.

as those made by Malevinsky with his "algebraic formula." Commenting on the length of the trial record, which ran to nearly two thousand pages, Hand's final opinion noted that this was due chiefly to the use of expert witnesses. "Argument is argument whether in the box or at the bar," Hand wrote, "and its proper place is the last."

> The testimony of an expert upon such issues, especially his cross-examination, greatly extends the trial and contributes nothing which cannot be better heard after the evidence is all submitted. It ought not to be allowed at all; and while its admission is not a ground for

reversal, it cumbers the case and tends to confusion, for the more the court is led into the intricacies of dramatic craftsmanship, the less likely it is to stand upon the firmer, if more naïve, ground of its considered impressions upon its own perusal. We hope that in this class of cases such evidence may in the future be entirely excluded, and the case confined to the actual issues; that is, whether the copyrighted work was original, and whether the defendant copied it, so far as the supposed infringement is identical.[42]

Hand's objections to the use of experts at trial were long-standing. As a young lawyer he had published an essay in the *Harvard Law Review* objecting to the use of expert testimony in all kinds of cases, not just copyright, on grounds of principle, maintaining, among other things, that experts usurped the jury's role as finder of fact.[43] This essay was part of a widespread but ultimately futile nineteenth-century reaction produced by the spectacle of warring experts. Experts, after all, were supposed to be disinterested repositories of knowledge, not partisans.[44] Now, three decades later, when Hand returned to the subject in *Nichols* he was arguing against experts specifically in literary cases. Even more specifically, when Hand spoke in *Nichols* about experts leading the court into "the intricacies of dramatic craftsmanship," he was evidently invoking Malevinsky's often obscure testimony. An educated and sophisticated man who prided himself on his literacy, his taste, and his ability to reach sound conclusions in matters of literary dispute, Hand did not need Malevinsky's theories about "basic emotions," "personifications," and "crucibles" to understand the issues in the case. Nor was he inclined, like Judge Goddard, to tip his hat politely to Malevinsky's "deep study of the technical construction of plays and motion pictures."

Nonetheless, the abstractness of Malevinsky's theory seems to have spurred Hand to think beyond his "general admonition" about "variances" and "concrete expression."[45] As he had remarked in his preliminary memo,

> I think we should not commit ourselves to the proposition that a plot taken alone cannot be protected; it depends upon how faithfully it has been copied. If you take it line upon line, it ought not to be a defense that you have changed the dialogue or the dramatis personae. But there is a point at which the plot becomes so abstract that it is

like the sequence of concept in a work of the reason, or the emotions of a poem, or the information in a work of science or history.[46]

Abstractness was precisely the problem. How was one to find a pragmatic framework to deal with the classic problem of the general in relation to the particular when it came to infringement analysis? Hand was willing to accept, at least for the sake of argument, Nichols's contention that Universal had used some details from *Abie's Irish Rose*, but nevertheless, he said, speaking for the panel, "we think the defendant's play"—*The Cohens and Kellys*—"too unlike the plaintiff's to be an infringement." Therefore, Hand said, it "becomes necessary to give an outline of the two plays."[47]

Hand, whose tastes ran to the classics rather than popular drama, was a perceptive critic and his summaries in *Nichols* quickly established the differences between the works. *Abie's Irish Rose*, he observed, focuses on "a religious zealot who insists upon his child's marrying no one outside his faith; opposed by another who is in this respect just like him, and is his foil. Their difference in race is merely an obbligato to the main theme, religion. They sink their differences through grandparental pride and affection."[48] In *The Cohens and Kellys*, on the other hand,

> zealotry is wholly absent; religion does not even appear. It is true that the parents are hostile to each other in part because they differ in race; but the marriage of their son to a Jew does not apparently offend the Irish family at all, and it exacerbates the existing animosity of the Jew, principally because he has become rich, when he learns it. They are reconciled through the honesty of the Jew and the generosity of the Irishman; the grandchild has nothing whatever to do with it.[49]

Perhaps silently echoing Harrison Steeves's testimony, Hand concluded that the only matter common between the play and the movie was the "quarrel between a Jewish and an Irish father, the marriage of their children, the birth of grandchildren and a reconciliation."[50]

How then was one to determine when, despite differences, infringement occurred? Building on his observations in his preliminary memo, Hand proposed what has come to be known as the "abstraction test." "Upon any work, and especially upon a play," Hand wrote, a great number of patterns of increasing generality will fit equally well, as more and more of the incident is left out. The last may perhaps be no more than the most general statement of what the play is about, and at times might consist only of its title; but there is a point in this series of abstractions where they are no longer protected, since otherwise the playwright could prevent the use of his "ideas," to which, apart from their expression, his property is never extended. Nobody has ever been able to fix that boundary, and nobody ever can.[51]

With respect to plays, Hand said, the matter "chiefly centers upon the characters and sequence of incident, these being the substance."[52]

The issue was how closely two works corresponded in particulars. Hand illustrated the point, characteristically, with an example from Shakespeare.

> If Twelfth Night were copyrighted, it is quite possible that a second comer might so closely imitate Sir Toby Belch or Malvolio as to infringe, but it would not be enough that for one of his characters he cast a riotous knight who kept wassail to the discomfort of the household, or a vain and foppish steward who became amorous of his mistress. These would be no more than Shakespeare's "ideas" in the play, as little capable of monopoly as Einstein's Doctrine of Relativity, or Darwin's theory of the Origin of Species. It follows that the less developed the characters, the less they can be copyrighted; that is the penalty that an author must bear for marking them too indistinctly.[53]

In the two works at issue, Hand continued, "we think both as to incident and character, the defendant took no more—assuming that it took anything at all—than the law allowed."[54] The stories were quite different. Universal may well have taken certain general plot elements such as the quarrel, marriage of children, and reconciliation from Nichols because the amazing success of *Abie's Irish Rose* proved their popularity. Nevertheless, even assuming these elements were original to Nichols, that Nichols had discovered this dramatic vein, she could not keep it to herself. The "theme," as Hand put it, "was too generalized an abstraction from what she wrote."[55] As to character, there were but two general types common to the play and the movie, the lovers and the fathers. Nichols's lovers were little more than "stage properties."

"They are loving and fertile," Hand remarked dryly, "that is really all that can be said of them, and anyone else is quite within his rights if he puts loving and fertile lovers in a play of his own, wherever he gets them."[56] As for the fathers, all that Universal might be said to have taken were the stock comic figures of the Jew and the Irishman. Insofar as the fathers were individuated, they were different. Nichols's Jewish father was an affectionate man who was obsessed with his religion. Universal's Jewish father was neither warm nor religious but ostentatious and vulgar, "only by misfortune redeemed into honesty." Nichols's Irishman was "a mere symbol for religious fanaticism and patriarchal pride, scarcely a character at all." The defendant's Irishman was merely "a grotesque hobbledehoy, used for low comedy of the most conventional sort."[57] Where, then, should one draw the line between what Nichols's copyright protected and what it did not? In theory, the placement of such a line might seem arbitrary, but in practice, Hand said, "we have no question on which side of the line this case falls. A comedy based on conflicts between Irish and Jews, into which the marriage of their children enters, is no more susceptible of copyright than the outline of *Romeo and Juliet*."[58]

Let us recall that Nichols's argument on appeal rested on the claim that infringement was essentially an action, a taking. Citing *Fisher v. Dillingham*, Nichols had maintained that it was irrelevant whether story elements such as the opposition between an Irishman and a Jew to the marriage of their children could be found in works before *Abie's Irish Rose*. Universal had taken these elements from Nichols. In his decision Hand reaffirmed the principle established in *Fisher* that one might infringe by copying even if there was precedent for an element in works prior to the plaintiff's. The question in *Nichols*, however, was whether Universal had taken anything that was protectable. This turned the discussion into a consideration of at what level of generality the works were similar. Hand's abstraction test provided—and many decades later still provides—a pragmatic framework to address this question. Irritated by Malevinsky's "algebraic" claims, Hand objected categorically to the use of expert testimony in copyright cases. But in fact Professor Steeves's expert testimony had been useful in exposing the commonplaces and conventions from which Nichols's play was built and thus in building a critical basis for Goddard's decision.

Hand's abstraction test contributed a framework for an act of literary judgment. Silently building on the foundation excavated by Professor Steeves, Learned Hand's decision in *Nichols* is an elegant piece of literary analysis. As we have seen, it was by no means novel to find a judge acting as a literary critic. More than two hundred years before *Nichols*, Daniel Defoe stood in the pillory because of the way his judges chose to interpret *The Shortest Way with the Dissenters*, taking it as a provocative libel. Likewise, Lord Chancellor Hardwicke acted as a critic when he declared that Pope's letters had social value and therefore were protected by the Statute of Anne. In a similar fashion the Supreme Court in *Burrow-Giles v. Sarony* affirmed that Sarony's portrait of Oscar Wilde was a work of authorship and protected by copyright. By 1930 copyright doctrine was no longer overtly concerned with discriminating between what was or was not worthy of protection. But as a result of the development of the scope of protection beyond the literal text—copyright's reach toward the metaphysical—the practice of making discriminations of a different order had become crucial. Inevitably these involved literary judgments. Adapting Hand's nicely turned dictum about argument from the witness box or the bar, one might point out that literary criticism is literary criticism whether delivered from the witness box or the bench.

* * *

Anne Nichols had good reason to believe that the popularity of her play was being exploited by Universal. Moreover, she had reason to be particularly annoyed because she had been in negotiation with Universal. Perhaps, too, she was concerned that the publicity for *The Cohens and Kellys* would adversely affect her ability to strike a bargain with another movie company. If so, this latter concern was unfounded. Within a year after initiating her suit, Nichols concluded a record-making contract with the Famous Players-Lasky Corporation, which later became Paramount Pictures. The movie was released in 1928 as a Paramount silent film starring Buddy Rogers as Abie Levy and Nancy Carroll as Rose Mary Murphy. At the same time Nichols produced a novelized version that was promoted as a movie tie-in.[59] Nichols consistently refused to discuss her profits from *Abie's Irish Rose*, but the sale of the movie rights set a record. According to the *New York Times*, Nichols's contract with Famous Players-Lasky was likely to yield considerably more than the $1 million she had reportedly been demanding, and it is possible that it finally yielded as much as $2 million.[60]

Although Nichols wrote and produced other plays after *Abie's Irish Rose*, in fact she spent most of the next quarter of a century managing and exploiting her great hit. For example, she made a point of following regional productions of *Abie*, including amateur performances at schools and elsewhere. "I had a compulsion to check up on the various companies," she told an interviewer in 1962. "And invariably I'd find that the minute my back was turned, the actors would start distorting the play by ad-libbing lines for laughs. I had to travel back and forth across the country constantly to keep them in check. I hardly found time to write anymore."[61] In 1942 Nichols developed *Abie* into a radio serial that reached five million homes and earned her $6,000 a week.[62] And in 1946 a sound film version was released by Bing Crosby Productions. By the late 1940s Nichols was exploring the possibility of developing her property for the new medium of television.

It was in response to the radio show that Nichols in the 1940s experienced a change in the reception of her work. Sophisticated critics had long enjoyed mocking *Abie's Irish Rose* as a silly play, but now in the context of World War II and Nazi racism a new note of dissent appeared specifically in relation to Nichols's use of Jewish stereotypes. The first sign came in complaints from the New York Anti-Defamation League about the radio show's representation of Jewish characters, particularly "Mamele" as played by the Yiddish character actor Anna Appel. These complaints contributed to the show's demise after Procter & Gamble withdrew its sponsorship. Then in December 1946, when Bing Crosby Productions was about to release its remake, Richard E. Gutstadt, the national director of the Anti-Defamation League, wrote directly to Crosby protesting the movie's portrayal of Jews. "We are convinced, Mr. Crosby, that this movie does more than merely perpetuate a false stereotype. It rivets that stereotype in the mass mind of millions of people who may laugh as they witness it, who will come to see it because you produced it; but who will carry away with them a deposit of unfactual distortion incalculably damaging."[63] Much the same point was made in an editorial "Thumbs Down on 'Abie'" published in the *National Jewish Monthly*, a B'nai B'rith journal. "Circumstances involving minority groups today are not what they were in the early 1920's," the editorial said, invoking the recent Nazi horrors. "We do believe that this film will reinforce, if it does not actually create, greater doubt and keener misconceptions, as well as outright prejudice."[64] Having been made, the movie was released but it does not appear to have been a success.

Nichols was both confused and outraged. Documents indicate that in 1952 she was planning to bring suit for damages alleging a continuing conspiracy against her in connection with attempts to persuade movie theaters not to show the new *Abie* movie as well as with the cancellation of the earlier *Abie* radio show and the blocking of a possible *Abie* television series. Among the alleged conspirators were various movie theater corporations, B'nai B'rith, the Anti-Defamation League, Walter Winchell, the U.S. Communist Party, and the *Daily Worker*. "It is well-known through recent Congressional hearings that Communist Party members and camp followers had great influence in the motion picture industry," the papers claim. One memo drafted as part of the preparation for the suit suggested that an analysis of Walter Winchell's columns—Winchell, a Jew, had been outspoken against ethnic comedy— would show that he was receptive to Communist propaganda.[65]

There is no evidence that the contemplated suit was filed. What is striking, however, is the transformation through which the onetime liberal who had written a play celebrating tolerance had become an angry reactionary who saw herself as the victim of a Jewish-Communist conspiracy. Writing in her late years, Nichols said that she now understood why *Abie's Irish Rose*, which had been well-received in Los Angeles, had come so close to failing when she brought it to New York. She recalled that in 1922 the manager of a discount ticket agency had explained to her that "it took organization to kill a play that had already begun to catch on." Now, reflecting on this comment and her later experiences, she realized that "the 'commies' had their busy little hands in it" because her play was a threat to their movement. "Divide and conquer was their hymn of hate and brotherly love had to go. Nothing was too small for them to overlook and *Abie* became a real menace to them when it was found that the play had every kind of love known to man in it. It was built on love."[66]

In this comment Nichols was recalling Moses Malevinsky's praise of *Abie's Irish Rose* in his book *The Science of Playwriting*. There

Malevinsky cited the "remarkable unity of thought and expression" in Nichols's comedy, declaring that the play exhibited no less than nine different forms of love, including love for a child, a race, a religion, and for humanity generally, as well as the love between the boy and the girl. "No wonder that audiences re-act to this play!" Malevinsky exclaimed, "Its metaphysical and psychological aspects are all-encompassing."[67] Malevinsky had died in 1932, years before Nichols became an aggrieved woman suspicious of communist plots, but a quarter of a century later Nichols still relished his admiration and praise. As a playwright who presented herself as an intuitive rather than a reflective artist—"I just write from the heart"—Nichols was ill-equipped to comprehend the social and historical changes that had transformed the reception of *Abie's Irish Rose* between 1922, when it was seen as a liberal plea for inclusiveness, and 1946, when the Anti-Defamation League protested the play's stereotypical portrayal of Jews. Of course a play, like any work of art, is not a stable, objective entity but, as some forty years of postmodern criticism have emphasized, an act of communication. Necessarily the significance of a work of art changes over time as its audience changes. *Hamlet* has come to be understood in very different ways from what it may have meant in 1601.

Criticism has not always taken the dynamic, interactive nature of works of art into account. Nor has copyright theory, which, commercial in lineage, has tended to treat plays and movies as commodities and therefore, implicitly, as objects. The most enduring legacy of *Nichols v. Universal* has been the abstraction test that Learned Hand formulated as an approach to distinguishing between protectable expression and unprotectable idea. Descriptions will become more and more abstract as more of the incident—the concrete expression—is left out. At some point we will pass the boundary between what is and what is not protected. Let us note that Hand's formulation does not consider the dynamic, interactive nature of works of art. Indeed, by imagining the works at issue as verbal constructions that may be described at various levels of detail, Hand, too, was implicitly treating Nichols's play as if it had a stable, fixed existence, as if it were a thing rather than an act of communication. Ironically, the change in the reception of *Abie's Irish Rose* from the 1920s to the 1950s also highlights the historical specificity of Hand's pragmatic approach.[68]

Hand's abstraction test was naturally the product of its time and circumstances. How could it be otherwise? But his approach continues to be influential today, even when we have come to think of literary works in more fluid and dynamic ways. One of the circumstances that contributed to Hand's formulation was his philosophical training at Harvard. Another, less obvious factor, was his having to contend with the frustrating, slippery abstraction of Malevinsky's "algebraic formula." Anne Nichols and Moses Malevinsky were, like the two components of a binary star, bound to each other in a complex but mutually satisfactory relationship. Charged with determining whether infringement had occurred, and compelled to grapple with Malevinsky's contentions, Learned Hand found he had to develop some principled way of dealing with the particular in relation to the general in connection with infringement analysis. Thus all three—Nichols, Malevinsky, and Hand—became interacting participants in a legal drama larger than any of them individually.

CHAPTER SIX

Prohibited Paraphrase

Salinger v. Random House (1987)

IN July 1983 Ian Hamilton, an English poet and critic who had recently published a well-received biography of Robert Lowell, wrote to J. D. Salinger explaining that he had been commissioned by Random House to write a book about him and his work. Would it be possible, Hamilton asked, to visit Salinger sometime in the fall to discuss the project? He knew that the famous recluse was unlikely to respond to this inquiry. But, as he later put it, "*not* getting a reply was the essential prologue to my plot," a scheme that involved a quest story in which the rebuffs from Salinger would be part of the narrative. "The idea—or one of the ideas—was to see what would happen if orthodox biographical procedures were to be applied to a subject who actively set himself to resist, and even to forestall, them."[1] Not expecting a response, Hamilton began his research by sending letters to all the Salingers in the Manhattan telephone directory asking for information. One of these turned out to be the writer's sister, another his son. It was perhaps these approaches that prompted Salinger's response.

> Dear Sir:
>
> You say you've been commissioned by Random House to write a book about me and my work (you put it, perhaps undeliberately, in just that order), and I have no good reason to doubt your word, I'm exceedingly sorry to say. I might just add, probably not at all wisely, that it has always been a most terrible and almost unassimilable wonder to me that it is evidently quite lawful, the world over, for a newspaper or a publishing house to "commission" somebody, in the not particularly fair name of good journalism or basic profitable academic research, to break into the privacy not only of a person not reasonably suspected of criminal activity but into the lives as well, however glancingly, of that person's relatives and friends. I've de-

spaired long ago of finding any justice in the common practise. Let alone any goodness or decency.

Speaking (as you may have gathered) from rather unspeakably bitter experience, I suppose I can't put you or Random House off, if the lot of you are determined to have your way, but I do feel I must tell you, for what very little it may be worth, that I think I've borne all the exploitation and loss of privacy I can possibly bear in a single lifetime.

Sincerely yours

J. D. Salinger[2]

Hamilton recalled that he found the letter touching but a little artificial, "somewhat too composed."[3] Artificial and composed it may be, but the rhetoric also seems to me conspicuously unstable in its mixture of aggrieved resentment ("unspeakably bitter experience"), half-hidden sneers ("profitable academic research"), and self-pitying representation of the writer as victim. All these strains come together in the passive-aggressive conclusion in which Salinger declares that although he cannot prevent "the lot of you" from proceeding, "I must tell you, for what very little it may be worth, that I think I've borne all the exploitation and loss of privacy I can possibly bear in a single lifetime." Given that Hamilton, as he later acknowledged, was trying to provoke Salinger into playing the role of the quarry in a literary fox hunt, one cannot merely dismiss Salinger's bitter response as unjustified. Nonetheless, its style suggests a person who might at once be pathetic and nasty, charming and dangerous.

Strange and difficult Salinger certainly was. At the time Hamilton contacted him in 1983, it had been more than eighteen years since he had published anything—"Hapworth 16, 1924," his last published piece, appeared in the New Yorker in January 1965—and many years, too, since he had made any kind of public appearance. Salinger was a World War II veteran who had served in many of the worst battles of the war including the Normandy assault, the nightmarish Hürtgen campaign, and the Battle of the Bulge. He was also involved in the opening of the concentration camp at Dachau. At the war's end, physically intact but psychologically devastated, he checked himself into a Nuremberg hospital for treatment. After a brief marriage to a German woman and his return to New York in 1946, Salinger began developing his career as a

J. D. Salinger (1951). The Lotte Jacobi Collection. © The University of New Hampshire.

writer, publishing regularly in the *New Yorker*. This phase of his career climaxed with the appearance of *The Catcher in the Rye* (1951), followed by *Nine Stories* (1953), still the two works for which he is best known. In 1953 Salinger retreated to the remote village of Cornish, New Hampshire, where he lived in semi-isolation for the rest of his life, accompanied at various times by women much younger than himself, including his second wife, Claire Douglas, whom he started dating in 1951 when she was sixteen and married in 1955, and his year-long affair with Joyce Maynard in 1972, a Yale freshman at the time they met. Salinger died in Cornish at the age of ninety-one in 2010.[4]

As his angry protest to Hamilton about "exploitation and loss of privacy" suggests, Salinger was unusually touchy about public attention, a sensitivity that went back to the start of his career. Thus he wanted the author photograph of himself removed from the back cover of *The Catcher in the Rye,* and he sailed to England in order to avoid being present in New York when the book was published. He was less than thrilled when the novel was chosen as a Book of the Month Club selection, and at first he insisted to his editor at Little, Brown that no advance galleys or review copies of the book be distributed. Shortly after moving to Cornish in 1953, Salinger allowed himself to be interviewed by Shirlie Blaney, a pretty high school girl who published an account of the meeting in the local newspaper, the *Daily Eagle.* Salinger, who thought the girl was talking with him as part of a school project, felt profoundly betrayed. He responded by withdrawing from the life of the village and building a fence around his isolated property.[5]

Salinger did maintain some relationships in Cornish and elsewhere. Indeed, one of his friends was Judge Learned Hand who had long owned a vacation home in Cornish. Dinner at the Hands' was a weekly ritual for Salinger when the judge was in residence, and Salinger corresponded regularly with Hand when the judge was in New York. Hand understood Salinger's aversion to public attention. When a *Newsweek* reporter attempted to interview Hand about Salinger in the 1950s, he refused. "I know that Mr. Salinger does not want any publicity, and as his friend I am certainly unwilling to impose upon him what he would regard as an invasion of his privacy."[6] Likewise, Salinger's other friends, most of whom he maintained contact with by mail, respected his desire for seclusion. When Salinger learned in the 1960s that the University of Texas had obtained a collection of more than forty of his letters from a New York manuscript dealer, he resolved that no letters should ever again fall into collectors' hands. Therefore, he asked his longtime agent, Dorothy Olding, to destroy her files, a collection of perhaps five hundred pieces of correspondence dating back to World War II that included personal observations as well as discussions related to his writing. Olding faithfully complied.[7]

By the late 1960s, after "Hapworth 16, 1924" received mixed reviews, Salinger had come to feel that publication of any kind was a violation of privacy. In 1972 he repaid with interest a $75,000 advance that he had received from Little, Brown for his next book.[8] "It's a goddam embarrassment publishing," Joyce Maynard reports him as saying to her that year. "The poor boob who lets himself in for it might as well walk down Madison Avenue with his pants down."[9] A year or two later, in the context of trying to avoid litigation to prevent distribution of an unauthorized reprint, *The Complete Uncollected Short Stories*, Salinger agreed to speak with Lacey Fosburgh, a *New York Times* reporter, by telephone. "There's a marvelous peace in not publishing," he told her. "It's peaceful. Still. Publishing is a terrible invasion of my privacy. I like to write. I love to write. But I write just for myself and my own pleasure."[10] Betty Eppes, a young woman who secured a brief meeting with Salinger in 1980 by describing herself as an aspiring writer, reported that he told her that "publishing" was "a vicious, vicious thing."[11]

Perhaps the most public event in Salinger's life after his move to Cornish and his retreat from publishing was the lawsuit he initiated against Random House and Hamilton in 1986. What distressed Salinger was the very idea of a biography. But what could he do, what recourse would he have, if, as he put it in the letter to Hamilton, "the lot of you are determined to have your way"? Initially Salinger may have felt powerless. But after examining advance galleys for Hamilton's book and consulting with his attorneys, Kay Collyer and Boose, Salinger authorized them to send threatening letters to Random House and Hamilton. Salinger demanded that all references to his unpublished correspondence be removed.

From early on in the Hamilton project, Random House had taken account of potential legal action, but the consensus was that Hamilton's comparatively brief quotations were permissible. Moreover, the letters themselves were neither secretly nor surreptitiously obtained. Hamilton had found many of them through a recently published Salinger bibliography that not only listed letters individually but provided substantial quotations from them.[12] He had gained access to the originals and to further letters in the Harvard, Princeton, and University of Texas libraries. Challenged by Salinger, however, Random House summoned Hamilton from London to New York to minimize their exposure. There Hamilton spent a week, as he put it, "hacking and juggling" his text, rephrasing passages so that very little of Salinger's language remained.[13] A fastidious and elegant writer, Hamilton found this unpleasant work. It flattened his own text and made Salinger seem dull. Did such a result really serve either his or Salinger's interests? After these revisions Hamilton's book employed only about two hundred words from the letters and no more than ten words from any one item. A new set of galley proofs was produced and sent to Salinger's lawyers. Nevertheless, the effort to avoid litigation failed. Within a week Salinger filed suit for infringement, and legal battle was joined.

* * *

The claim in *Salinger v. Random House* was infringement.[14] But it was evident that the real issue was Salinger's concern with privacy. As Hamilton put it in his affidavit, "In the light of Mr. Salinger's hostility to this work, which dates back to its inception, I cannot believe that he is actually concerned about the copyright question at all. It is clear to me that he has simply seized upon the copyright issue as a means of interfering with publication of a work which he opposes for personal reasons."[15] The Salinger case thus returns us to issues similar to those that emerged some two hundred and fifty years earlier in *Pope v. Curll*. In that case, too, the works immediately at issue were letters. Furthermore, in *Pope* as in *Salinger* the legal battle involved a celebrity author who was attempting to use copyright for purposes related to privacy.

The law of copyright had of course developed substantially. *Pope* turned on the question of whether private letters were protected at all. Did they properly fall under the statute's goal of "the encouragement of learning?" By the time of *Salinger* there was no question about the protection of letters. The U.S. Copyright Act of 1976 declared that every "work of authorship fixed in any tangible medium of expression" was protected from the moment of fixation, a formula that undoubtedly included letters.[16] Equally important, the institution of authorship had also developed. *Pope*, as I have discussed, constructed his career in a transitional moment when the notion of professional authorship was not quite respectable. Moreover, Pope lived in a culture that understood identity as social and performative rather than as a fixed core of selfhood, the formation that emerged in the later eighteenth and early nineteenth centuries. Nonetheless, Salinger's concerns both as an author and as a litigant curiously refract, sometimes in inverted form, those of Pope.

Pope's great subject, as I have suggested, was finally himself. His letters, like his poetic epistles and his satirical works, were in effect portraits of his gentility and integrity in contrast to a world of knaves and fools. Part of Pope's control of his persona involved oversight of the presentation of his publications—the choice of formats and types among other things—and he was concerned too with his visual representation, taking care that flattering images of himself were publicly available. Salinger also cared about the physical presentation of his writings. He struggled fiercely over the details of book covers and over matters related to the presentation of him personally. When he came to publish *Nine Stories* (1953), for example, he demanded both a front cover without a pictorial illustration and a back cover without biographical notes. After the publication of a tawdry paperback edition of his short stories that showed a sultry blonde staring seductively at the reader, Salinger demanded that every publishing contract give him final say over the details of presentation. Among other things he required that no author picture appear on any of his books.[17] Whereas Pope took care to ensure that flattering images of him were available, Salinger did his best to prevent any images at all from circulating.

Part of Pope's strategy of self-promotion was his portrayal of himself in the *Epistle to Dr. Arbuthnot* as besieged by suitors in his Twickenham country retreat. "What walls can guard me, or what shades can hide? / They pierce my thickets, through my grot they glide." This was, of course, largely a matter of genteel posturing. Salinger, however, really was besieged in his Cornish retreat where reporters and admirers stalked him seeking an interview or a photograph. Moreover, like Pope, Salinger's material was also in a sense his own life and experience. Thus, as many have noted, Pencey Prep, the private school from which Holden Caulfield flees, resembles Valley Forge Military Academy, the school that Salinger attended in the mid-1930s, and the English setting of "For Esmé—with Love and Squalor" resembles Tiverton, the Devon town where Salinger's army unit was headquartered in 1944 while awaiting D-day and the invasion of France.

Being autobiographically grounded, Salinger's fiction naturally, if somewhat quixotically, dramatizes his concern with privacy. Thus *The Catcher in the Rye* famously opens with Holden Caulfield telling us what he is *not* going to reveal: "If you really want to hear about it, the

Cover art: *For Esmé—with Love and Squalor* (1959 ed.). New York: Ace Books, Inc., no. H235. Artwork by Enric Sio. Image reproduction courtesy of Steven Strelan.

first thing you'll probably want to know is where I was born, and what my lousy childhood was like, and how my parents were occupied and all before they had me, and all that David Copperfield kind of crap, but I don't feel like going into it, if you want to know the truth." Holden goes on to explain that not only does autobiography bore him but "my parents would have about two hemorrhages apiece if I told anything personal about them"—a statement that apparently reflects the attitudes of Salinger's own parents.[18] Salinger introduced deliberate falsehoods on legal documents such as his marriage certificate. Likewise, Holden misrepresents the facts of his life, especially when speaking to adults. For example, on a New York-bound train he introduces himself to the mother of a Pencey classmate, as "Rudolf Schmidt," explaining that he is returning home because he is suffering from a brain tumor. "I didn't feel like giving her my whole life history."[19] Inquisitive figures such as Mr. Spencer, the teacher at Pencey who is genuinely disturbed by Holden's failure, or Ackley, the "nosy bastard" who lives in the next room at Pencey, are portrayed as insensitive and irritating.

Along with inquisitiveness, Holden rejects "phoniness," by which he seems to mean social posturing. Holden's characteristic repetitions and emphases—"I could tell you more," he says at the end of the novel, "but I don't feel like it. I really don't"—reflect his desire to demonstrate scrupulous honesty.[20] "Honesty," a quality beyond social skill, perhaps even incompatible with social skill, is the unnamed opposite of "phoniness" in Holden's moral universe. It is also the value that Salinger, according to Joyce Maynard, insisted upon. "Good writing has got to be unblinkingly honest," he told Maynard.[21] One must not write to please others but only to say what is "real and true." But honesty is dangerous, Salinger somewhat melodramatically insisted. "Honest writing always makes people nervous, and they'll think of all kinds of ways to make your life hell."[22] For Salinger honesty also seems to have become associated with silence. Thus in "Raise High the Roofbeam, Carpenters," Seymour, reflecting on the horrors of the Battle of Gettysburg, remarks that Lincoln's address was "dishonest." If someone "*had* to speak at the anniversary of the event, he should simply have come forward and shaken his fist at his audience and then walked off."[23] Writing was for Salinger a good thing. But he came to understand publishing as inherently "phony," inherently dishonest.

We recall that dishonesty was an issue raised by the nineteenth-century scholars who discovered that Alexander Pope edited and sometimes even reassigned his letters when preparing them for publication. But for Pope, as I have suggested, the idea of presenting a raw and unedited picture of himself and his relationships would have seemed unacceptably crude. Pope was not trying to reveal an essential inner self—such a concept might have been meaningless to him—so much as to portray himself in the context of his eminent social circle. In the terms expounded by Lionel Trilling in his seminal *Sincerity and Authenticity*, Pope was "sincere" insofar as he understood himself to be accurately representing the values and virtues that he and his friends embodied.[24] Salinger, on the other hand, like his character Holden Caulfield, aspired to the later, inner-directed concept of "authenticity."

We have seen how tensions related to the drama of authorship played themselves out in Alexander Pope's complex schemes concerning the publication of his letters. Salinger's drive to "honesty," his commitment to be true to his inner self, was part of the imperative that shaped his retreat to New Hampshire. Part may also have been Salinger's urge to flee his own egotism, his desire to escape the burdens of selfhood. This impulse, perhaps related to his engagement with Buddhism, helps to explain his discomfort with any form of personal display. Moreover, seeing his personal letters exhibited in public must have touched a particularly sensitive nerve because for Salinger letters really were—to use the phrase that Pope adapted from Lucian—windows into his bosom. Some sense of what letters seem to have meant to Salinger may be gathered by noting the somewhat unusual way in which letters figure in Salinger's fiction. As Daniel Pecchenino notes in an excellent essay about Salinger's concern with authenticity, Salinger's characters, like Salinger himself, are frequent letter writers. Letters in fiction, Pecchenino observes, generally serve to further or shift the plot, but in Salinger's stories letters have little relation to the turns of the narrative. Instead, letters in Salinger typically serve to authenticate the voices of particular characters, as for example, the excited letter from Franny to her boyfriend that Salinger prints at the start of her story in *Franny and Zooey*. As Pecchenino notes, one might even argue that *The Catcher in the Rye* is a kind of extended letter from Caulfield to the reader.[25]

Torn between the drive to be true to his inner self regardless of convention and a contrary drive to escape the burdens of selfhood, Salinger appears to have suffered from a peculiarly intense and idiosyncratic case of authenticity, one that made any kind of exposure painful. Given his idiosyncrasies, the lawyers for Random House may have thought it unlikely that Salinger would proceed with his suit. To do so would mean exposing himself to a deposition in which he would be subjected to questioning under oath. But Salinger did proceed, filing a complaint dated October 3, 1986, in which he charged Random House and Hamilton with infringing his rights in his unpublished letters "by quotation and by excessive paraphrasing" and seeking to reap an "unfair benefit" from Salinger's "creativity."[26] Salinger asked for preliminary and permanent injunctions to prevent the publication of the biography.

* * *

Publication of Hamilton's book was imminent, and therefore matters proceeded very quickly. On the day that Salinger filed, District Judge Pierre N. Leval convened a meeting in chambers in which he surveyed the matter with the attorneys. At issue was whether Hamilton's references to Salinger's unpublished letters were permissible under the doctrine of "fair use." As a principle, fair use is often traced back to the eighteenth-century case of *Gyles v. Wilcox* (1740), decided one year before *Pope*, in which Lord Chancellor Hardwicke ruled that an abridgment should not be considered piracy. After all, if the purpose of copyright was the encouragement of learning, it was necessary to allow one author to build upon and develop the work of another. In *Gyles*, which involved two legal treatises, the issue was whether the defendant's treatise was really the same as that of the plaintiff, merely "colourably" shortened so as to appear different. Rather than ruling on the matter himself or sending it to a jury, as had been requested, Hardwicke referred the issue to a special master who found the defendant's work to be noninfringing.[27]

In U.S. law fair use is generally traced to the landmark case of *Folsom v. Marsh* (1841), which I have already mentioned in Chapter 3. In *Folsom*, which involved the use of George Washington's letters in a new biography, Justice Joseph Story specified that in deciding whether use of protected materials was fair, the factors to be considered included "the nature and objects of the selections made, the quantity and value of the materials used, and the degree in which the use may prejudice the sale, or diminish the profits, or supersede the objects, of the original work."[28] The principles sketched by Story were eventually codified in the Copyright Act of 1976, which identifies four factors to be considered in determining whether a challenged use is fair: (1) the purpose and character of the use; (2) the nature of the copyrighted work; (3) the amount and substantiality of the portion used in relation to the copyrighted work as a whole; and (4) the effect of the use upon the potential market for or value of the copyrighted work.[29]

But would fair use apply to unpublished materials such as Salinger's letters? Prior to the Copyright Act of 1976 this issue did not arise in federal courts because copyright protected only registered and published materials. Unpublished materials were subject to the common-law principle, known as common-law copyright, which recognized that the author had the right to control the first publication or to withhold a work from publication. Such issues were from time to time litigated in state courts, not at the federal bar. The 1976 act, however, preempted common-law copyright, which meant that Salinger's case would be heard in federal court. A year and a half earlier in *Harper & Row v. Nation*, the first federal case to deal with the matter of fair use with respect to unpublished works, the U.S. Supreme Court had affirmed the author's right to control first publication. It seems likely that this conspicuous precedent influenced Salinger's decision to proceed.

Decided in 1985, the *Nation* case involved excerpts from former president Gerald Ford's unpublished memoirs in which Ford described his pardoning of Richard Nixon. Ford's text had been surreptitiously obtained by the *Nation*, which published an article on the forthcoming memoir quoting about three hundred words from the book, thereby scooping *Time*, which had contracted with Harpers and was about to print an excerpt related to the pardon. When Harpers sued for infringement, the magazine claimed fair use, contending that the material it published was of national importance and could not be protected. The District Court observed that the magazine had taken the "heart" of a valuable work that was about to be published and rejected the fair use claim. But a divided panel of the Court of Appeals reversed, citing among other things the political significance of the subject matter. The Supreme Court then overruled the reversal. The final word was that of Justice Sandra Day O'Connor who wrote the majority opinion, noting among other things the importance of the fact that the Ford memoir was as yet unpublished. A dissenting opinion by Justice William Brennan stressed the importance of public debate, rejecting what Brennan called a "constricted reading of the fair use doctrine."[30]

The controverted nature of the *Nation* matter—the two lower courts disagreeing and the Supreme Court divided—signaled how difficult the fair use question might prove in the *Salinger* matter. Nonetheless,

Salinger's attorneys relied heavily on Justice O'Connor's opinion and particularly on the passage stating that "Under ordinary circumstances, the author's right to control the first public appearance of his undisseminated expression will outweigh a claim of fair use."[31] In the October 3 meeting in Judge Leval's chambers, Marcia Paul stated Salinger's position: "We believe that when dealing with the right of first publication with unpublished letters under the authority of the *Nation* case, that the fair use doctrine has little, if any, relevance."[32] Salinger's letters were privileged and protected. Salinger had the right to prevent them from being published in any form.

Judge Leval questioned Paul on the key differences between the *Nation* case and the present matter. The *Nation* had obtained a copy of Ford's memoirs surreptitiously; but Hamilton had found Salinger's letters in publicly accessible archives. Ford's memoirs were soon to be published; the *Nation* had merely jumped the gun by publishing them sooner. Salinger, on the other hand, intended never to have the letters published in his lifetime. Was there a difference between "gun jumping" and an attempt "to deny the public whatever the public might receive from the publication?"[33] Leval remarked that Salinger was after all a famous author and that the public had an interest in his thoughts. Even at this early stage in the proceedings, Leval was perhaps signaling the weight he accorded to the public interest.

To some degree, of course, Salinger's concern with privacy was self-defeating. One of the ironies of the case is that in order to pursue the matter Salinger had to register the letters, sending copies to the Library of Congress where they became available for anyone to examine for a modest fee. Of course the letters were already publicly available in the Texas, Princeton, and Harvard libraries, where Hamilton had read them and, as noted, interesting excerpts had appeared in the published Salinger bibliography. To tie this loose thread, Salinger's attorneys wrote the publisher of the bibliography demanding assurances that all paraphrases and quotes from unpublished material be deleted before further copies were distributed. But since copies of the bibliography could already be found in libraries around the world, the request was mostly symbolic. Salinger's letters might be unpublished, but they were not quite private.

These ironies were apparent at the October 3 meeting in Judge Leval's chambers. Salinger's attorneys presented Leval with a copy of

Judge Pierre N. Leval. Courtesy of The U.S. Court of Appeals, Second Circuit.

their comparative analysis of the letters and the book, requesting that it be placed under seal because it included quotations. This was consistent with Salinger's position on the protected nature of the materials. Judge Leval granted the request, observing that the defendants could in no way be injured by sealing the documents. As for the general public, he remarked that although the court files would be sealed, the public would have access to Salinger's letters through archives and depositories. It is worth noting that the seal on the legal materials containing the contested quotations continues to the present day, more than a quarter of a century after the case was resolved. Interestingly, although Salinger's lawyers were adamant about even fragmentary quotations from his personal letters, they did not raise similar issues about quotations from unpublished fiction that Hamilton had located at Princeton. Marcia Paul said that Salinger had "no desire to take the same position with regard to unpublished stories as with regard to his private correspondence."[34] The only works at issue were the letters. In his affidavit Hamilton had asserted that Salinger was not in fact concerned with the copyright question at all but with his privacy. Now in the meeting in chambers, the defendants' attorney Robert Callagy remarked, "What is really behind this case is an attempt to use the copyright law to achieve another purpose."[35]

One issue on which the parties agreed was quantitative. The revised page proofs of Hamilton's book contained 217 words of actual quotation from Salinger's letters, no more and no less. This was a very small percentage either of Salinger's text or of Hamilton's. But Leval, who throughout the proceedings showed an impressive grasp of the subtleties of dealing with literary matters, remarked that merely quantifying the defendants' use was not to the point. "I think these matters are not to be decided by accountants based on percentages."[36] In fact the issue came to turn not on direct quotation but on paraphrase, a much more subtle and elusive matter. When is a paraphrase so close to the original that it becomes an infringement? At the October 3 meeting, Marcia Paul, asserting that "paraphrase of expression is as much protected under the copyright laws" as direct quotation, observed that the defendants' brief did not speak to that issue.[37]

Before the meeting ended, one final matter was addressed. Callagy indicated that the defendants intended to subpoena Salinger for a deposition. Paul objected that the request for a deposition was little more than harassment; Salinger's aversion to public appearance was well-known. Nonetheless, she agreed to produce Salinger if the judge required it. Leval ruled that the defendants were entitled to a deposition. One week later on the afternoon of October 10, 1986, Salinger and Paul sat in a conference room in the Helmsley Building on Park Avenue and for six hours Salinger answered Callagy's questions about his life and work. Large portions of the deposition are under seal, among other things because Callagy led Salinger methodically through an identification of the letters asking him to identify the "expressive heart" of each—the term came from the decision in the *Nation* case—and say how much he thought Hamilton had taken. As Paul Alexander, who provides an account of the deposition, has remarked, this must have been one of the worst days of Salinger's life.[38] According to report, Salinger's hands shook so violently that Marcia Paul held them firmly under the conference table throughout the proceeding.[39]

The following week Hamilton was also deposed. Salinger's attorney pressed him as to his understanding of fair use and also pressed on the matter of paraphrase. Hamilton acknowledged that paraphrase was "a very troubled question." "I knew that I had to avoid, as it were, appropriating the expressive part of any letter by which I took to mean the literary devices that make that letter distinctively by J. D. Salinger. So I had that in mind. It was a great temptation, of course, because he is a very witty, stylish writer."[40] Asked why he copied a passage from one of the letters, Hamilton responded, "I wanted to convey the fact that [Salinger] was adopting an ironic term." "Couldn't you have stated that he had an ironic tone?" the attorney asked. Hamilton responded, "That would make a pedestrian sentence I didn't want to put my name to." Likewise, when pressed as to why he closely paraphrased Salinger's comment that Wendell Wilkie "looks to me like a guy who makes his wife keep a scrapbook for him" instead of just reporting that Salinger thought Wilkie was vain, Hamilton replied "Because that is, again, laborious, pedestrian."[41] A punctilious stylist himself, for Hamilton one of the appeals of Salinger as a subject was the vitality of his language.

Several weeks later, Judge Leval denied Salinger's application for an injunction, finding that Hamilton's use of Salinger's materials was not infringing. After factoring out ideas, commonplaces, and historical facts—elements not protected by copyright—Leval identified about thirty instances in which Hamilton had taken a word, a phrase or an image. "In the rarest case, a complete sentence is taken." There can be no doubt, he remarked, that these takings improve Hamilton's book. "It certainly tells us more about Salinger to read his acid quip that anyone who has worked for 'a good upholsterer' considers himself qualified to edit a short story anthology . . . than to be told that he resented the presumption of unqualified editors."[42] But brief excerpts such as these did not interfere with Salinger's control over initial publication and would have no effect on the marketability of the letters. They were legitimate instances of fair use. Salinger had claimed that the fair use doctrine did not apply to unpublished materials, but Leval rejected this position as "exaggerated and unreasonable."[43] In any case,

Leval concluded, "Hamilton's use of copyrighted expression is so minimal, it is difficult to perceive any harm to Salinger. The wound he has suffered is not from infringement of his copyright but from the publication of a biography that trespasses on his wish for privacy. The copyright law does not give him protection against that form of injury."[44]

Salinger promptly appealed and less than three months later the Second Circuit Court of Appeals reversed, sending the case back to the District Court with directions to issue an injunction. The decision was written by Judge Jon O. Newman who was joined by Judge Roger L. Miner in a truncated panel of two, the third member having died during the course of the proceedings. Judge Newman's approach was different from Leval's. Leval had brusquely rejected Salinger's interpretation of the *Nation* ruling to mean that no use of an unpublished work was permissible. Newman did not quite affirm Salinger's reading, however, he did declare that "the tenor of the Court's entire discussion of unpublished works conveys the idea that such works normally enjoy complete protection against copying any protected expression."[45] This interpretation clearly tilted the matter toward Salinger. Newman took issue as well with Leval's assessment of the magnitude of Hamilton's use of protected expression, expressing doubts as to whether Leval had taken sufficient account of Hamilton's close paraphrases as well as his verbatim quotes. Counting paraphrases as well as quotations, Newman concluded that Hamilton's biography had taken a much more substantial portion of the letters than Leval acknowledged. He also concluded that the Hamilton biography might indeed have some negative effect on the commercial value of Salinger's letters. Salinger might have no present intention of publishing the letters; nonetheless, he had the right to protect their value in the event that he changed his mind.

The Supreme Court declined to review Newman's reversal of Leval, and so the formal legal matter ended at the Second Circuit Court of Appeals. Hamilton's biography, *J. D. Salinger: A Writing Life*, was withdrawn, and a year later Random House published an expurgated substitute, titled *In Search of J. D. Salinger*, which concluded with Hamilton's report of the law case. Hamilton also turned his experiences with Salinger to account by writing *Keepers of the Flame*, a historical study of

Judge Jon O. Newman. Courtesy of The U.S. Court of Appeals, Second Circuit.

the protection of reputations and management of literary estates ranging from early modern figures such as John Donne to moderns such as James Joyce. In this characteristically literary way Hamilton sought to make sense of his frustrating experience in the Salinger matter.

* * *

But the important legal issues raised by *Salinger v. Random House* did not end with the formal conclusion of the case. The question of the use of unpublished materials was revisited the following year in *New Era v. Holt*. In this case the publishing arm of the Church of Scientology sued to suppress an unflattering biography titled *Bare-Faced Messiah: The True Story of L. Ron Hubbard* on the grounds that it quoted biographical materials that were protected because unpublished. Citing *Salinger* as well as the *Nation* case, New Era contended "that the holder of a copyright in unpublished matter enjoys virtually complete protection against claims of fair use."[46]

Once again the case came before Judge Leval who used the occasion to revisit *Salinger* and elaborate on the relation of language to fact. To make the protection of an author's right to first publication prevail over all competing considerations, Leval said, would mean that public figures could use copyright as "an aggressive weapon" to obstruct criticism. This was of course precisely what the Church of Scientology was doing in seeking to suppress Russell Miller's biography of Hubbard. "It is not a satisfactory answer," Leval said, "that the world remains free to use the facts and ideas" to be found in such writings. "Often it is the words used by the public figure (or the particular manner of expression) that are the facts calling for comment."[47] In the case at hand, Leval noted, one of the biographer's purposes was to establish Hubbard's unattractive character. "It is a principal objective of Miller's biography to argue and prove that Hubbard's dominating traits of character included dishonesty, boastfulness and pretention, paranoia, bigotry and snobbery, cruelty and disloyalty, aggressiveness, cynicism and derangement at times approaching insanity. The vast majority of Miller's takings of Hubbard's words are to demonstrate these observations."[48] Leval went on to an exhaustive examination of particular passages arranged under headings according to the specific traits Miller was seeking to demonstrate. As a striking example of the use of language to display character, Leval cited Miller's quotation of Hubbard's sneer in one of his journals, "The trouble with China is, there are too many Chinks here." It was, Leval remarked, the choice of words that revealed Hubbard's character.[49] There was no "fact" to report apart from the phrase itself.

Leval concluded that, taking into account the book as a whole, the defendant had demonstrated fair use. Comparing the *New Era* matter to *Salinger*, Leval acknowledged that some takings of Salinger's expression were for the purpose of enlivening Hamilton's study. "That is not the case here. Hubbard's expression is taken primarily to show character flaws in a manner that cannot be accomplished without use of his words." Nonetheless, Leval continued, given the Second Circuit's ruling in *Salinger,* "I cannot conclude that the Court of Appeals would accord fair use protection to all of Miller's quotations, or that the biography as a whole would be considered non-infringing."[50] Therefore, obeying the mandate of the *Salinger* decision, he felt compelled to conclude that *Bare-Faced Messiah* did to some degree infringe Hubbard's copyrights.

Normally a finding of infringement would lead to an injunction against publication as the Church of Scientology had requested. But Leval concluded that such an order would suppress an important study of an influential public figure. As he saw it, copyright interests had been brought into direct conflict with constitutional guarantees of free speech. On first amendment grounds, Leval denied New Era's request for an injunction. As Mark A. Fowler, one of the attorneys in both *Salinger* and *New Era,* put it in an important article, "In essence, Judge Leval was politely telling the higher court that it was dead wrong in *Salinger* and that it had unnecessarily created a circumstance where copyright was impinging on free speech values."[51]

The Church of Scientology appealed, and once again the issue of fair use in unpublished materials came before the Circuit Court. In a stern opinion, Roger J. Miner, the judge who had joined with Jon Newman in overturning the *Salinger* opinion, rejected the idea that first amendment concerns were relevant at all given that Leval had found that the biography did to some degree infringe. Facts were indeed unprotected, and the public had a right to know facts; it was not necessary to use protected expression to communicate facts. Thus Miner also rejected Leval's contention that sometimes in biographical studies the precise language used by the subject *was* the fact. If Miller's biography of Hubbard was suppressed, the public would not necessarily be deprived of an " 'interesting and valuable historical study,' Miner said, but only of an infringing one."[52] The logic of Judge Miner's blunt opinion, with its very restrictive reading of *Salinger,* seemed to point to a complete over-turning of Leval's decision on the grounds that quotation of unpublished material was never permissible. Surprisingly, however, Miner did not issue an injunction. But he refrained, as he put it, "for a reason wholly different from any of those set forth in the district court's opinion."[53] The plaintiff had unreasonably delayed bringing its action against Holt and therefore forfeited any claim to an injunction on the grounds of laches or neglect. Thus, while completely rejecting Leval's reasoning, Judge Miner invoked a flaw in the plaintiff's claim that allowed the court to deny an injunction.

Miner was joined in his opinion by Judge Frank X. Altimari. The third member of the panel, however, Chief Judge James L. Oakes, issued a separate opinion. Oakes concurred that no injunction should issue. Nevertheless, he sought to make clear that he dissented from Miner's restrictive application of *Salinger*. "I do not think," he said, "that *Harper & Row*, as glossed by *Salinger*, leads to the inevitable conclusion that all copying from unpublished work is *per se* infringement."[54] Oakes noted that Miner's opinion went "out of its way to take issue with Judge Leval's opinion" and that this tended "to cast in concrete" the decision in *Salinger* and confine the concept of fair use.[55] To Oakes it seemed necessary only to affirm the denial of an injunction for laches.

The disagreements in *New Era* led Henry Holt, the publisher of the Hubbard biography, to call for a rehearing of the case en banc—that is, consideration of the matter by a panel of all the active members of the Circuit Court of Appeals. The motion did not gain the necessary majority of the active judges. But, significantly, Jon Newman, who had overruled Leval in *Salinger*, not only supported the motion for rehearing but issued a dissenting opinion. Joined by three other judges including Oakes, Newman expressed concern that the language of *New Era* might lead to misunderstandings that could deter authors and publishers. The court's holding, Newman said, should be understood as limited to the finding that, given the particular circumstances of the case, the doctrine of laches barred issuance of a preliminary injunction. The panel had not committed the Circuit as a whole, he insisted, to the proposition that "the copying of some small amounts of unpublished expression to report facts accurately and fairly can never be fair use."[56]

The *New Era* case concluded with the question of fair use in unpublished material less than firmly settled. Was it ever acceptable to employ unpublished material in a critical or biographical work and if so under what circumstances? *Salinger* and *New Era* produced considerable anxiety. An article in *Newsweek* titled "The End of History?" reported that publishers and authors were assuming that quoting almost anything unpublished was a violation of copyright. "If the law were this way when I wrote the three volumes of 'The Age of Roosevelt,'" Arthur Schlesinger reportedly said, "I might be two volumes short."[57]

In response, Judge Newman wrote a brief piece titled "Not the End of History," in which he stated that in his view "the quotation of expressive content for the purpose of fairly and accurately conveying factual information" was permitted. Newman suggested that rather than censoring all dubious passages, publishers should be prepared to litigate to establish their rights. Legally, this suggestion made perfect sense, but was it practicable? Would publishers really take on such risks and expenses?[58]

Newman's article appeared at the same time that Congress began hearings on the question of fair use. Had the Second Circuit in fact created a virtual per se rule prohibiting any publication of unpublished material? Was legislative intervention needed? The argument in favor of legislation was the need to correct the impression left by *Salinger* and *New Era*. The principal argument against was that action was unnecessary because no per se rule had in fact been established. Moreover, such an amendment would be a threat to the "bedrock" copyright principle that the author has the right of first publication. After lengthy hearings, a one-sentence amendment was recommended and passed stating that if a finding of fair use was based on consideration of the codified factors for analysis, the "fact that a work is unpublished shall not itself bar a finding of fair use."[59]

* * *

The Second Circuit's struggle with the question of fair use in unpublished works concluded with legislative intervention. The issues were difficult because they reached deep into the history of copyright. Is copyright a property right or a privilege? Has it been instituted to benefit authors and publishers or the public at large? Moreover, when the subject matter of law is something as fluid and protean as language, how are lines to be drawn and distinctions made?

Leval and Newman had engaged each other on the legal issues raised by *Salinger* in a formal conversation through their judicial opinions. They also engaged each other in discussion outside the courtroom. Newman initiated the conversation on March 24, 1988, with a lecture at Columbia University titled "Copyright Law and the Protection of Privacy," in which he complained about the difficulties that fair use creates for a writer who simply wishes to maintain his privacy. This was of course exactly the situation in *Salinger*, which involved an obviously sincere and sympathetic plaintiff. *New Era*, in which the plaintiff's motives were more problematic, had not yet been initiated. Newman insisted that his conclusions in *Salinger* were not based on privacy interests but solely on "traditional principles governing the scope and application of the fair use defense."[60] But he complained about the situation created by the 1976 statute in which the common-law protection of unpublished writings was preempted by statutory copyright. Because of the preemption, the defense of an author's right to prevent publication depended on whether privacy interests could be presented in conjunction with economic interests. (We recall Newman's comment that although Salinger might have no intention of publishing his letters, nevertheless, he had the right to protect their commercial value in case he changed his mind.) Moreover, since the author's right not to publish was now subject to copyright analysis, an author such as Salinger who wished to maintain his privacy had to "fend off claims of fair use."[61]

Distressed by the situation that the preemption of common-law copyright had produced, Newman declared that he would give almost total protection to an unpublished private writing. Indeed, he would go so far as to prevent the disclosure of facts revealed in unpublished texts unless of course the facts were discovered independently. This would, he acknowledged, significantly alter the idea/expression dichotomy, but it would restore the recognition of privacy. "I do not doubt the high public interest in knowing the factual content of a private writing by a well-known person," he wrote. "But in the balance between the right to know and the right of privacy I would weigh the scales in favor of disclosure only when the private matters sought to be disclosed are important to the public's business. Satisfaction of the public's curiosity alone should not suffice."[62]

The following year, Judge Leval responded in a lecture titled "Fair Use or Foul?" delivered at New York University. "Members of the Jury," Leval began, as if reading jury instructions. "Defendant contends that she is not liable for copyright infringement because her quotations made fair use of the plaintiff's writings. It is now my duty to explain to you what we mean by fair use. And do you know what, ladies and gentlemen of the jury, I can't. No one can. We don't know."[63] Leval went on to trace the confusing pattern of reversals in fair use cases, noting the foundational *Nation* case in which the District Court was reversed by the Court of Appeals, which in turn was reversed by the Supreme Court. In *Salinger* Leval's own findings of fair use were overturned. Most recently in *New Era* Leval's findings were again overturned. "It has been exhilarating to find myself at the cutting edge of the law," Leval quipped, "even though in the role of the salami."[64]

Perhaps, Leval argued, the confusion with respect to fair use might be clarified by returning to first principles in the English Statute of Anne (1710) and the U.S. Constitution. Copyright was not a matter of moral right but a utilitarian provision designed, as the English statute put it for the "encouragement of learning," or, as the constitutional clause put it, "to promote the progress of science and useful arts." But all creative activity is necessarily derivative; writing begets further writing that uses its sources productively. Therefore fair use must not be considered a "bizarre, occasionally tolerated exception" to the author's monopoly but a necessary part of the design of the law framed to take account of the way cultural production in fact occurs.

Leval went on to make a further point in which he implicitly invoked Newman's proposals about the recognition of privacy interests in copyright doctrine. "Much confusion in fair use analysis, I believe, has resulted from the temptation of judges to import extraneous, often sentimental, considerations that are not a part of the goals of copyright law." Serious distortions would occur, he said, if copyright were pressed into the service of privacy interests, which were already the subject of a developed body of law. Moreover, copyright law was not fashioned to serve as the defense of privacy and was grossly inappropriate as an instrument to that end. Among other things, he noted, copyright enforcement required a public filing in the Library of Congress. Thus, "the very act required to preserve privacy would insure its violation."[65]

Discussing the four factors specified by the 1976 statute for fair use analysis, Leval suggested that in connection with the first, the purpose and character of the use, the crucial issue was whether the secondary work was merely a repackaging of the original or whether the quoted matter was used productively as raw material for the creation of new information or new understandings. Productive use was the core issue. Here Leval issued a mea culpa, acknowledging, as he had done earlier in his *New Era* decision, that some of the quotations that Hamilton had taken from Salinger were not "productive" but merely served to improve the literary quality of Hamilton's text by using Salinger's expression. Nonetheless, the Appeals Court in *Salinger* and *New Era* had set a far-reaching and problematic rule. "Never mind justification. Unpublished matter simply may not be quoted."[66]

In reaching back to the Statue of Anne and the Constitution in search of first principles, Leval indicated how deep into the history of copyright the debate extended. In his Columbia lecture, Newman, too, had reached back to early copyright history, citing among other things the mingling of property and privacy interests in *Pope v. Curll* (1741). "There is a strong indication in the early cases," he said, "that while the right being articulated was one of property, the interest being protected was one of privacy." Why was copyright used in this way? Protection against copying required an injunction, Newman pointed out, and the equity courts doubted their power to issue injunctions to protect personal as distinct from property rights. "And so the law of literary property was enlisted in the service of privacy." Furthermore, over time courts came to acknowledge "that not only was a literary property right being protected, but an interest in one's personality as well."[67]

Newman was correct about the early mingling of copyright and privacy interests. Pope's motives in suing Curll were complex, but he certainly was seeking to establish, among other things, a gentleman's right to privacy. More than a quarter of a century later, Pope's attorney, now Lord Mansfield, carried the blending of property and privacy interests a step further. In *Millar v. Taylor* (1767), Mansfield argued for the common-law right that underlay the statutory grant of copyright protection. From what source was the common-law right drawn? From principles of justness and fitness, he answered, noting among other things that it is fitting that the author should judge "when to publish, or whether he ever will publish."[68] Moreover, as Mansfield saw it, if an author had such a common-law right in his writing before publication, he must clearly maintain it after publication. The common-law right was the foundation of the statutory right, not vice versa.

At issue throughout the eighteenth century was the question of whether copyright was indeed founded on the common-law right and therefore was perpetual, as Mansfield held, or whether it was a limited grant as the statute specified. The great case of *Donaldson v. Beckett* (1774) settled the practical question of the perpetuity—protection was limited in term—by what amounted to fiat. A majority of the House of Lords voted to overturn the injunction that was at issue. But *Donaldson* never entirely put to rest the conviction on the part of many that copyright was a property not merely a grant. And even in the United States, where the foundational case of *Wheaton v. Peters* (1834) confirmed copyright as a grant rather than a right, the claim that copyright really *should* be regarded as a property never disappeared. As Eaton S. Drone, the author of the most important American copyright treatise of the nineteenth century, wrote in 1879 on the matter of the limited term of protection, "The law which puts an arbitrary terminus on the ownership of literary property is the same in principle with one that would abridge the farmer's right to his orchards and grainfields." Speaking of the way literary works eventually become part of the public domain, Drone went on angrily, "To take from one and give to all is not less communism in the case of literary property than it is in that of any other kind of property."[69]

Private right and public policy—copyright has developed within the magnetic field of these two poles. Both in his decision and in his writings Pierre Leval emphatically aligned himself with the claims of public policy and the utilitarian conception of copyright. Newman acknowledged these as well; nonetheless, he also acknowledged his sympathy for Salinger's desire for privacy. But how was the established doctrine of fair use to be applied in the concrete case at hand, Hamilton's use of Salinger's letters? Neither Leval nor Newman believed that the unpublished nature of the letters was itself dispositive under current law. Nor was there disagreement on the extent of verbatim quotation in Hamilton's biography. But ever since the statute of 1870, enacted after the *Uncle Tom's Cabin* case, established that copyright was not limited to the literal text, infringement analysis had become more problematic. In *Nichols v. Universal*, as we have seen, Learned Hand ruled for the defendants, declaring that Universal's movie may have used elements that proved popular in *Abie's Irish Rose* but that the movie did not infringe Nichols's copyright. Nonetheless, even while finding against infringement, Hand noted that copyright protection went beyond verbatim appropriation; otherwise "a plagiarist would escape by immaterial variations."[70] In *Nichols* the issue revolved around story elements: character, plot, setting, sequence of events, and so forth. At what point would the plot and characters of a new work follow an earlier one so closely that it would be found infringing? In *Salinger* the issue was language. At what point would a paraphrase follow the original text so closely that it would be found infringing?

From early on in *Salinger* there were indications that the question of paraphrase would be crucial. When Salinger's lawyers objected to the use of quotations in the original galleys of the biography, Random House summoned Hamilton back to New York to spend an unpleasant week turning lively quotations into awkward paraphrases. Although the revised text did not satisfy Salinger, Random House believed that the doctrine of fair use would protect them. They noted that no more than 10 words remained from any single letter and that the 217 words quoted represented a very small portion of Salinger's originals. But Salinger's attorneys claimed infringement "by extensive paraphrasing" as well as by quotation. And at the initial meeting in Judge Leval's chambers, Salinger's attorney objected that Random House was ignoring the issue of paraphrase. Leval's decision emphasized the minimal nature of Hamilton's quotations, remarking that most were fragmentary, but Newman, taking into account paraphrases as well as quotations, found the appropriation more substantial. "If the District Judge had included paraphrases," Newman wrote, "he would have noticed numerous instances where the quantity of material taken from a single letter greatly exceeded a single sentence."[71]

In fact Judge Leval *had* taken account of paraphrase as well as verbatim quotation and the record was eventually clarified to make this explicit.[72] The issue between Leval and Newman was not so much a question of whether Leval and Newman had taken account of the same passages as a matter of interpretation and literary judgment. Leval was inclined to allow Hamilton to sail more closely to Salinger's text than Newman. For example, in one of his letters Salinger remarked, "I suspect that money is a far greater distraction for the artist than hunger." Hamilton paraphrased: "Money, on the other hand is a serious obstacle to creativity." Did this paraphrase infringe? Leval held it did not, Newman that it did. In another example, Salinger acidly responded to an editor who rejected one of his pieces, calling it "competent handling."

This, Salinger remarked, was "Like saying, She's a beautiful girl, except for her face." Salinger's response to rejection was a taut sneer. Hamilton's paraphrase was wordy and vague: "How would a girl feel if you told her she was stunning to look at but that facially there was something not quite right about her?" As Hamilton acknowledged, it was painful to flatten Salinger's sparkling language in this way. He might well be charged with representing a lively stylist as dull, but did his paraphrase infringe? Leval held that it did not, Newman that it did.[73]

One of the most extensive passages cited was Hamilton's version of Salinger's satirical description of Charlie Chaplin and Oona O'Neill. Salinger had dated Oona and was disturbed that the beautiful young girl had married a man much older than herself. "I can see them at home evenings," Salinger wrote to his friend Whit Burnett in 1943. "Chaplin squatting grey and nude, atop his chiffonier, swinging his thyroid around his head by his bamboo cane, like a dead rat. Oona in an aquamarine gown, applauding madly from the bathroom. Agnes (her mother) in a Jantzen bathing suit, passing between them with cocktails. I'm facetious, but I'm sorry. Sorry for anyone with a profile as young and lovely as Oona's." Hamilton reported:

> [Salinger] provides a pen portrait of the Happy Hour Chez Chaplin: the comedian, ancient and unclothed, is brandishing his walking stick—attached to the stick, and horribly resembling a lifeless rodent, is one of Chaplin's vital organs. Oona claps her hands in appreciation and Agnes, togged out in a bathing suit, pours drinks. Salinger goes on to say he's sorry—sorry not for what he has just written, but for Oona: far too youthful and exquisite for such a dreadful fate.

Did Hamilton's paraphrase infringe? Leval held that it did not, Newman that it did.[74]

Leval observed that the use of letters posed a peculiar dilemma for a biographer. "To the extent he quotes (or closely paraphrases), he risks a finding of infringement and an injunction effectively destroying his biographical work. To the extent he departs from the words of the letters, he distorts, sacrificing both accuracy and vividness of description."[75] Newman rejected this characterization of the situation, noting somewhat acidly, "This dilemma is not faced by the biographer who elects to copy only the factual content of letters."[76] Speaking in reference to

Salinger's fantasy of Oona O'Neil and Charlie Chaplin at home, Newman suggested that Hamilton might simply have reported "the fact that Salinger was distressed that O'Neill had married Chaplin or that in his mind he imagined how disastrous their life together must be."[77] So of course Hamilton might have done, but to do so would be to fail to indicate that Salinger's imaginary portrait of O'Neil and Chaplin is not just a description but, like much of his writing about people and things of which he disapproves, an action—in this case both mockery and emotional exorcism. How does one weigh the balance of "fact" and "expression" in such a passage?

Both Leval and Newman are sophisticated and literate judges in the tradition of Learned Hand. Leval in particular is, like Hand, something of a stylist who leans toward playfulness and irony, as for example when in his NYU lecture he compares himself to a salami. Newman is perhaps less playful but he is certainly interested in language. Indeed, he has published in *Verbatim*, a literary magazine concerned with linguistic issues.[78] Let us note that when the subject matter of law is something as fluid and protean as language, distinctions and judgments may involve unspoken assumptions about the nature of language. Is language transparent, a window onto an objective world of fact, or is language itself partially constitutive of the world we see? Classical and early modern rhetoricians tended to think of language as an active agent, an instrument to persuade or influence others. Enlightenment and modern thinkers on the other hand tended to treat language as a medium to be made as transparent as possible. As a precursor of the Enlightenment view, think of Francis Bacon in the *Novum Organum* attempting to purge language of the distortions and errors that it introduces into thought. Again and again, in his writing on the issues in *Salinger* and *New Era*, Leval emphasizes the degree to which language is not transparent, not merely a window onto a world of fact. Thus his reiterated insistence on the importance of accurate quotation in historical and biographical work. Newman, on the other hand, seems somewhat more inclined to accept the idea of a world of independent fact. Thus his curt rejection of the biographer's dilemma as formulated by Leval: "The biographer who copies only facts incurs no risk of an injunction."[79]

Nonetheless, as the difficult issues embedded in *Salinger* took a somewhat different shape in the case centered on the less appealing figure of L. Ron Hubbard, the distance between Leval and Newman with respect to a biographer's paraphrase or quotation of unpublished material shrank. In his NYU lecture Leval acknowledged that his concern for the public interest perhaps made him too disposed to find fair use in certain passages.[80] Meanwhile in his dissent from the refusal to grant a rehearing en banc in the *New Era* case, Newman made clear his position that even as to unpublished writings, the doctrine of fair use might permit some modest copying of an author's expression when it was necessary to report a fact fairly and accurately.[81]

While hearings on the copyright statute were pending in Congress, Judge Leval developed his NYU lecture into an important *Harvard Law Review* article, "Toward a Fair Use Standard."[82] The modest title signaled both Leval's sense of the prevailing confusion with respect to fair use and his doubts about the possibility of any bright-line criterion for determining when unauthorized quotation or close paraphrase was appropriate. Again Leval emphasized the degree to which facts and ideas cannot always be separated from the words in which they are expressed. "Can ideas be correctly reported, discussed, or challenged if the commentator is obliged to express the idea in her own different words? The subject will, of course, reply. 'That's not what I said.'" Such a principle, he suggested, should be particularly apparent to jurists because after all the law, too, was embodied in words. Imagine a requirement that "judges, in passing on the applicability of a statute or contract, describe the provisions in their own words rather than quoting it directly."[83]

Bright-line rules with respect to fair use might be impracticable, but the four factors set out in the statute did provide a framework for analysis. Traditionally, the fourth factor, the effect on the market, had been considered the most important, but Leval suggested that it was the first factor, the purpose and character of the use, that was the "soul" of fair use. In his NYU lecture Leval had spoken of this factor in terms of productivity. Was the taken expression used as raw material for the creation of something new? In the *Harvard Law Review* article Leval introduced a new term, "transformative."[84] Did the secondary work employ the quoted material in a different manner or for a different purpose from the original? The identification of a transformative purpose did not in itself result in a finding of fair use, the other factors, including the nature of the work used and the quantity and importance of the material used, also had to be taken into account. But the first factor was the indispensable element in a fair use defense.[85] The judgment as to fair use necessarily involved a subtle and perhaps to some degree subjective literary judgment.

Judge Roger J. Miner who had irritably rejected Leval's findings in the *New Era* case questioned whether it was the proper role of judges to "decide whether literary material is used to enliven a text or demonstrate truth."[86] Such distinctions should be left to literary critics. Judge Miner, who published his own contribution to the conversation about fair use in unpublished materials—"Exploiting Stolen Text: Fair Use or Foul Play?"—took a much harder line on the matter than either Newman or Leval.[87] His essay, perhaps written in anticipation of the congressional hearings on the question of fair use in unpublished works, argued that "outright theft of intellectual property ought not to be condoned by Congress." When "an author has not published or publicly disseminated his or her copyright material, there simply is no reason to allow the use of that material without the author's consent."[88] Miner advocated a return to the total elimination of any claim of fair use in material that is "unpublished or undisseminated."[89] As for the delicate question, pressed by Leval, as to when it becomes impossible to separate fact from expression, when language *becomes* fact, Miner recognized no such possibility. Facts were facts and expression was expression. "The freedom of access to facts and ideas is the history of democracy. The right of ownership in intellectual property is quite another thing."[90]

Miner's blunt approach to writing as property and his unqualified rejection of the notion of judges making literary distinctions are not anomalous. Many jurists have taken similar positions. Leval himself remarked in *New Era* that it is "an uncomfortable role for courts to serve as literary critics."[91] But as we have seen, jurists from the time of the stern judges analyzing Defoe's *Shortest Way with the Dissenters* to that of Learned Hand analyzing *Abie's Irish Rose* have necessarily been involved in making literary judgments. Undoubtedly judges have also been influenced by their perception of the plaintiffs and defendants who have appeared before them. Defoe was not a sympathetic figure to his judges. Pope the gentleman clearly had an advantage in Chancery over the notoriously scurrilous bookseller Curll. And Pope's advantage was particularly strong in Lord Chancellor Hardwicke's court, given that some thirteen years earlier Hardwicke had been the agent to prosecute Curll for libel. Likewise, Harriet Beecher Stowe was at a disadvantage in the court of an avowed supporter of the Fugitive Slave Act. Salinger, on the other hand, was clearly a sincere and sympathetic plaintiff.

To what degree do the personal dramas of individuals—in the matter of copyright, the courtroom dramas of authors—influence the development of the law? Judge Newman insisted that he was merely following traditional copyright principles in overturning Leval's decision in *Salinger*, and that may be true. But, given his impassioned article on copyright and the protection of privacy, Newman also seems to have been influenced by Salinger's intense and genuine dread of public exposure. What if the precedent-setting case on letters and fair use had involved a less sympathetic figure? Salinger's suit was followed by the Church of Scientology's attempt to suppress an unflattering biography of L. Ron Hubbard. Would the same precedent have been set if the L. Ron Hubbard case had been tried first?

[CHAPTER SEVEN]

Purloined Puppies

Rogers v. Koons (1992)

In fall 1980, Art Rogers, a professional photographer based in Point Reyes, California, made a portrait of Jim and Mary Scanlon seated on a bench, holding between them a litter of eight German Shepherd puppies. It was, Rogers believed, one of the best photographs he had ever made. Several years later Rogers licensed *Puppies* to Museum Graphics, a publishing company founded by Ansel Adams that produces high-quality note cards and posters both of Adams's work and that of other photographers. In early summer 1989 Scanlon phoned Rogers to report that a colorized version of the photograph was on display at the Museum of Contemporary Art in Los Angeles and that a picture of it had appeared in the *Los Angeles Times.* The "colorized version" turned out to be a polychrome wood sculpture, *String of Puppies.* This had originally been shown the previous fall at the Sonnabend Gallery in New York as part of well-known artist Jeff Koons's *Banality* show.

Shortly thereafter, Rogers, assisted by a San Francisco attorney, registered the *Puppies* copyright and sent a letter to Koons and Sonnabend threatening litigation but offering to settle the matter for $175,000. John Koegel, the attorney for Koons and Sonnabend, rejected Rogers's proposal. In response Rogers's New York attorney L. Donald Prutzman filed a complaint in District Court in New York charging that Koons's sculpture was illegally copied from Rogers's photograph. Thus in fall 1989 *Rogers v. Koons*, a major case both in copyright and in contemporary art history, was initiated.[1]

Sometimes rather awkwardly called "postmodernism," the artistic movement with which Koons is associated became prominent in the latter part of the twentieth century. Among other things, postmodern artists—a group that includes diverse figures such as Andy Warhol, Robert Rauschenberg, Jasper Johns, and Sherrie Levine—challenge received notions of "authorship" and "originality." For example, in 1980 Levine famously exhibited a series of iconic Walker Evans images that she had rephotographed from a catalog and signed with her own name. The show was called, provocatively, *After Walker Evans*. Sometimes postmodern artists employ "readymades" or appropriated objects—the urinal exhibited by Marcel Duchamp in 1917 as *Fountain* is an often-cited prototype—and sometimes they recycle material from commerce and popular culture such as Andy Warhol's *Campbell's Soup Cans* and *Brillo Box*. The movement, which through readymades and recycling also puts the notion of the "work" under pressure, has literary parallels in writers such as Roland Barthes and Jacques Derrida as well as in the fables of Jorge Luis Borges. Borges's "Pierre Menard, Author of the *Quixote*" (1939), which describes the fictive lifework of a writer who sought to reproduce, not from memory but freshly and anew, every word in Cervantes's novel, may be regarded as a witty anticipation of these kinds of problematizing acts of appropriation.[2]

"Authorship" and "originality" are fundamental concepts in copyright. Given that postmodern art challenges copyright doctrine at its foundations, it is not surprising that developments in postmodern art have prompted legal controversies. It is notable, however, that so many matters, like *Rogers v. Koons*, have involved photographers suing painters and sculptors. Even a full century after Napoleon Sarony established that commercial photographs might be considered works of art, it appears that professional photographers still experience a sense of exclusion from the institution of authorship and that there is an element of professional resentment that contributes to litigation in this area.[3] In one of the best known of the mid-twentieth-century cases, Patricia Caulfield, a nature photographer, sued Andy Warhol who had adapted her 1964 photograph of hibiscus flowers published in *Modern Photography* into *Flowers*, his very successful series of silkscreen paintings, prints, and posters. Caulfield obtained a settlement but nonetheless remained upset. "What's irritating," she said, "is to have someone like an image enough to use it, but then denigrate the original talent."[4] Likewise, photographers Charles Moore and Fred Ward found that Warhol had used their pictures, in the one case an image of a man being attacked by police dogs in the Birmingham riots and in the other a famous shot of Jacqueline Kennedy taken shortly after President

Kennedy's assassination. Like the Caulfield matter, both the Moore and Ward complaints were settled.

Other instances of prominent artists challenged by photographers include Larry Rivers and Robert Rauschenberg. Rivers was accused by Arnold Newman of appropriating part of Newman's iconic photograph of Pablo Picasso in his 1975 print portfolio *Homage to Picasso.* "Some art necessitates the use of photography," Rivers responded. "In this case, it was just to give information about Picasso. I didn't even use the whole thing, only across the forehead and down to the nose. The rest is drawn in. It's like a quote, that's all."[5] The following year San Francisco-based photographer Morton Beebe sued Rauschenberg who had incorporated an image of a young man, arms outspread in a swan dive, into one of his collage prints. Beebe was particularly upset because Rauschenberg was known as a defender of artists' rights. Rauschenberg protested that he had been making collage prints for decades and had never felt that he was infringing on anyone's rights. He had transformed the images, presenting them to be reconsidered in totally new contexts.[6] Like the other appropriation cases, both the Rivers and Rauschenberg matters were settled out of court.

Rogers's suit, then, was merely the latest in a series of controversies in which photographers claimed that their works had been illicitly appropriated. In the Rogers matter, however, rather than settling, the defendants, Koons and Sonnabend, represented by their attorney John Koegel, chose to resist, claiming that Koons's sculpture constituted a "fair use" of Rogers's photograph. Perhaps Koons and Sonnabend were influenced by the substantial sum that Rogers was demanding, but it is also likely that they decided the time had come to make a stand on principle. Koegel responded to Rogers' settlement offer by quoting Justice Joseph Story's famous remark in *Emerson v. Davies* (1845), where Story acknowledged the need of all creators to borrow from the work of others: "Every book in literature, science and art, borrows and must necessarily borrow, and use much which was well known and used before."[7] Moreover, as the case developed, the documents filed on behalf of Koons and Sonnabend stressed the cultural importance of the issue, describing the postmodern art tradition and asserting that no less than the future of art was at stake.

The legal attempt to establish the legitimacy of Koons's postmodern practices failed spectacularly. Both the District Court and the Second Circuit Court of Appeals found for Rogers. Moreover, the Second Circuit refused Koons's appeal for reconsideration en banc, and the U.S. Supreme Court also refused to review the case.[8] Koons was not only held liable for infringement, but on a related matter that concerned his shipping a copy of *String of Puppies* for exhibition in Germany he was held in contempt of court. For Koons and Sonnabend the loss had other ramifications as well. While *Rogers* was pending, three additional cases related to works exhibited in the *Banality* show were filed. One involved Koons's use of "Odie," a copyrighted comic strip character, in a sculpture called *Wild Boy with Puppy*.[9] The second involved his use of a photograph titled *Boys with Pig* in a sculpture called *Ushering in Banality*.[10] The decisions in these cases closely followed *Rogers* in analysis. The third, which involved Koons's use of the Pink Panther character, was settled before proceeding to judgment. Thus, by April 1993, Koons had been found guilty of infringement three times.

But the three judgments of the early 1990s were not the end of the story. Some twelve years later another suit was filed, this one by a prominent fashion photographer, Andrea Blanch. She claimed that Koons had infringed her published magazine photograph *Silk Sandals by Gucci* by incorporating elements in a painting titled *Niagara*. Blanch's suit invoked the judgments of the 1990s, representing Koons as an incorrigible predator who had been found guilty of infringement on multiple occasions.[11] This was of course literally true if somewhat tendentious. But the outcome of the *Blanch* case was very different from that of *Rogers:* Koons prevailed. Clearly something had happened to change legal analysis with respect to fair use. The sources of that change can be traced directly to Judge Pierre N. Leval, the litigation in *Salinger v. Random House*, the ensuing debate over fair use, and the incorporation of Leval's concept of "transformative use" in the Supreme Court's landmark decision in *Campbell v. Acuff-Rose* in 1994, the year after the last of the three Koons cases.

* * *

Jeff Koons was in some respects not the most strategic candidate to employ in making a principled stand on behalf of fair use in postmodern art. Hardly a conventional figure of unworldly genius toiling in a garret, Koons was and is a canny self-promoter who has proved conspicuously adept at marketing his paintings and sculptures. The works themselves, which now sell for millions of dollars, are generally produced by employees or contracted artisans. "I'm basically the idea person," Koons says. "I'm not physically involved in production. I don't have the necessary abilities, so I go to the top people."[12] The scale of Koons's enterprise is formidable. In his factory-sized New York studio, Koons currently employs more than 120 assistants, some in his painting department, others in the sculpture department, others doing digital or purely administrative work.[13] Where Koons excels is not in making objects but in conception and promotion. Confirming his remarkable success, Koons recently received a version of artistic canonization in the form of a huge retrospective at the Whitney Museum of American Art. As the Whitney's director remarked in his forward to the show's catalog, since the 1980s, Koons's work has been so omnipresent that "it is now hard to imagine a pre-Koonsian age." Controversial, polarizing, and often criticized, it was surprising, Adam D. Weinberg said, that Koons had never before had a retrospective in the city in which he lives and works. The time had come for a comprehensive assessment of his career.[14]

Born in 1955 in York, Pennsylvania, where his father, an interior decorator, owned a furniture store, Jeff Koons became interested in art early in life. He began art lessons at eight and, encouraged by his father, produced imitations of Old Master paintings that were exhibited in the store where they sold for several hundred dollars apiece. After high school, Koons attended the Maryland Institute College of Art in Baltimore. As he put it, "I didn't know anything else than art to do."[15] In his first year, Koons heard that Salvador Dali, whose work he knew from a coffee-table book, was staying at the St. Regis hotel in New York. With characteristic enthusiasm, Koons telephoned, rode a bus to Manhattan, and met Dali in the hotel lobby. Later, at the Knoedler gallery, the artist invited Koons to photograph him in front of one of his paintings. Koons, who recalled that Dali was wearing "that majestic fur coat and carrying a black cane with a silver handle," would later develop images referencing the flamboyant artist. "I just remember leaving New York that day feeling that this type of life"—presumably a life of wealth and fame through art—"was accessible."[16]

In Baltimore Koons's student work was subjective and surrealist, his paintings typically filled with dream imagery. But he spent his senior year in Chicago where he came under the influence of Ed Pasche, a postmodernist who collected magazine and newspaper images for use in paintings. Pasche pointed Koons away from the psychological toward the outward world of circulating commercial images. "Ed really revealed to me that everything is already here in the world and you just have to look for it."[17]

Moving to New York, Koons supported himself with a day job selling tickets and memberships at the Museum of Modern Art. Here, perhaps recalling Dali's theatricality, Koons turned himself into a clown-like character, attracting attention by dying his hair red, sporting a pencil mustache, and wearing polka-dot shirts, comic bowties, and sometimes an inflatable plastic flower. "People loved me," Koons reported, "and I doubled the membership rolls. The trick is to be outrageous but not offensive."[18] But eventually Koons directed his promotional talent in a more lucrative direction, acquiring a broker's license and selling mutual funds and commodities at a series of trading companies and brokerage houses. Koons, a natural salesman, evidently did well. According to report, his telephone pitch was so effective that he often convinced himself to invest, buying commodity shares that ended up losing him money.[19]

While working as a broker in the early 1980s, Koons began to establish himself on the contemporary art scene in New York and elsewhere. His first show, *The New* (1980), featured readymades, immaculate vacuum cleaners encased in vitrines. His second, *Equilibrium* (1985), displayed, among other things, Spalding basketballs mysteriously suspended in tanks of water. This effect was achieved by carefully layering salt and freshwater so that the two did not mix and the basketball floated on a bed of the heavier salt water. His third, *Luxury and Degradation* (1986), employed images from the marketing of alcohol such as ads for Dewar's scotch and Gordon's gin along with related objects such as a stainless steel travel bar and, most elaborately, a stainless steel model train set, with each miniature car actually filled with Jim Beam whiskey.

These shows, at once sensual and satirical, were followed in 1988 by *Banality*, the exhibition that prompted Art Rogers's lawsuit as well as the cases involving "Odie," the comic strip character, and Barbara Campbell's *Boys with Pig*. *Banality* was Koons's breakthrough exhibition, the show that established him at thirty-four, according to *People* magazine, as "the hottest young artist in America."[20] The show consisted of twenty pieces, although only eighteen were ready for the November opening at Sonnabend in New York. Each piece was produced in an edition of three with a fourth "artist's proof" reserved for Koons. Since the sculptures were multiples, it was possible to mount the show simultaneously in three venues, and, along with the Sonnabend exhibition, versions of *Banality* appeared at the Max Hetzler gallery in Cologne and the Donald Young gallery in Chicago. In addition to *String of Puppies*, *Wild Boy and Puppy*, *Ushering in Banality*, and *Pink Panther*, the pieces that figured in litigation, the show included a large white and gold porcelain piece showing a blond Michael Jackson cradling Bubbles, his pet chimpanzee; a pretty prepubescent boy and girl gazing at a large tropical flower with a conspicuously erect stamen; a figure of Buster Keaton riding a donkey that Koons identified as an allusion to Christ; and a pair of goofy male and female toy bears smiling and waving to the viewer while holding a red love-heart between them.

Banality was the first show in which, rather than exhibiting readymades such as the suspended basketballs, Koons employed a collage technique, using photographs, magazine clippings, and other media materials to produce designs that his fabricators—woodcarvers, porcelain workers, and glassworkers—turned into large, often greater-than-life-sized sculptures. The show's title suggests a satirical intent, but in fact Koons's purposes seem more equivocal. Combining eroticism, cloying cuteness, and religious symbolism, the exhibition was finely balanced between satire and celebration, between "banal" as contemptible and "banal" as commonplace. "The thing the bourgeois respond to at the present time is really banality," Koons told Richard Lacayo. "They feel a lot of guilt about this, too. I was trying to remove the guilt and shame of the bourgeoisie. [To do that] it's necessary to be baptized in banality."[21] The purpose of the show was to relieve the bourgeoisie of their shame about vulgarity.

Was Koons being ironic when he spoke of "baptism in banality?" To what degree was the *Banality* show celebratory and to what degree satiric? It is of course impossible to say. Koons can be both oracular and opaque in ways that suggest he is often unaware of the tensions and contradictions in his self-presentation. Some of his statements are outrageously self-promoting, as for example when he claims that the only figures equal to himself in twentieth-century art are Duchamp and Picasso or when he calls the *Banality* show "probably the most important exhibition held at the end of the twentieth century."[22] Is Koons sincere or, as some have suggested, a canny and theatrical charlatan? "I decided long ago that Koons believes what he says," Calvin Tomkins remarks, adding that he suspects that Koons's "convincing (and obsessive) sincerity" is a factor in the magnetic power that some of his "absurd images" can exert.[23]

Koons's theatricality, which manifested itself in the clown-like costumes he wore at the Museum of Modern Art, was also evident in relation to the promotion for *Banality*. Offered the choice of an exhibition catalog or an advertising budget, Koons chose a series of four advertisements in major art magazines each presenting himself as a Hollywood-style celebrity. In the ad for *Art* he appears, in Katie Siegel's phrase, as a "swanky but vulgar master of the universe," seated in front of a pavilion tent wearing a monogrammed robe.[24] In *Art in America* he appears in a flowery field between two bikini-clad models, one of whom is offering him a sugary red-and-white cake, an image he associated with the temptations of Christ. In *Flash Art* he appears with a sow and a piglet. "I wanted to debase myself and call myself a pig before the viewer had a chance to," he explained.[25] In *Artforum*, the most academic and intellectual of the journals, he presented himself as a handsome, hip teacher in front of a class with "Exploit the Masses" and "Banality as Saviour" written on the blackboard behind him. In these ads Koons asserted his arrival on the art scene as a kind of media star. "I've made what the Beatles would have made if they had made sculpture," he said. "Nobody ever said that the Beatles' music was not on a high level, but it appealed to a mass audience."[26]

Although *Banality* was, at least as Koons described it, targeted at the middle class, the prices for individual works were anything but bourgeois. These ranged from $50,000 for a small piece, to $250,000 for

Michael Jackson and Bubbles, which Koons claimed was the largest porcelain ever made. *String of Puppies* was priced at $125,000. Reviewing the exhibition in the *New York Times* under the title "Greed Plus Glitz, with a Dollop of Innocence," Michael Brenson described the show as suggesting "an art gallery turned into a department store or Disneyland." Brenson remarked that "Koons seems to want more money than any artist his age has ever made for art." Perhaps the high prices could be seen as symptomatic of tensions generated by the link between art and money in an era of grossly inflated art values. Nonetheless, Brenson found Koons's posture objectionable, suggesting that with his prices Koons was "pushing the relationship between art and money to the point where everyone involved—artist, dealer and collectors— seems to come out looking slightly absurd." Perhaps picking up on the show's conceptual equivocation, its unstable balance between satire and celebration, Brenson remarked, "The blend of sincerity and scheming, cleanness and crassness, chastity and corruption, presents as impossible contradiction."[27]

Brenson accused Koons of "thinking strategically" and making "art in which profit seems to come first."[28] But the prices that Brenson found objectionable twenty-five years ago seem paltry compared to what Koons's works would eventually fetch at auction. Koons's prices began to skyrocket in 1999 when billionaire industrialist and art collector Peter Brant paid a then record $1.8 million at auction for one copy of *Pink Panther* from the *Banality* show. More recently, in 2012, one of five versions of *Tulips* sold at auction for $33.6 million. And a year later, *Balloon Dog (Orange)*, again one of five versions, sold for $58.4 million.[29] According to an *Art News* article published in 2005, several years after Koons's prices had begun to soar, Koons "masterminded his fame and fortune through a combination of charm, guile, and a talent for creating expensive art that inspires critical debate." He did so with the help of a close circle of dealers, collectors, and museums such as the Guggenheim and the Whitney. "As Koons likes to point out," one museum curator has remarked, "someone in every generation has to be held up as a shining example of what is wrong with current art. It's a dirty job, but Koons, who has the single-mindedness of a missile, has taken on the duty."[30]

Koons's high prices, industrial methods of production, and frank embrace of commercial values may have influenced the decisions in *Rogers v. Koons*. The 1992 Circuit Court decision against Koons, for example, cited the Michael Brenson review of the *Banality* show, quoting the passage about Koons "pushing the relationship between art and money so far that everyone involved comes out looking slightly absurd."[31] It seems likely, too, that Koons's theatricality, his penchant for self-promotion and self-display, played a subtle if unacknowledged role in shaping the judges' sympathies. At the same time as *Rogers v. Koons* was making its way through the courts, Koons was developing and realizing his notorious *Made in Heaven* show in which he appeared with Ilona Staller—better known as "Cicciolina," an Italian porn star— in a series of sexually explicit paintings and sculptures.

The *Made in Heaven* project began in 1989—about the same time that *Rogers* was initiated—when the Whitney invited Koons to create a billboard display in connection with *Image World*, an exhibition exploring ways in which contemporary artists have responded to mass media. Having seen pictures of Staller in magazines, Koons, enthralled, traveled to Italy and arranged to be photographed with her. This resulted in a billboard erected in lower Manhattan showing an apparently naked Koons and a barely clothed Staller advertising what appeared to be a forthcoming movie, *Made in Heaven: Starring Jeff Koons and Cicciolina*. The *Banality* advertisements had presented Koons as a Hollywood-style celebrity. The billboard took the conceit a step further, presenting him as costarring in a steamy movie. As Scott Rothkopf, curator of the 2014 Koons retrospective at the Whitney, remarks, "Seen from the streets of Manhattan, the billboard represented a particularly brazen form of self-promotion." In it Koons "cast himself as a bona fide star with an even more famous heroine, claiming his proper place in the network of publicity and mass attention that many artists had long coveted while pretending to scorn."[32]

After producing the billboard image, Koons had further photographs taken of himself and Staller. He turned these into erotic paintings and sculpture that he exhibited in May 1990 at the Venice Biennale. By this time Koons's relationship with Staller had developed into a romance that was generating enormous publicity for them both. As Rothkopf reports, the couple appeared daily at the Biennale installation to pose "before legions of paparazzi in front of their graven images" while rumors of an impending marriage—on, then off, then on again—spawned still further publicity. A year later, in June 1991, Koons and Staller were married in Budapest, her native city, with official pictures from the wedding reaching millions of readers all over the world.[33]

The movie was never produced. But the related *Made in Heaven* exhibition that developed from the billboard and Biennale installation opened at the Sonnabend Gallery in November 1991.[34] At this time the Circuit Court decision in *Rogers* was pending. In this show Koons portrayed himself and Staller in a series of sexually explicit paintings and sculptures. Reviewing the exhibition in the *New York Times*, Michael Kimmelman described Koons's paintings as "not fundamentally different from what one might see in *Hustler* magazine, translated almost to the scale of a movie screen." "Just when it looked as if the 80's were finally over," Kimmelman said, "Jeff Koons has provided one last, pathetic gasp of the sort of self-promoting hype and sensationalism that characterized the worst of the decade." Like Salvador Dali, Kimmelman remarked, Koons appeared to have become "an opportunistic publicity monger whose conflation of himself and his work" portended self-destruction.[35] Perhaps because the exhibition was so blatantly transgressive in conception and execution, it provoked wry humor as well as outrage, as for example in Paul Taylor's observation, also in the *New York Times*, that the show's "hard-core sexual tableaux" display an "anatomical prowess that looks like a mix of Hieronymus Bosch and Dr. Seuss."[36]

Koons himself described the *Made in Heaven* paintings and sculptures in quasi-religious language. Interviewed by Andrew Renton in 1990 while the works were in production, Koons remarked that in the *Banality* show he had dealt with familiar commercial images: "I was trying to remove guilt and shame of the bourgeois class." The new works, he said, were also dealing with the removal of guilt and shame, "but it's really starting back much farther, and Ilona and I are really a contemporary Adam and Eve." Staller, he explained somewhat paradoxically, was the "eternal virgin," a woman totally pure and without shame. "Because of having no guilt and shame, nothing sticks to her." His purposes in the show were not pornographic. "Pornography is just performing a sexual act. It really has no interest to me. I'm interested in love. I'm interested in reunion. I'm interested in the spiritual, to be able to show people that they can have impact, to achieve their desires. Ilona is my desire." At this time Koons was training some three hours a day to transform his body. "I don't know if you've seen me recently, Andrew," he told Renton, "but the aspect of the eternal has already been implanted in me. I am getting younger and younger, and every day I look like a boy coming out of the shell of the man the day before." His life and his art, Koons insisted, were inseparable, "totally one." "I've been able to direct my life into a course to be able to do exactly what I want, and I want to let other people know that they can do that too in their own lives. Everything is obtainable to them. Absolutely everything." Asked whether he expected then to live forever, Koons replied portentously, "I feel totally part of the eternal. I am in the eternal."[37]

Naturally, neither the District Court nor the Circuit Court decisions in *Rogers* mentioned *Made in Heaven* or Koons's relationship with Ilona Staller. These were not at issue. Nonetheless, it is difficult to imagine that the judges were unaware of Koons's notoriety and the wide publicity that his current show was generating. The Circuit Court described him as a "controversial artist, hailed by some as a 'modern Michelangelo,' while others find his art 'truly offensive.'"[38]

* * *

Rogers's Complaint, filed on October 11, 1989, charged that *String of Puppies* was "substantially copied" from Rogers's copyrighted photograph.[39] Asserting that three copies of the sculpture had been sold or offered for sale at $125,000 each, Rogers demanded $375,000 in compensatory damages and an additional $2.5 million in punitive damages. Koons's Answer, filed a month later, declared that the "portion" of the photograph that Koons was alleged to have infringed was "not an original work of authorship." Koons's response denied the claim of substantial similarity and, further, contended that any use made of the photograph was privileged as "fair use."

Rogers and Koons both made motions for summary judgment. Rogers argued that there were no genuine issues of fact, Koons's appropriation of *Puppies* was obvious, and Rogers was entitled to judgment as a matter of law. Appended to his motion was an affidavit in which Rogers traced his career as a professional photographer first in North

Art Rogers, *Puppies* (1980). Courtesy of Art Rogers, Art Rogers Photography.

Carolina and then in California, noting that he regularly exhibited at galleries and museums, that his work was held in several museum collections, including the San Francisco Museum of Modern Art, and that he had received a Guggenheim Fellowship among other honors. Rogers described the making of *Puppies* in detail, including the selection of a location that would allow him to take advantage of the "beautiful, creamy, soft but crisp light" that he needed in order to achieve the effect he wanted. Such images were not "snapshots," he insisted. "They do not simply capture something that 'happened'; they have to be carefully created." The photo session involved sixty shots, which included various compositional ideas, although only one was finally used. Several years after producing the image, Rogers said, he contracted with Museum Graphics for note-card reproductions of *Puppies* and other works. He also licensed the image for reproduction in an anthology of photographs called *Dog Days* and he was planning to use it in a series of hand-tinted photographs. Rogers described how he first learned about Koons's use of his photograph in 1989. "The more I thought about the matter, the more upset and outraged I became that my work had been exploited—essentially 'ripped off'—by Mr. Koons, without my permission and with no compensation or credit to me." Koons was both competing with him and "falsely representing" that the image was his original work. "I consider that both immoral and unfair."[40]

In addition to his own affidavit, Rogers submitted statements from expert witnesses, two from prominent photographers—Cornell Capa and Arnold Newman—and one from Jane Kinne, an executive at an agency dealing in image rights. Capa testified as to substantial similarity between the works in question. Koons, he declared, "has used—I would say plagiarized—the work of another artist to enhance his reputation and, not incidentally, to make a substantial amount of money, without any credit or any compensation for what was taken."[41] Newman, a very distinguished photographer, known among other things for his celebrity portraits, discussed photographers' practice of granting licenses for "art renderings." Presumably, Koons's sculpture was just such a "rendering" produced without license. Kinne also discussed licenses for "art renderings," mentioning that she had represented photographers who had licensed their work to Andy Warhol.

Koons's opposing motion focused on two principal issues: protectability and fair use. As to the first, Koons argued that while the sculpture admittedly employed the photograph, all it used was unprotectable "fact," the fact that two people sat on a bench with eight puppies. None of the specifically artistic qualities such as light and tone appeared in the sculpture. The photograph was black and white, taken in natural light. The sculpture was carved, colored, and included none of the background. No "lay observer" could conceivably find the "expressive elements" in the sculpture to be substantially similar to those in the note card. The second argument concerned "fair use." Koons did not consider his sculpture to be substantially similar to the photograph, but, even if that were not the case, the doctrine of fair use protected his work. Going through the four factors specified in the statute, Koons quoted at length Pierre N. Leval's discussion of "transformative use"—a use that employs the taken material "in a different manner or for a different purpose from the original"—as it had been presented only months earlier in the *Harvard Law Review*. Clearly Koons's sculpture represented a "transformation" of the photograph and the important first factor favored Koons as did, he argued, the other three. As to the fourth factor, for example, the effect on the potential market for Rogers's photograph, it was clear that the sculpture did not substitute for or compete with the note-card image.[42]

Koons also submitted affidavits from experts, two from museum officials, one from a professional photographer, and one from a gallery owner. Brenda Richardson, associated with the Baltimore Museum of Art, and Kathy Halbreich, associated with the Boston Museum of Fine Arts, each discussed the differences between the photograph and the sculpture, making the point that Koons had produced something quite different from Rogers's photograph. The subject might be similar—a couple holding puppies—but, as Halbreich put it, "artistic expression is not about the subject of the work." The photograph presented a "pleasant pastoral scene" but there was nothing pleasant or cute about the sculpture, which was "cold" and "unsettling."[43] Jan Groover, a distinguished still-life photographer, also discussed the differences between the "cute" photograph and the sculpture. These, she declared, turned Rogers's "pleasing scene" into a "nightmare." "A reproduction right is a right to reproduce the photograph," Groover said. "It has nothing to do with a transformative use such as the Koons sculpture in this lawsuit." Responding to the matter of the right to license an "art rendering" of a photograph, an issue raised by Rogers's experts, Groover declared that she had never heard of the term.[44] Ronald Feldman, the owner of an important SoHo gallery, specifically countered Jane Kinne's claims about Andy Warhol's supposed purchases of photographic rights, saying the term "art rendering" was never used when he purchased photographs from Kinne for use in a Warhol project. Warhol's prints, Feldman testified, were not "art renderings" but distinctive and "transformative" works of art.[45]

While the parties were preparing their cases, depositions of the principals were taken. On February 14, 1990, Rogers's attorney led Koons through testimony about his education, employment, and financial arrangement with Sonnabend as well as through the details of the manufacture of the *String of Puppies* sculpture. This was produced by the

Demetz Art Studio, a long-established Italian workshop in the Dolomites that specializes in ecclesiastical art works. Koons testified that he closely oversaw the carving of the piece from the *Puppies* note card, visiting the studio regularly, sending faxes, and making sure that every detail from the coloring to the exact shape and size of the puppies' noses corresponded to his conception of what the final sculpture should be. Some of these notes and instructions, including multiple directives to reproduce the image "as per photo," figured prominently in the court's decision.

Attempting to establish that Koons's interests were at least in part commercial, Prutzman noted a recent *Wall Street Journal* article that quoted the artist saying, "I like the idea of my work selling for a lot of money."[46] Koons rejected the implication that he was interested in money for its own sake, insisting that high prices were important to him primarily because they would insure a work's impact and preservation. "The more it sells for, the more automatic protection and the more political power it has, as far as its placement. That is important to me, that my work can survive for the future."[47] Pressing him further, Prutzman asked whether Koons had ever used the phrase "market share" in relation to his work, as a quote in the *Wall Street Journal* article suggested. Koons acknowledged the phrase but insisted that his principal interest was in communicating his ideas broadly. "Money really isn't important in art. When you do great things, money automatically comes to you because of the value of the greatness of the actions that you're doing."[48] "Is it fair to say that your works have great value because they're great?" Prutzman asked. "I think so, absolutely. They are great," Koons answered.[49]

Perhaps impoliticly, Koons was dismissive of Rogers's claims as an artist. Asked whether he had felt the need to secure permission to use the *Puppies* photograph, Koons responded that if he had regarded the picture as "in the realm of art" he would have sought legal permission. "If I'm dealing with aspects of art and I feel that I need legal permission or something, I get it or I go about trying to get legal permission. If I'm dealing with something that is not art to me, I don't of course—there is no reason for me to have tried to obtain legal permission from something that to me just is not art."[50] "So in your view if it isn't art, you don't need permission to copy it?" Prutzman summarized. "No, no, that is not what I'm saying," Koons replied, but in fact that was quite clearly what he *was* saying. "To me that is not art," he repeated, referring to *Puppies.* "To me it is a post card." "Art," he went on, "is a gesture you don't take lightly. It doesn't present itself lightly. It doesn't present itself as a cupcake. . . . To me this photograph post card is a cupcake."[51]

From a legal point of view the matter of the photograph's artistic status was irrelevant. Rogers's image was protected whatever its aesthetic value. But the question of Koons's understanding of art recurred as a motif throughout his deposition. What in his opinion made a work of art? Since Koons's work, typically produced by employees and craftsmen, conspicuously lacks the "hand of the master"—to use the phrase from traditional connoisseurship—this was not an easy subject for him to address. We recall the prominent stamped signature with which Napoleon Sarony branded his celebrity photographs. Likewise, Koons emphasized the importance of signature. A piece was not "finished," he said, until he was satisfied. Until he signed the bottom of a work, it "could be anything" but it had no existence as art. "It has no place in this world till I sign the piece on the bottom."[52] The matter of signature returned later in the deposition. Would Koons feel free, Prutzman asked, to use Disney's Snow White in one of his works? Koons equivocated but added:

> Now, if Walt was right there and Walt did a drawing for me and signed it Walt Disney and gave it to me I would think again Snow White is in some realm that has to be looked at as art in some level, not that it is great art or anything, but if he signed it there in front of me and did a drawing for me, you know, it is just—it is, I think, enough.[53]

Art Rogers was deposed by John Koegel about a month after Koons's deposition and Rogers may well have had the advantage of reading a transcript of Koons's appearance. After taking Rogers through the narrative of how he became aware of Koons's sculpture and establishing that Rogers had never seen the sculpture itself, Koegel led Rogers into the treacherous area of art theory. Did Rogers regard Koons's sculpture as a work of art? Did Rogers have a definition of art? "I don't care. It is not something I'm concerned with. I don't define it," Rogers responded. The only thing he could discuss, he insisted, was his own art. He considered himself an artist and he considered his work original. Rogers accepted that there were some differences between the sculpture and the photograph but insisted that Koons's piece was a reproduction of his portrait. "Koons' piece to me is a copy of my photograph."[54]

Koegel questioned Rogers about the kinds of photographs he had made, the forms in which he had sold and published his pieces, and the details of how the *Puppies* photograph was produced. Asked how he came up with the idea of having the puppies lined up and held between the Scanlons on the bench, Rogers responded, "That's kind of hard to say, because that's what we call, an artist calls inspiration. Those are things that just come from inside of you, those things develop in your creative evolution."[55] Koegel pressed Rogers to acknowledge that, apart from anything else, his camera merely recorded what was before it, but Rogers rejected the term "recorded" saying that as an artist and photographer he had a problem with the word because it implied "a cold, unconscious, just mechanical event."[56] Throughout the questioning Rogers consistently presented himself as an artist but he refused to characterize his style in any detail, insisting that his pictures speak for themselves. People "see things in my art that I may not have necessarily intended in the beginning," he said. "I strive for some universal appeal in my work. I want everyone, regardless of who they are, their background, to look at it and to enjoy it, to respond to it."[57]

Whereas Koons came off in deposition as arrogant and dismissive, Rogers came off as modest, matter-of-fact, and genuinely upset by Koons's use of his picture. Whether their very different performances in deposition influenced District Judge Charles S. Haight Jr. is not evident from the substance of his decision in favor of Rogers, filed on December 12, 1990. Nonetheless, there is perhaps a hint of sympathy for Rogers, and perhaps a hint of the judge's aesthetic taste as well, in his description of Rogers succeeding "in getting two adults and eight puppies to hold still long enough to produce a charming photograph."[58] Judge Haight did not characterize Koons's sculpture in any comparable way, either positively or negatively. Indeed, the sculpture itself was never introduced into evidence. All that was presented for the court to consider were the various descriptions of the works in question offered by the parties and their experts and a pair of photographs, the black and white *Puppies*, and a color image of *String of Puppies*.[59]

In fact Koons's sculpture differs from Rogers's black-and-white photograph in a number of conspicuous ways. The carved wood sculpture is large, more than life-size, and it is of course colored. Indeed the coloring is striking: the dogs are painted blue with large white dots on their bulbous noses—a detail derived, as one of Koons's experts noted, from cartoon imagery not photographic reality—and the two figures are wearing pink and orange shirts, with the woman wearing yellow pants as well. Koons has added daisies on each side of the woman's head and a third daisy is balanced on the crown of the man's head. Perhaps these allude to the rustic setting of the original photograph; certainly they contribute an air of goofiness, making the woman's face reminiscent of the jug-eared *Mad* magazine character Alfred E. Neuman. More subtly, the figures' expressions are changed, especially about the mouths, which become rather thin and taut in the sculpture. Whereas Rogers's husband and wife look straight at the viewer, smiling with pride and pleasure, in the sculpture the figures do not meet the viewer's eye. The blue dogs, on the other hand, do stare at the viewer, their dark eyes emphasized by surrounding whites that echo the round dots of their noses. Indeed, the sculpture seems designed so that, seen from directly in front, four dogs—the odd-numbered figures—watch the observer. But moving in an arc before the piece, the viewer is followed by the gaze of each of the other dogs in turn. The effect is unsettling. The photo's background of grass, fence, and woods is completely gone; the sculpture merely stands on a pedestal. So too is the particular quality of light—"beautiful, creamy, soft but crisp"—that Rogers was proud of achieving in his image.

Despite differences, the basic composition of the sculpture was obviously derived from the photograph. Was this sufficient to produce a finding of infringement? John Koegel had argued that Koons had taken only unprotectable facts, but Judge Haight rejected this argument noting that the manner in which Rogers had arranged his subjects—the man and the woman seated on the bench with the eight puppies carried in their arms before them—constituted "a protectable original act of expression."[60] This was a principle that went back to *Burrow-Giles v. Sarony* (1884) in which the court's decision, as we have seen, emphasized the way Sarony had posed and arranged Oscar Wilde. Nor did Haight accept that, given the differences in size, texture, and color between the sculpture and the photograph, Rogers should be required to perform a substantial similarity analysis to demonstrate infringement. "Questions of size and color aside," Haight declared, "the sculpture is as exact a copy of the photograph as Koons' hired artisans could fashion."[61] There was no question that "an average lay observer"—the final authority for a judgment of substantial similarity in the Second Circuit—would find the sculpture to be taken from the photograph. In making this categorical statement, Haight was evidently dismissing as trivial details such as the added daisies and the puppies' noses. He was also leaving no room for discussion of the different effects that the photograph and the sculpture might be calculated to produce. Perhaps he considered this aspect of effect—the "rhetoric" of the two works, as it were—irrelevant.

The judge also rejected Koons's argument based on fair use. There was a "faint suggestion" in Koons's argument, Haight observed, that *String of Puppies,* along with the other works in the *Banality* show, was "intended to comment satirically upon contemporary values." But Haight found no evidence that *String of Puppies* was specifically addressed to the copyrighted work. "Koons' sculpture does not criticize or comment upon Rogers' photograph. It simply appropriates it."[62] Turning to the four factors specified in the statute, Haight remarked that the first, the purpose of the use, involved consideration of whether Koons's use was of a commercial or nonprofit nature. Here Koons's notoriously high prices and perhaps his reputation for self-promotion may have influenced the judge. Notwithstanding its "unquestioned status as a work of art," Haight remarked dryly, "the sculpture is not unsullied by considerations of commerce."[63] As to the second factor, the nature of the copyrighted work, Haight termed the photograph "a creative work, more closely akin to fiction" than to fact.[64] This, too, disfavored Koons. The third factor, the amount and substantiality of what was taken, also told against Koons, given that he had, as Haight saw it, "appropriated the entire photograph."[65] Finally, the fourth factor, the effect on the potential market for the copyrighted work, turned on the question of "art rendering" rights that emerged in the expert affidavits. Siding with Rogers's position that Koons's sculpture undermined the plaintiff's right to license his own "art renderings," the judge concluded that this factor too militated against fair use. Haight

thus granted Rogers's motion for summary judgment on the legal issue
of infringement, but he declined to specify a money award, saying that
Koons retained the right to prove at trial the expenses incurred in production of the sculptures.[66]

Koons appealed Haight's judgment of infringement to the Second
Circuit. He also appealed the District Court's order to turn over his
reserved copy of *String of Puppies* to Rogers, an order that had turned
into a messy contempt citation. In his brief, Koons argued a number of
specifically legal issues, among them questioning whether the court
had properly determined infringement without undertaking a formal
analysis of substantial similarity or even viewing the actual sculpture.
Koons also emphasized that the stakes in the case went well beyond
the particular issue of the note card and the sculpture. "The chilling
effect on creative art from a procedure which allows expedited infringement liability by a judge who may not know or appreciate art is obvious."[67] Placing himself in the postmodern art tradition from Marcel
Duchamp through Jasper Johns, Robert Rauschenberg, and Andy Warhol,
Koons discussed the social and artistic importance of preserving the
freedom to employ materials from popular culture in the service of
social commentary. Not just Koons's work but an entire art historical
tradition was jeopardized by the District Court's decision. The fair
use doctrine, he argued, "must be flexible enough to encompass and
thereby not discourage these new and legitimate art forms."[68]

Koons framed his appeals argument in part in terms of the character of his work as social commentary and the need of contemporary
artists to employ materials from popular and commercial culture. This
was not an inaccurate characterization but it was perhaps incomplete.
The pieces in the *Banality* show were, as I have remarked, equivocally
balanced between satire and celebration of popular culture. Responding
to Koons, Rogers recalled that Koons himself had stated that the "message or artistic statement" of the *Banality* show was not critical but
liberational: the point was "to remove the guilt and shame of the bourgeois."[69] Seeking to discredit Koons's claim to be commenting on the
photograph, Rogers cited Koons's own experts. Jan Groover, a photographer familiar with Rogers's work, had declared that Koons's "sculpture
is not about the photograph." Likewise, Brenda Richardson, a museum
curator, had declared, "I do not see how anyone can say that there is a

reference to a photograph in the *String of Puppies* sculpture."[70] At bottom, Rogers said, Koons was asking the court to extend the parody branch of fair use to embrace any claim of criticism or social commentary no matter how tenuous. "If fair use is extended to allow Koons to do that here," Rogers warned, "there will be very little left to copyright law."[71]

Rogers then proceeded to use Koons's experts against him in a second way, suggesting that in fact they were being less than candid in claiming that there was no similarity between *String of Puppies* and the photograph. "These art cognoscenti may theorize that, from their standpoint, the sculpture 'bears absolutely no artistic relationship with or similarity to the photograph,'" Rogers said, "but that opinion cannot change what is obvious to everyone else (and indeed must be obvious to them as well), that 'String of Puppies' copies substantially all of 'Puppies.'"[72] Rogers's slightly sneering term "art cognoscenti" perhaps betrays something of the sort of professional resentment between commercial photographers and "legitimate" artists that, as I have noted, contributed to litigation in the 1960s and 1970s. When Koons's rhetoric of social criticism was stripped away, Rogers declared, his copying of the photograph was "nothing more than a self-proclaimed 'internationally important visual artist's' inequitable misappropriation of a lesser known visual artist's work, without permission, payment, or even attribution."[73]

There was perhaps a hint of sympathy for the plaintiff in District Judge Haight's remark about Rogers's "charming photograph." The sympathies of the Circuit Court were blatant. The key to the case, wrote Judge Richard J. Cardamone, was Koons's

> borrowing of plaintiff's expression of a typical American scene—a smiling husband and wife holding a litter of charming puppies. The copying was so deliberate as to suggest that defendants resolved so long as they were significant players in the art business, and the copies they produced bettered the price of the copied work by a thousand to one, their piracy of a less well-known artist's work would escape being sullied by an accusation of plagiarism.[74]

Judge Cardamone characterized Rogers as a widely exhibited "artist-photographer" whose work is held in multiple collections. He noted that "substantial creative effort" went into the composition and production of *Puppies*, a process in which "Rogers drew on his years of artistic development." He remarked that Rogers "selected the light, the location, the bench on which the Scanlons are seated and the arrangement of the small dogs. He also made creative judgments concerning technical matters with his camera and the use of natural light." After copies of the finished print were delivered to the Scanlons, *Puppies* became part of Rogers's catalog of images "from which he, like many professional photographers, makes his living." The image had been used and exhibited a number of times and licensed to Museum Graphics. Rogers also planned to use the image in a series of hand-tinted prints.[75]

Turning to the defendant, Cardamone noted that while pursuing his career as an artist Koons had worked as a mutual funds salesman, a commodities salesman and broker, and a commodities futures broker. He described Koons's numerous exhibitions and extensive bibliography, observing that his "works sell at very substantial prices, over $100,000." Reporting that Koons was a "controversial" figure, Cardamone quoted Michael Brenson's *New York Times* review of the *Banality* show—"Greed Plus Glitz, with a Dollop of Innocence"—in which Brenson commented on Koons's prices and cunning. He then described the making of *String of Puppies*, noting that Koons regarded Rogers's photograph as part of mass culture and that after buying the card Koons "tore off that portion showing Rogers' copyright of 'Puppies.'" Quoting extensively from the production notes that Koons gave to the Demetz studio in Italy, Cardamone emphasized the extent to which Koons was concerned that the photograph be faithfully copied in the carving.[76]

The general effect, then, of Judge Cardamone's discussion was to portray Rogers as a serious, hardworking artist while hinting that the better-known Koons was something of a scoundrel interested primarily in money. Not surprisingly, the judge's legal analysis confirmed the lower court's finding of infringement. He also confirmed its order that Koons turn over his proof copy of *String of Puppies* to Rogers. Koons had claimed the sculpture was parody, a form of social criticism. Cardamone roughly rejected this claim, saying "it is not really the parody flag that appellants are sailing under, but rather the flag of piracy."[77] Koons's purposes were not high-minded. "Here there is simply nothing in the record to support a view that Koons produced 'String of Puppies' for anything other than sale as high-priced art."[78] Furthermore, Koons's conduct, especially his tearing the copyright notice off of Rogers's note card, suggested that he had acted in bad faith. Cardamone agreed with the court below that on the matter of damages due to Rogers, Koons retained the right to prove his expenses. Nonetheless, he suggested that Rogers remained at liberty to elect statutory damages in lieu of further litigation. "In fact," he added, "given Koons's willful and egregious behavior, we think Rogers may be a good candidate for enhanced statutory damages."[79]

Koons reacted angrily to the decision. "Since when did judges qualify as art critics?" he told the New York Times, adding that the ruling would have a chilling effect on artistic freedom and that he would appeal.[80] Shortly after, Koons petitioned the Second Circuit for reconsideration en banc arguing, among other things, that there was no evidence that Koons had acted in bad faith as Cardamone's decision asserted. The removal of the back flap of the Puppies note card containing Rogers's copyright notice, Koons observed, was "entirely innocent." It had nothing to do with removing the copyright notice but, as explained at oral argument, was "simply a physical consequence of inserting the card in a notebook of images that Koons was using to develop the Banality show.[81] The petition for rehearing was rejected as was the subsequent petition for consideration by the U.S. Supreme Court.

After denial of certiorari in Rogers on October 13, 1992, the other two cases stemming from the Banality show moved forward swiftly. Motions in United Feature Syndicate v. Koons, filed about two months after Rogers, had been stayed pending the resolution of the String of Puppies case. United Feature Syndicate concerned Koons's use of the comic strip character "Odie" in his sculpture Wild Boy with Puppy. The issues in this case generally paralleled those in Rogers and, not surprisingly, the court ruled against Koons on March 24, 1993.[82] The following week Barbara Campbell v. Koons, involving Campbell's Boys with Pig photograph and Koons's sculpture Ushering in Banality was also decided against Koons. As the court noted in its brief decision, Campbell required little discussion since the issues were substantially identical to those in Rogers v. Koons.[83] Thus for a third time Koons was found to be an infringer. Ultimately, Koons settled all of the cases that arose from the *Banality* show, including the charge brought by MGM in response to his use of the Pink Panther character.[84]

* * *

In the years after *Rogers*, Koons apparently sought and secured permission whenever he used an image or an object that he considered recognizable.[85] Nonetheless, in 2004 Koons again found himself in court responding to a professional photographer's charges of infringement. Commissioned by Deutsche Bank to create a series of paintings for the Deutsche Guggenheim, an exhibition space located on the ground floor of the bank building in Berlin, Koons had produced a series of seven monumental paintings, *Easyfun-Ethereal*. These incorporated layered imagery drawn from commercial advertising and mass-produced food products. One of the paintings, *Niagara*, depicted four pairs of shapely female legs dangling in a kind of cascade over sugary images of food including a tray of frosted donuts, an ice-cream-topped fudge brownie, and a tray of sugared-apple Danish pastries. In the background was an image of Niagara Falls. The sleek legs and feet hanging down through the top two-thirds of the painting echo the waterfall, suggesting a torrent of female limbs suspended over a field of cloying sweets. The composition thus creates a contrast between the cascade of legs and the natural cascade in the background as well as an association between the sensuality of the legs and feet and the sugary confections below.[86]

The source of the second pair of cascading legs in *Niagara* was a photograph titled *Silk Sandals by Gucci* that had appeared in the August 2000 issue of *Allure*, a women's beauty magazine. Andrea Blanch, who had been commissioned by *Allure* to make the photograph, was an established fashion and portrait photographer whose work had appeared in prominent magazines including *Vogue* and *Harper's Bazaar*. Blanch saw Koons's painting when it was exhibited at the Guggenheim Museum in New York in 2002. Recollecting the experience, Blanch reported that her first reaction was excitement that Koons had incorporated her work in his painting. Flattered, she telephoned friends who to her surprise recommended legal action. "The thought of suing never crossed my mind," Blanch said. "I wanted to give him the benefit of the doubt, but then something happened a couple of weeks later." A friend met Koons at a party and told him that Andrea Blanch was ex-

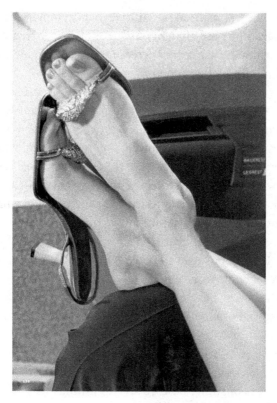

Andrea Blanch, *Silk Sandals by Gucci.* Courtesy of Andrea Blanch, Andrea Blanch Studio.

cited that he had used her photograph. The friend reported that Koons had turned "gray." Blanch's response was indignation: "He knew that he'd done it, and he didn't bother to ask permission. I thought, 'Yeah, I'm suing.' That's how it happened."[87]

As this anecdote suggests, Blanch's suit, like those of the photographers who sued Warhol, Rivers, and Rauschenberg, was at least in part a matter of professional pride. Filing suit in 2004, Blanch's complaint invoked the three judgments of the early 1990s. She termed Koons "a notorious infringer" who had "consistently manifested the utmost of disregard and contempt for the intellectual property rights of others." Reporting that part of the imagery in *Niagara* was "slavishly copied" from her *Allure* photograph and citing Koons's history of "willful, deliberate, malicious and repeated acts of copyright infringement,"

Blanch demanded $1 million in punitive and exemplary damages.[88] In deposition she admitted that Koons's use of her photograph did not cause any harm to her career or decrease the market value of her photograph. She had suffered no economic harm.

Koons's response acknowledged that he had used Blanch's photograph but maintained that his reference to the original was "limited and transformative."[89] The picture in *Allure*, published as part of a feature on metallic cosmetics, showed a pair of sandal-clad feet displaying shiny toenails. The feet were shot at close range with the legs slanting upward at a forty-five degree angle from the lower-right-hand corner of the image and the feet resting on a man's lap in what appeared to be a first-class airplane cabin. Remarking that the impulse for *Niagara* had come from a billboard in Rome that consisted of several sets of women's legs, Koons said that the legs of the model in the *Allure* picture represented to him "a particular type of woman frequently presented in advertising."[90] He extracted the legs from the airplane context, inverted the orientation, changed the coloring, and added them to other contrasting images of legs, floating them, along with ice cream, donuts, and pastries, above a landscape of grass, waterfall, and sky. "I thus suggest," Koons explained, "how commercial images like these intersect in our consumer culture and simultaneously promote appetites, like sex, and confine other desires, like playfulness."[91] The original photograph was "typical of a certain style of mass communication," Koons said. He acknowledged that it would have been possible to make a similar photograph himself, but using an existing image ensured "a certain authenticity or veracity." It was, he added, "the difference between quoting and paraphrasing."[92]

We recall that in the *String of Puppies* case Koons's attorney invoked the principle of "transformative use," quoting at length from Pierre Leval's recent *Harvard Law Review* article "Toward a Fair Use Standard," written in the aftermath of the *Salinger* and *New Era* decisions. Leval's article had revisited the traditional four-factor procedure of fair use analysis, suggesting that the most important factor was not, as had been generally held, the effect of the use on the potential market or value of the copyrighted work, but rather the purpose and character of the allegedly infringing use. Bearing in mind the utilitarian goal of copyright as an incentive to the advancement of learning, Leval proposed that the crucial issue in fair use analysis should be the degree to which the subsequent work could be understood as "transformative." Was the appropriated expression used as "raw material" that was then "transformed in the creation of new information, new aesthetics, new insights, and understandings"?[93]

The issues that Leval raised had been ignored both by the District Court and by the Circuit Court in *Rogers v. Koons*. But while *Rogers* was under consideration another fair use case, *Campbell v. Acuff-Rose*, was making its way through the courts. *Campbell*, which involved the hip-hop band 2 Live Crew's rap version of Roy Orbison's rock ballad "Oh, Pretty Woman," reached the U.S. Supreme Court after differing opinions in the District Court, which granted summary judgment for 2 Live Crew, and the Court of Appeals, which reversed, holding the defense of fair use barred, among other things, by the song's commercial character. Prominently citing Leval's *Harvard Law Review* article, the Supreme Court in a unanimous decision ruled that it was an error for the Court of Appeals to conclude that the commercial nature of 2 Live Crew's parody rendered it presumptively unfair. The central objective of an examination of the purpose and character of an allegedly infringing use, the court said, was to determine whether and to what extent the new work was "transformative." Such "transformative" works, Justice David Souter wrote, "lie at the heart of the fair use doctrine's guarantee of breathing space within the confines of copyright." The more "transformative" the new work might be, the less will be the significance of other factors such as whether or not the allegedly infringing work was commercial in nature.[94]

Koons's response to Blanch's claim was crafted to invoke Leval's concept of "transformative use." So, too, had been his attorney's argument a dozen years earlier in the *String of Puppies* case. But now, after *Campbell v. Acuff-Rose*, Koons spoke with the authority of the U.S. Supreme Court supporting Leval's concept. On the other hand, Blanch's opposition to Koons's claim of fair use defense rested less on specifically legal argument than, as District Court Judge Louis L. Stanton noted, on the three earlier cases in which Koons was found liable for willful infringement of copyright. In effect Blanch was merely saying, "Look, he's done it again!" The earlier cases all involved works from Koons's *Banality* show and were, as Judge Stanton observed, different on their facts. "Each case of alleged infringement involving different works must be decided on its own merits."[95] Stanton accepted Koons's argument that his use of Blanch's photograph was "transformative" and endorsed his claim of fair use. At the same time, by emphasizing that each case must be decided on its own merits, Stanton made clear that he was not implicitly reversing or even questioning the outcome in *Rogers v. Koons*.

Andrea Blanch appealed and the Circuit Court, in a unanimous opinion written by Judge Robert D. Sack, affirmed, citing Judge Leval's "seminal" law review article and agreeing that Koons's use of Blanch's photograph was "transformative." Whereas the Circuit Court in the *String of Puppies* case was conspicuously hostile to Koons implying that he was something of a scoundrel, the Circuit Court in *Blanch* accepted at face value Koons's statements about the social and critical purpose of his work, noting that these were very different from Blanch's purposes in making her photograph. The test for whether a secondary work is to be considered "transformative"—that is, whether it "adds something new" to the original, with a "further purpose or different character"—almost "perfectly describes Koons's adaptation of 'Silk Sandals,'" Judge Sack wrote. He added in a note that "Koons's clear conception of his reasons for using 'Silk Sandals,' and his ability to articulate those reasons, ease our analysis in this case."[96] Judge Robert Katzman, a member of the three-judge panel, added a concurring opinion in which he made several qualifying comments and noted that the facts in *Blanch* were "quite distinguishable" from those in *Rogers v. Koons*. "This is our Circuit's second encounter with Koons' work," Judge Katzman remarked. "His work, like that of other appropriation artists, inherently raises difficult questions about the proper scope of copyright protection and the fair-use doctrine. I would continue to answer those questions as necessary to decide particular cases, mindful that the fair-use inquiry is a fact-specific one that is 'not to be simplified with bright-line rules.'"[97]

Reflecting on her unsuccessful lawsuit several years later, Andrea Blanch observed that since the conclusion of the suit against Koons she had "spent more time looking at his work; and I've gained an appreciation for it. It's conceptual—so either you like the concept or not. Some of the things I like, and others are kind of silly." Asked about "appropriation art" as a movement, Blanch remarked that in her opinion "there should be more consideration for the original artist and the art that is appropriated. It's very possible that Koons' honest intention was to make a cultural statement," she added, "but I still believe that it's not good enough. If I were dead, fine. But I'm a living person, and he should have asked my permission. Bottom line."[98]

Why was the outcome in *Blanch* so different from that in *Rogers*? It is not inappropriate to note the change in tone between the *Blanch* and *Rogers* decisions. The *Rogers* courts—especially the Circuit Court, which spoke disdainfully of Koons and Sonnabend, his gallery, as "players in the art business"—were clearly less sympathetic with Koons than with Rogers, the earnest "artist-photographer" from Point Reyes, California. One thinks of Edmund Curll's disadvantage in defending himself in Lord Chancellor Hardwicke's court. A dozen years later Koons stature had risen and he had become more respectable. Of course the two cases also presented different fact patterns, even though both involved the appropriation of a photograph. In *Rogers* the central subject of Rogers's portrait was turned into a polychrome sculpture. In *Blanch* an excerpt from the plaintiff's photograph was rotated and manipulated and then included in a photo-collage painting. The plaintiff's image of legs represented only one element among many in *Niagara*, whereas Koons's sculpture, like Rogers's photograph, showed a man and a woman seated on a bench holding a string of puppies. These facts made it easier to conclude that *Niagara* rather than *String of Puppies* represented a fair use of the plaintiff's work.

The difference in media between the three-dimensional sculpture and the two-dimensional painting may also have been consequential. One might think that the court would have more readily perceived differences between a three-dimensional sculpture and a photograph than between a painting and a photograph. As already noted, however, the *Rogers* court never saw Koons's sculpture. Nor did the *Blanch* court see his painting, only a photograph of it. In both *Rogers* and *Blanch*, then, the court was comparing photographs to photographs. In such circumstances what was most apparent was the overall composition of the works in question. At a glance it was obvious that *String of Puppies* was more like *Puppies* than *Niagara* was like *Silk Sandals by Gucci*.

Would the result in *Rogers* have been different if the sculpture itself had been put in evidence? It is of course impossible to say, but I suspect not. Despite their copyright-protected status, photographs are still commonly regarded as more or less transparent records of objective materials that appeared before the camera. John Koegel argued that the man and the woman holding the eight puppies between them were merely "facts" not "expression" and therefore not protected, but the courts did not accept this claim, drawing on the principle that a photographer's arrangement of the subject matter constitutes part of the protected expression. Ironically, Koegel's argument may have served to draw attention to the compositional similarity between the photograph and the sculpture. As obvious as it was that the composition of *Niagara* was different from *Silk Sandals* so it was obvious that the composition of *String of Puppies* was similar to that of *Puppies*. If the *Rogers* court had seen the polychromed wood sculpture they might have shown greater appreciation for the differences between the sculpture and the photograph in tone and scale, but they still, I think, would have seen *String of Puppies* as appropriating the "expressive heart" of Rogers's portrait.

The facts in the two cases were indeed different. But the most obvious way to explain the difference in outcome was that between *Rogers* and *Blanch* the law had changed: *Campbell v. Acuff-Rose*, ratifying Pierre Leval's idea of "transformative use," had altered the way courts approached questions of fair use.[99] John Koegel had invoked Leval in *Rogers* to no avail. Perhaps if "Oh, Pretty Woman" had preceded *String of Puppies*, the Koons case would have been resolved differently. But this raises a related question: why was *Rogers* rather than *Campbell* not the precedent-setting case that sanctioned "transformative use"? The Supreme Court gives no reasons for agreeing to review one case and denying another. It is worth noting, however, that, unlike *Rogers*, *Campbell* involved a disagreement between courts. It is also worth noting that *Campbell* posed a clear and well-defined legal issue. Was a fair use defense effectively barred by the commercial character of a defendant's use? The interpretive issues in *Rogers*, which were visual rather than verbal, were also arguably more difficult than those in *Campbell* and more closely tied to exactly how one chooses to understand the meaning and purposes of the works in question. In

the case of Jeff Koons's equivocal work arriving at such an understanding is frequently challenging.

Of course Leval's notion of transformative use did not "solve" the
issue of fair use but merely led it back from the brink of determinism.
Neither a calculation of how much of a protected work a second comer
had taken nor an accounting of which side was favored by a majority
of the statutory factors should, according to Leval, resolve a contro-
versy. As Leval said in his meeting with opposing attorneys at the
start of *Salinger*, "I think these matters are not to be decided by accountants based on percentages."[100] Sometimes it might be easier to
decide whether a second comer's use was indeed "transformative" and
sometimes it might be more difficult, requiring considerable literary
or visual or musical sophistication and judgment. What was inescap-
able was the need to exercise judgment. So, too, in questions of "substantial similarity" it would be desirable to have an algorithm like
Moses Malevinsky's algebraic formula to decide whether one work in-
fringes upon another. But finally, as Learned Hand understood, the best
the law can provide—in matters of fair use as well as in matters of
substantial similarity—is a framework for acts of informed criticism.

CHAPTER EIGHT

Afterword

Metamorphoses of Authorship

I began this study by invoking Daniel Defoe's public humiliation for the crime of seditious libel by being exhibited in the pillory. As I suggested, the goal of this form of punishment was to shame the criminal and reaffirm the social norm. Defoe's pillorying was a theatrical event designed by the court. But in this case Defoe, rallying his friends to protect him from violence and to distribute copies of his mocking *Hymn to the Pillory*, transformed the official drama of humiliation into a kind of triumph. Alexander Pope, too, designed a role for himself, presenting himself as a gentleman poet besieged by fools and rapacious scoundrels like Curll. In Pope's case the drama helped to obscure the tension between his status as a gentleman and his career as an author who made a fortune from his writings. A century later, under very different circumstances, Harriet Beecher Stowe, the wife and daughter of eminent clergymen, also experienced a tension between gentility and professional authorship, one that in her case was inflected by gender and liberal Christian conviction. She, too, found herself cast in a role as a professional that she could neither wholly embrace nor wholly reject.

Napoleon Sarony, on the other hand, does not seem to have been a man ambivalent about commerce. Like the burgeoning cult of celebrity that provided the raw material for his trade in cabinet cards, Sarony happily constructed himself as a celebrity, employing his own dramatic persona as a warrant to underwrite the value of his products and to establish his legal status as an artist. True, Sarony complained from time to time that photography kept him from painting and sketching, from "something that is truly art," but whether this was a serious regret or merely another element in the construction of his persona is not clear.[1]

Anne Nichols, too, played her role as an artist and entrepreneur without apparent ambivalence. Nichols conspicuously embraced the stereotype of the author who writes from inspiration and depth of feeling, but she revealed no evidence of tension between inspiration and commerce. When a true author has an idea, Nichols said, she does her best "to put it on paper and to get it to Washington and copyright it so it cannot be taken."[2] Both Sarony and Nichols played versions of the specially gifted person, happy to profit from his or her talent to the maximum degree possible. But Nichols's performance was perhaps inflected by her symbiotic relationship with her lawyer, Moses Malevinsky. This seems to have involved a mutually acceptable differentiation of roles. Malevinsky was the intellectual, the man with theories who could explain what Nichols's play was about and why it was a work of genius. She was the intuitive artist, the playwright who instinctively understood how to dramatize emotions such as love. He was the intellectual man, she was the intuitive woman. In this role she was able to preserve her femininity even while acting as a professional.

J. D. Salinger also constructed a drama of authorship, but an idiosyncratic one, centered on "honesty." Having achieved financial independence as a result of his early successes, Salinger turned his back on the literary marketplace. For Salinger, publication itself came to seem a violation; the only honest enactment of integrity was silence and withdrawal. Ironically, Salinger was compelled to step into a public forum and submit to deposition precisely in order to protect his desire to withdraw.

Jeff Koons, displaying himself on billboards and in advertisements, readily appears as the polar opposite of Salinger. But Koons enacts a dialectic of his own, a struggle between a conspicuous impulse toward narcissistic self-display and a desire to escape into objectivity through the use of impersonal, recirculated cultural materials. In many respects, the figure Koons most emphatically recalls is Napoleon Sarony. Like Sarony in his Union Square studio, a factory for the production of celebrity images, Koons's sculptures and paintings are produced by an army of assistants in his Chelsea studio. Like Sarony, too, Koons assigns the mere execution of works to others. And, again like Sarony, the tension between industrial methods and assertions of genius is resolved in the emphasis that Koons places on signature. Both Sarony and Koons entangle art, celebrity, and commerce, as indeed did Alexander Pope centuries earlier. It was perhaps precisely this kind of entanglement that Salinger, in the name of authenticity, was seeking to escape.

The dramas of authorship sketched in this study thus reveal certain continuities even as the social contexts change and develop. So, of course, do the legal contexts in which these dramas are performed. Defoe's trial and punishment took place at the end of the old legal regime before the empowering of the author in the Statute of Anne. Pope's suit against Curll was one of the earliest in which an author appeared in court as a legally recognized plaintiff, but at this time it was not yet clear whether writings such as letters were protected and if so exactly what protection entailed. In *Pope v. Curll* the lord chancellor suggested a distinction between the ink and paper of the physical letter and the language or sentiments that formed the specifically literary property, and thus began the process of abstraction, extension, and generalization that has characterized the large-scale history of copyright. *Stowe v. Thomas*, which eventually led to the legislative recognition of the translation right, represented a major change in theory. No longer was protection limited to a particular piece of language; now copyright protected the "substance" of a work, a concept significantly more elusive and difficult to define. *Burrow-Giles v. Sarony* took the process of abstraction further, identifying "mental conception" as the ghostly source of a protected work. And Jeff Koons's practices show how "mental conception" still operates today, even in relation to traditional forms such as sculpture and painting.

When does one author trespass on the "intellectual property" of another? One observation that emerges from this study is the difficulty of establishing "bright-line" principles. As early as 1704, in his *Essay on the Regulation of the Press*, published in the wake of his conviction for libel, Daniel Defoe called for an act that would specify exactly what topics writers should avoid in order to protect themselves from prosecution. Some two hundred years later, Moses L. Malevinsky conceived his "algebraic formula" in a similar quest for objectivity and certainty. But in copyright matters, as I have suggested, the quest for objectivity and certainty is chimerical. The law can provide a useful framework for analysis but it cannot do away with the need for critical judgment. One reason this is the case is that the law, like other forms of writing, is, as Pierre Leval pointed out, embodied in words. Indeed, sometimes the law is embodied in metaphors. The notion of "concrete" expression is one such metaphor. "Transformative," Leval's influential contribution to fair use analysis, is another. Inevitably the determination of what is or is not "transformative" is subject to critical discrimination.

Even in the earliest days of hard thinking about copyright, language and metaphor were crucial in attempting to articulate the shape and limits of the law. Thus William Blackstone, seeking to frame a formula that would define the subject of copyright in such a way as to prevent copyright from becoming a monopoly on ideas or subjects, reached back to the ancient trope of language as the "dress of thought," a metaphor going back at least as far as the Roman rhetorician Quintilian. Copyright, Blackstone said, did not protect general ideas but only the "same conceptions, cloathed in the same words."[3] Justice Robert Grier employed Blackstone's metaphor when he ruled that Harriet Beecher Stowe's copyright in *Uncle Tom's Cabin* was limited to the specific language in which she had clothed her conceptions. But a metaphor is, as the songwriter Paul Simon might say, a slip-sliding sort of thing. In his discussion of translation, George Ticknor Curtis, the authority on whom Stowe's attorneys relied, invoked the trope to very different effect, dismissing the idea that a mere "change of dress" annihilates the author's property in a work.[4] Likewise Eaton Drone, the leading copyright authority of the latter part of the nineteenth century, invoked the trope to argue that a translator was not an author. An author creates something new, Drone said, but a translator merely "takes the entire creation of another" and "clothes it in a new dress."[5] Thus the valence of Blackstone's metaphor was silently inverted and a new doctrine was promulgated. And this could happen so smoothly, I suspect, precisely because the traditional doctrine forged by Blackstone was lodged in a metaphor.

Hardheaded observers will sometimes express the opinion that copyright is finally all about money: litigate or settle, these matters come down to money. Hollywood, as I noted in my discussion of *Nichols v. Universal*, imitates; successful film formulas and subjects proliferate, providing opportunities for litigation. It is not irrelevant to observe that a profitable movie such as *Avatar* is more likely to attract lawsuits than a dud. But copyright litigation is not always solely or even primarily about money. Alexander Pope's suit against Edmund Curll mingled financial interests with Pope's desire to establish that a gentleman had the right to prevent the unauthorized publication of his correspondence. J. D. Salinger's suit against Random House had no financial motivation at all. Likewise, the photographers who sued Warhol, Rivers, Rauschenberg, and later Koons did so at least in part because they were offended by the unacknowledged use of their work. Constructing something like a property right founded on personality, copyright adjudicates the boundary between the private and the public by setting rules about printing and publishing and by creating private incentives to foster public purposes, the production and circulation of knowledge. Put one way, the right not to publish can be understood as the foundation of the right to privacy. Put another way, it can be understood as the right to limit public discourse. Thus the tension between privacy and publicity can also become the tension between censorship and speech, as Pierre Leval was acutely aware in both the *Salinger* and *New Era* matters.

This book has focused on case studies of individual authors involved in copyright litigation. Informing any such study is the assumption that the author, either as plaintiff or defendant, is the central figure in the drama of copyright. This is clearly true: both the Statute of Anne and the U.S. Copyright Act of 1790 place authors and their works at the heart of the copyright doctrine. Nonetheless, some qualification is necessary. Although the Statute of Anne was influenced by the concerns of Defoe and other authors, it can be argued that the principal driving force was the lobbying of the great booksellers whose business had been thrown into disorder by the lapse of licensing. As I have noted, Pope was exceptional in his day in his use of the statute; most of the early copyright cases did not directly involve authors. The two most important British cases of the eighteenth century were *Millar v. Taylor* (1769) and *Donaldson v. Beckett* (1774), which together determined that copyright was not perpetual but limited in term. These cases were litigated in the name of authors' rights, but in fact both involved booksellers suing booksellers. James Thomson, the poet whose works were the subject of both *Millar* and *Donaldson*, was long dead.

Nineteenth-century authors such as Wordsworth and Dickens in Britain and Stowe and Twain in the United States were actively involved in copyright matters. But a major social and economic change began in the latter part of the nineteenth century, a process of corporate consolidation and transformation that in the United States started with the railroads and spread to other industries, including the media. In "Metamorphoses of Authorship," an important essay published some years ago, Peter Jaszi identified the way that, in the context of the nineteenth and twentieth centuries, the legal concept of authorship underwent a hollowing out as the emphasis in copyright law shifted from the author to the work.[6] The first U.S. copyright statute, the act of 1790, modeled on the Statute of Anne, spoke of securing rights to authors. The current statute, the Copyright Act of 1976, speaks of providing copyright protection for "original works of authorship." This shift relates to the emergence of "work-for-hire" doctrine, that is, the principle that, in an industrial context, copyright belongs to the employer who commissions a project rather than to the worker who executes it. Twentieth- and twenty-first-century authors—including J. D. Salinger and Jeff Koons—have continued to be involved in copyright matters both as plaintiffs and defendants. But no longer is the legal author necessarily a living, breathing, mortal human being. Indeed, in the case of many of the most valuable literary properties today—blockbuster movies, for example, and corporate franchises built around protected figures such as Mickey Mouse or James Bond—the legal author is rarely a human being. We still have writers, artists, and composers of course, but work-for-hire doctrine extends the process of abstraction and generalization that has characterized the large-scale history of copyright to the point that, not infrequently, the foundational figure of the author has itself become metaphysical.

Notes

I. DEFOE IN THE PILLORY

1. The two authoritative biographies of Defoe are Paula R. Backsheider, *Daniel Defoe: His Life* (Baltimore: Johns Hopkins University Press, 1989) and Maximillian E. Novak, *Daniel Defoe: Master of Fictions* (New York: Oxford University Press, 2001). For their discussions of *The Shortest Way* and Defoe's subsequent trial and punishment on which I have relied for factual information, see Backsheider, *Daniel Defoe*, 94–134, and Novak, *Daniel Defoe*, 168–198. See also John Robert Moore, "Defoe in the Pillory: A New Interpretation," in *Defoe in the Pillory and Other Studies* (Bloomington: Indiana University Press, 1939), 3–32. Jody Greene provides an interesting discussion of Defoe's pillorying in *The Trouble with Ownership: Literary Property and Authorial Liability in England, 1660–1730* (Philadelphia: University of Pennsylvania Press, 2001), 107–149.

2. William Fuller, *Mr. William Fuller's trip to Bridewell, with a true account of his barbarous usage in the pillory* (London, 1703), 2–3. The standard account of Fuller is George Campbell, *Imposter at the Bar: William Fuller, 1670–1733* (London: Hodder and Stoughton, 1961).

3. Daniel Defoe, *A Hymn to the Pillory*, 2nd ed. (London, 1703), 1, 4, 11, 13.

4. *Hercules Ridens*, no. 2, August 3–7, 1703.

5. See Ethyn Williams Kirby, *William Prynne: A Study in Puritanism* (Cambridge, MA: Harvard University Press, 1931), 20–50.

6. Daniel Defoe, *Twenty-Six Depositions* (1702) and *Original Letters* (1702); see Campbell, *Imposter*, 193–195.

7. These points are famously made by Michel Foucault in "What Is an Author?" Foucault noted that the modern conception of texts as objects of individual appropriation began with the establishment of the author as a figure subject to punishment. He also observed that before writing—as distinguished from books—became a commodity, it was conceived as an "act," one "placed in the bipolar field of the sacred and the profane, the licit and the illicit, the religious and the blasphemous." See Michel Foucault, "What Is an Author?" trans. J. V. Harari, *The Foucault Reader*, ed. Paul Rabinow (New York: Pantheon, 1984), 108.

8. Daniel Defoe, "A Brief Explanation of a Late Pamphlet," in *A True Collection of the Writings of the Author of the True Born English-man* (London, 1703), 435.

9. Jonathan Swift, *A Modest Proposal* (Dublin, 1729), 6.

10. Daniel Defoe, *An Essay on the Regulation of the Press* (London, 1704), 19.

11. Ibid., 28.

12. Jürgen Habermas, *The Structural Transformation of the Public Sphere*, trans. Thomas Burger (Cambridge, MA: Harvard University Press, 1989), 28. On the lapse of licensing see Raymond Astbury, "The Renewal of the Licensing

[187]

Act in 1693 and Its Lapse in 1695," *Library* 33 (1978): 296–322. I have discussed the early history of copyright in relation to Habermas's conception of the public sphere in Mark Rose, "The Public Sphere and the Emergence of Copyright: *Areopagitica*, the Stationers' Company, and the Statute of Anne," in *Privilege and Property: Essays on the History of Copyright*, ed. Ronan Deazley, Martin Kretschmer, and Lionel Bently (Cambridge: Open Book Publishers, 2010), 67–88.

13. Defoe, *Essay on the Regulation of the Press*, 25.

14. *Review*, December 3, 1709. See also my discussion of Defoe's agitation on behalf of authorial rights and the copyright bill in Mark Rose, *Authors and Owners: The Invention of Copyright* (Cambridge, MA: Harvard University Press, 1993), 34–38.

2. GENTEEL WRATH

1. *Pope v. Curll*, 2 Atk 342, 26 ER 608 (1741).

2. Alexander Pope, "An Epistle to Dr. Arbuthnot," ll. 128–132; *The Twickenham Edition of the Poems of Alexander Pope*, ed. John Butt, vol. 1, ed. John Butt (London: Routledge, 1993), 105. The standard biography of Pope is Maynard Mack, *Alexander Pope: A Life* (New York: W. W. Norton in association with Yale University Press, 1985). Pope's active engagement in his various publishing ventures is discussed in David Foxon, *Pope and the Early Eighteenth-Century Book Trade*, rev. and ed. James McLaverty (Oxford: Oxford University Press, 1991). McLaverty provides an excellent appendix on "Pope and Copyright" in which he details, among other things, the various literary property cases in which Pope was involved. See also McLaverty's excellent *Pope, Print, and Meaning* (Oxford: Oxford University Press, 2001).

3. Curll's life and activities as a bookseller are the subject of Paul Baines and Pat Rogers, *Edmund Curll, Bookseller* (Oxford: Oxford University Press, 2007). See 63–90 for their excellent treatment of the origins of the quarrel. Baines and Rogers note that Curll had been giving offense to Pope's friends for years before the incident of the emetic in 1716. Still worth consulting in relation to Curll is Ralph Straus, *The Unspeakable Curll* (London: Chapman and Hall, 1927).

4. Robert Halsband, "Pope, Lady Mary, and the *Court Poems* (1716)," *PMLA* 68 (1953): 237–250, discusses the *Court Poems* and Pope's motives for attacking Curll.

5. Alexander Pope, *A Full and True Account of a Horrid and Barbarous Revenge by Poison on the Body of Mr. Edmund Curll, Bookseller* (n.d.), 6.

6. Unsigned pamphlet, dated 1716. Like a periodical or newssheet, the pamphlet comically states that it is "To be publish'd Weekly" and is to be sold "by all the Publishers, Mercuries, and Hawkers within the Bills of Mortality."

7. Unsigned pamphlet, reprinted in Alexander Pope, *Miscellanies, the Third Volume* (London: Mott and Gilliver, 1732).

8. Ibid., 47.

9. Ibid., 50.

10. Ibid.

11. Pope, *Dunciad Variorum*, Book II, ll. 171–172; *Twickenham Edition of Alexander Pope*, ed. Butt, vol. 5, ed. James Sutherland, 386.

12. Pope, *Dunciad Variorum*, Book III, l. 356; *Twickenham Edition of Alexander Pope*, ed. Butt, vol. 5, ed. Sutherland, 425.

13. Baines and Rogers, *Edmund Curll*, 86.

14. For a discussion of these publications see Baines and Rogers, *Edmund Curll*, 86–89.

15. Mack, *Alexander Pope*, 660. Mack discusses the Cromwell correspondence, 148–152. As noted, Curll had purchased the letters from Cromwell's former mistress, Elizabeth Thomas. Speaking of her as "Corinna," Pope mentions Thomas in *The Dunciad* and includes a note excusing her as "a decent woman and in misfortunes" in *The Dunciad Variorum*; see *Twickenham Edition of Alexander Pope*, ed. Butt, vol. 5, ed. Sutherland, 105–106.

16. The story is told by George Sherburn in the introduction to his *The Correspondence of Alexander Pope*, 5 vols. (Oxford: Oxford University Press, 1956), 1:xi–xiv. See also Mack, *Alexander Pope*, 652–657, and Baines and Rogers, *Edmund Curll*, 246–276, who provide the fullest version of the narrative I know.

17. James McLaverty, "The First Printing and Publication of Pope's letters," *Library*, 6th ser., 2 (1980), 264–280.

18. Alexander Pope, *A Narrative of the Method* (London, 1735), 1, 36.

19. Edmund Curll, "To the Reader," *Mr. Pope's Literary Correspondence* (London, 1735), 2:iv–v.

20. Ronald Paulson, *Hogarth's Graphic Works*, rev. ed., vol. 1 (New Haven, CT: Yale University Press, 1970), 175. Paulson first identified the dominant figure as Pope, but in "addenda and corrigenda" in the revised edition he suggests that the dominant figure is Curll. Paulson adds, "It is likely that most contemporaries who were aware of the unsavory tussle over the publication of Pope's letters considered that Curll emerged the victor" (1:323).

21. Mack, *Alexander Pope*, 664; Sherburn provides a comprehensive bibliographical analysis of the early editions; *Correspondence of Alexander Pope*, 1:xviii–xxv.

22. Reprinted in Sherburn, *Correspondence of Alexander Pope*, 1:xxxix–xl.

23. Curll, *Mr. Pope's Literary Correspondence*, 2:xvi.

24. Mack, *Alexander Pope*, 665–671.

25. Sherburn, *Correspondence of Alexander Pope*, 1:xxiv. Sherburn notes that the Dublin edition was actually published later than the London edition, but nobody involved in the legal issue seems to have realized this at the time.

26. See Sherburn, *Correspondence of Alexander Pope*, 4:343 (letter to R. Allen) May 14, 1741. In this letter Pope informs Allen that he will not be able to visit him in June because he expects a visit from Warburton and because "another Incident" may prevent him from traveling. Sherburn suggests that Pope foresees the probability of the suit against Curll (4:343n2).

27. Thus shortly after securing a preliminary injunction against Curll, Pope reported to Ralph Allen on the affair in a letter in which he explained that Curll's piracy "would have ruin'd half my Edition," adding that he had secured

an injunction to prohibit Curll from selling the letters "tho doubtless he'l do it clandestinely." Sherburn, *Correspondence of Alexander Pope*, 4:350 (letter to R. Allen), July 14, 1741(?).

28. The standard biography is still C. H. S. Fifoot, *Lord Mansfield* (Oxford: Oxford University Press, 1936). See also Edmund Heward, *Lord Mansfield* (Chicester: Sweet and Maxwell, 1979).

29. Pope's *Complaint*, Curll's *Answer*, and Lord Chancellor Hardwicke's *Decision* are reprinted in Mark Rose, *Authors and Owners: The Invention of Copyright* (Cambridge, MA: Harvard University Press, 1993), 145–153.

30. In fact Curll used Pope's own edition as copy-text. Pat Rogers observes that Pope probably did not realize this. It might have been an effective point to make against Curll. See Pat Rogers, "The Case of *Pope v. Curll*," *Library* 27 (1972): 326–331, here 329.

31. See Baines and Rogers, *Edmund Curll*, 157.

32. Hardwicke, *Decision*, reprinted in Rose, *Authors and Owners*, 152–153.

33. Keith Stewart provides an excellent discussion of critical wisdom with respect to familiar letters; see "Towards Defining an Aesthetic for the Familiar Letter in Eighteenth-Century England," *Prose Studies* 5 (1982): 179–192.

34. Hardwicke, *Decision*, reprinted in Rose, *Authors and Owners*, 152–153. Ronan Deazley notes that Lord Campbell, the author of *Lives of the Lord Chancellors*, working from manuscripts in his own possession reported Hardwicke's decision on the matter of ownership in more specific terms, saying that the "receiver only acquires a qualified interest" in the letter. "The paper on which it is written may belong to him, but the composition does not become vested in him as property, and he cannot publish against the consent of the writer"; Deazley, *On the Origin of the Right to Copy* (Oxford: Hart Publishing, 2004), 72. For an excellent discussion of *Pope v. Curll*, see also Simon Stern, "From Author's Right to Property Right," *University of Toronto Law Journal* 62 (2012): 29–91, esp. 59–69.

35. 8 Anne ch. 19.The full text of the statute can be found online at the very useful site, *Primary Sources on Copyright (1450–1900)*, ed. Lionel Bently and Martin Kretchmer (www.copyrighthistory.org). This site provides extensive primary material as well as commentary on materials from Italy, Germany, France, Britain, and the United States.

36. Benjamin Kaplan, *An Unhurried View of Copyright* (New York: Columbia University Press, 1967), 9.

37. Sherburn, *Correspondence of Alexander Pope*, 3:309; Pope's letter is quoted in a letter from Gay and the Duchess of Queensbury to Swift, August 28, 1732.

38. See Howard Robinson, *The British Post Office: A History* (Princeton, NJ: Princeton University Press, 1948), 64–76.

39. Sherburn, *Correspondence of Alexander Pope*, 2:23. Pope had used the same metaphor in an elaborated form several years earlier writing to Lady Mary Wortley Montagu; see *Correspondence of Alexander Pope*, 1:353. James Anderson Winn uses this phrase as the title of his excellent study, *A Window*

in the Bosom: The Letters of Alexander Pope (Hamden, CT: Archon Books, 1977).

40. Sherburn, *Correspondence of Alexander Pope*, 1:xxxviii.

41. McLaverty, *Pope, Print, and Meaning*, 12. McLaverty provides an extended discussion of the 1717 *Works*, 46–81.

42. William Kurtz Wimsatt, *The Portraits of Alexander Pope* (New Haven, CT: Yale University Press, 1965), xv.

43. Sherburn summarizes the changes Pope made in preparing his letters for publications, *Correspondence of Alexander Pope*, 1:xv.

44. Charles Dilke, *The Papers of a Critic*, 2 vols. (London: John Murray, 1875), 1:106.

45. Whitwell Elwin, "Introduction to Pope's Correspondence," in *The Works of Alexander Pope*, 10 vols. (London, 1871), 6:xxx, xxxii.

46. Lionel Trilling, *Sincerity and Authenticity* (Cambridge, MA: Harvard University Press, 1971), 54.

47. Charles Taylor, *Sources of the Self* (Cambridge, MA: Harvard University Press, 1989).

48. Dror Wahrman, *The Making of the Modern Self: Identity and Culture in Eighteenth-Century England* (New Haven, CT: Yale University Press, 2006), 198, 275.

49. Brook Thomas, *American Literary Realism and the Failed Promise of Contract* (Berkeley: University of California Press, 1997), 18. Thomas's chapter on "Henry James and the Construction of Privacy," pp. 53–87, is particularly relevant.

50. The observation is Thomas's, made to me "privately."

51. See Mack's discussion of Pope's reassignment of letters, *Alexander Pope*, 662–663. Mack remarks, for example, that Pope was anxious to use his letters to refute the charges that he had shown ingratitude toward Addison. He was anxious to establish "the truth about this episode" and to do so "even if establishing it meant inventing a partly fictional scenario" (662).

52. Winn, *A Window in the Bosom*, 200.

53. Sherburn, *Correspondence of Alexander Pope*, 1:105 (November 25, 1710). Wendy L. Jones identifies Seneca as the source of the phrase; see *Talking on Paper: Alexander Pope's Letters* (Victoria: University of Victoria English Literary Studies, 1990), 16.

54. Sören C. Hammerschmidt, "Pope, Curll, and the Intermediality of Eighteenth-Century Character," *Word and Image* 28 (2012): 273–286.

55. *Pope v. Ilive* (1742) and *Pope v. Lintot* (1742) both concerned the *Dunciad*. *Pope v. Bickham* (1743) involved the *Essay on Man*. These suits are described by McLaverty in his appendix on "Pope and Copyright," in David Foxon, *Pope and the Early Eighteenth-Century Book Trade*, rev. ed. (Oxford: Oxford University Press, 1991).

56. "Pope's Preface," in Sherburn, *Correspondence of Alexander Pope*, 1:xl.

57. Mansfield's speech in *Millar v. Taylor* is reported by James Burrow, *The Question Concerning Literary Property* (London, 1773), 115.

58. Samuel D. Warren and Louis D. Brandeis, "The Right to Privacy," *Harvard Law Review* 4 (1890): 193–220. Warren and Brandeis take a passage from *Millar v. Taylor* as their epigraph and also cite Justice Joseph Yates: "It is certain that every man has a right to keep his own sentiments, if he pleases. He has certainly a right to judge whether he will make them public, or commit them only to the sight of his friends" (198n2).

59. Francis Hargrave, *An Argument in Defence of Literary Property*, 2nd ed. (London, 1774), 6–7.

3. EMANCIPATION AND TRANSLATION

1. *Stowe v. Thomas*, 23 F Cas. 201 (C.C.E.D. Pa. 1853). The case was originally reported by John William Wallace, the reporter for the Third Circuit (12 Wall. Jr. 547). In the discussion that follows I am greatly indebted to Melissa J. Homestead's groundbreaking study of *Stowe v. Thomas* published in her excellent *American Women Authors and Literary Property, 1822–1869* (Cambridge: Cambridge University Press, 2005), 105–149. An earlier version of Homestead's study was published as " 'When I Can Read My Title Clear': Harriet Beecher Stowe and the *Stowe v. Thomas* Copyright Infringement Case," *Prospects: An Annual of American Cultural Studies* 27 (2002): 201–245. Documents related to *Stowe v. Thomas*, including Stowe's *Affidavit* and *Complaint* and Thomas's *Answer*, can be found online at *Primary Sources on Copyright (1450–1900)*, ed. Lionel Bently and Martin Kretchmer (www.copyrighthistory.org). The *Primary Sources* commentary on *Stowe* by Oren Bracha, the national editor for U.S. materials, is excellent, and I am much indebted to it for the way it situates the case in relation to the development of U.S. copyright law; see "Commentary on *Stowe v. Thomas* (1853)." Joan D. Hedrick's superb biography, *Harriet Beecher Stowe: A Life* (New York: Oxford University Press, 1994) is an invaluable source of information.

2. On the classical republican values of early antebellum attitudes toward copyright see Meredith L. McGill's important *American Literature and the Culture of Reprinting, 1834–1853* (Philadelphia: University of Pennsylvania Press, 2003). The American resistance to international copyright has been much discussed; see James J. Barnes, *Authors, Publishers, Politicians: The Quest for an Anglo-American Copyright Agreement 1815–1854* (Columbus: Ohio State University Press, 1974) and Catherine Seville, *The Internationalisation of Copyright Law: Books, Buccaneers and the Black Flag in the Nineteenth Century* (Cambridge: Cambridge University Press, 2006), esp. 146–252.

3. On the transformation of the U.S. to an expanding capitalist society, see Charles Sellers, *The Market Revolution: Jacksonian America, 1815–1846* (New York: Oxford University Press, 1991).

4. On advertising and promotion, see Claire Parfait, *The Publishing History of Uncle Tom's Cabin, 1852–2002* (Aldershot: Ashgate, 2007), 47–66. Parfait also discusses Phillips, Sampson's decision not to publish the novel, 33–34. On the general subject, see also Michael Winship, "The Greatest

Book of Its Kind," *Proceedings of the American Antiquarian Society* 109, no. 2 (1999): 309–332.

5. "Uncle Tom's Cabin," *National Era*, April 15, 1852, 62.

6. *Norton's Literary Gazette*, June 15, 1852, 120; reproduced in Parfait, *Publishing History*, 55.

7. In around one year Jewett printed a total of about 310,000 copies in several editions: about 125,000 copies of the initial two-volume edition, about 180,000 copies of a cheaper one-volume edition, and about 5,000 copies of an expensive illustrated edition. Sales of the book appear to have dropped sharply by the middle of 1853, probably because by this point the market was saturated. See Parfait, *Publishing History*, 67–89, and Winship, "'Greatest Book of Its Kind.'"

8. The *Liberator*, December 23, 1853, quoted by Stephen A. Hirsch, "Uncle To-mitudes: The Popular Reaction to *Uncle Tom's Cabin*," *Studies in the American Renaissance* (1978): 303–330, here 316. Hirsch provides an extensive discussion of spinoffs and commercial exploitations of Stowe's novel as does David S. Reynolds, *Mightier Than the Sword:* Uncle Tom's Cabin *and the Battle for America* (New York: Norton, 2011), 132–136. On Jewett's commissioning and selling of Whittier's Little Eva song, see Parfait, *Publishing History*, 63–64.

9. On British editions, see Parfait, *Publishing History*, 106–108. The estimate of a million and a half copies in Britain and the colonies comes from a statement made by the London publisher Sampson Low quoted by Stowe's son, Charles Edward Stowe, in his *Harriet Beecher Stowe* (Boston: Houghton, Mifflin and Co., 1889), 190. Hedrick, *Harriet Beecher Stowe*, 233, gives a similar figure but speaks of Britain alone.

10. "A Mistake in Literary History," *National Era*, June 21, 1855, 96.

11. Upon meeting Stowe at the White House in 1862, Lincoln supposedly asked, "Is this the little woman who made this great war?" For this widely reported but undocumented remark, see, for example, Reynolds, *Mightier Than the Sword*, x. Reynolds argues persuasively that Stowe's novel did indeed contribute to bringing on the Civil War.

12. Parfait, *Publishing History*, 92.

13. "Uncle Tomitudes," *Putnam's Monthly Magazine* (1853), vol. I, 97–98; see Parfait *Publishing History*, 67, who identifies the author as Briggs.

14. On the extraordinary literacy rate in the United States, see David Dowling, *Capital Letters: Authorship in the Antebellum Literary Market* (Iowa City: University of Iowa Press, 2009), 11.

15. "News by the Mails," *New York Times*, July 12, 1852, 2, reporting a story in the *Boston Traveller*. This notice of Stowe's enormous royalty payment probably originated with Jewett who chose to publicize it as part of his campaign to promote interest in the novel. On Stowe's payment for serial publication, see Winship, "'The Greatest Book of Its Kind,'" 313.

16. Calculated by Hedrick, *Harriet Beecher Stowe*, 246. On the various payments to Stowe, see Parfait, *Publishing History*, 104–108, and Hedrick, *Harriet Beecher Stowe*, 445n64.

17. For the statement about less than 1 percent of Americans earning more than $5,000 annually in the mid-nineteenth century, see Reynolds, *Mightier Than the Sword*, 298.

18. Harriet Beecher Stowe, *Uncle Tom's Cabin* (New York: Modern Library, 2001), 136.

19. Ibid., 256–257.

20. Elizabeth Ammons argues that Stowe represents motherhood as the "ethical and structural model for all American life." "Stowe's Dream of the Mother-Savior: *Uncle Tom's Cabin* and American Women Writers before the 1920s," in *New Essays on Uncle Tom's Cabin*, ed. Eric J. Sundquist (New York: Cambridge University Press, 1986), 155–195,159. I have also been influenced by Gillian Brown's discussion of Stowe in her important *Domestic Individualism: Imagining Self in Nineteenth-Century America* (Berkeley: University of California Press, 1990), 13–60. Brown argues that for Stowe, right feeling is a nurturing attitude toward one's possessions and responsibilities. Thus Stowe domesticates ownership, making it a nexus of affective relations. She replaces the master–slave relationship with the loving relationship figured in mother and child. Maternal supervision thus becomes the ideal form of possession and home becomes a prefiguration of heaven. See also Martin T. Buinicki's excellent discussion of Stowe and "sentimental possession" in *Negotiating Copyright: Authorship and the Discourse of Literary Property Rights in Nineteenth-Century America* (New York: Routledge, 2006), 63–106.

21. James Cephas Derby, *Fifty Years among Authors, Books, and Publishers* (New York: G. W. Carleton & Company, 1884), 521; quoted by Homestead, *American Women Authors*, 117n30.

22. The letter, dated December 4, 1852, was read at an abolitionist meeting in Glasgow and subsequently published in the *New York Times*, February 17, 1853.

23. *Uncle Tom's Cabin* (Boston: Houghton, Mifflin and Co., 1889), xii–xiv.

24. Annie Fields, *Life and Letters of Harriet Beecher Stowe* (Boston: Houghton, Mifflin and Co., 1898), 377.

25. Miguel Cervantes, *Don Quixote*, trans. Walter Starkie (New York: Signet, 1964), 41. On the trope of writing as a child, see Mark Rose, "Copyright and Its Metaphors," *UCLA Law Review* 50 (2002): 1–15, here 3–6.

26. *Review*, February 2, 1710; quoted in Mark Rose, *Authors and Owners: The Invention of Copyright* (Cambridge, MA: Harvard University Press, 1993), 39.

27. On Stowe's early career as an author, see Hedrick, *Harriet Beecher Stowe*, 133–142.

28. See Homestead, *American Women Authors*, 118. E. Bruce Kirkham suggests that publication of the serial may have been deferred while Stowe was registering her copyright; see *The Building of Uncle Tom's Cabin* (Knoxville: University of Tennessee Press, 1977), 70.

29. On the contract for *Uncle Tom's Cabin*, see Hedrick, *Harriet Beecher Stowe*, 223–225, and Parfait, *Publishing History*, 35–46.

30. The letter to Bailey is widely reprinted. I cite from Susan Belasco, ed., *Stowe in Her Own Time* (Iowa City: University of Iowa Press, 2009), 53.

31. The letter to Follen is also widely reprinted. See ibid., 62–69.

32. See, for example, Daniel Defoe, *Moll Flanders* (Oxford: Oxford University Press, 2011), "my stock was but low" (65); "I ordered a part of my stock to be left behind me" (258); "I gave him an account of my stock" (259).

33. William J. Grayson, *The Hireling and the Slave* (Charleston, SC: John Russell, 1854), 44.

34. "Black Letters; or Uncle Tom-Foolery in Literature," *Graham's Magazine* 42 (February 1853), 209. In a second essay a month later, Graham repeated his objections, noting that Stowe had been reported as having received $20,000 from her publishers. "Are the wounds inflicted upon our common country paid for," he asked, "with so small a sum in gold?" "Editor's Table," *Graham's Magazine* 42 (March 1853), 365. The attacks on Stowe by Graham and others are discussed by Buinicki, *Negotiating Copyright*, 71–76.

35. Otto Reventlow, writing in *Atlantis*, a monthly German-language magazine published in Detroit; quoted and translated by Homestead, *American Women Authors*, 128.

36. August Becker, also writing in *Atlantis*; quoted and translated in ibid., 129.

37. See Robert E. Cazden, *A Social History of the German Book Trade in America to the Civil War* (Columbia, SC: Camden House, 1984), 370n24, citing a contemporary article reporting that Stowe rejected the offer of the Strodtmann translation. Cazden provides the standard account of the German-language book trade in the antebellum period.

38. "'Uncle Tom' at Law," *New York Weekly Tribune*, April 16, 1853, 10.

39. In the 1740 case of *Gyles v. Wilcox* (2 Atk 141, 3 Atk 269), Lord Chancellor Hardwicke ruled that a genuine abridgment was a new work and not an infringement.

40. *Burnet v. Chetwood* (2 Mer 441, 35).

41. George Ticknor Curtis, *A Treatise on the Law of Copyright* (Boston: Charles C. Little and James Brown, 1847), 290–293.

42. William Blackstone, *Commentaries on the Laws of England*, 4 vols. (Oxford: Clarendon Press, 1766), 2:406.

43. See Oren Bracha's important article, "The Ideology of Authorship Revisited: Authors, Markets, and Liberal Values in Early American Copyright," *Yale Law Journal* 118 (2008): 186–271. Bracha's work has greatly influenced my understanding of the history of nineteenth-century American copyright.

44. *Folsom v. Marsh*, 9 F. Cas. 342 (C.C.D. Mass. 1841), 348.

45. Curtis, *Treatise*, 293.

46. "S. H. and S. C. Perkins, for Mrs. Stowe," 23 Fed. Cas. 201–205.

47. "Mr. Goepp and B. H. Brewster, contra," 23 Fed. Cas. 205–206. The treatise cited by the defendant was Richard Godson, *A Practical Treatise on the Law of Patents for Inventions and of Copyright* (London: Joseph Butterworth and Son, 1823). Godson does not discuss translations at length but notes that in one recent case the Lord Chancellor had ruled that translations, if original, could not be distinguished from other works (241–242).

48. "On Monopolies," Godson, *Practical Treatise*, 1–41.

49. "Theory of the Rights of Authors," Curtis, *Treatise*, 1–25.

50. For biographical accounts of Justice Grier, see Carl B. Swisher, *History of the Supreme Court of the United States: The Taney Period, 1836–64* (New York: Macmillan, 1974), 229–233, and Frank Otto Gatell, "Robert C. Grier," in *The Justices of the United States Supreme Court*, ed. Leon Friedman and Fred L. Israel, 5 vols. (New York: Chelsea House, 1980) 2:873–892.

51. Swisher, *Taney Period*, 232. Grier justified these assurances in 1857 when, a Northerner in a majority Southern court, he supported the majority position in the Dred Scott case.

52. Homestead, *American Women Authors*, 133.

53. *Oliver v. Kauffman*, 18 F. Cas. 657, 661; U.S. App. LEXIS 226, **17 (C.C.E.D.Pa. 1850). Despite Justice Grier's charge, the jury in *Oliver* finally failed to agree.

54. Without the one Northern vote that Grier provided, the five Southern justices, led by Chief Justice Taney, would probably have decided the case on more narrow grounds. See Don E. Fehrenbacher, *The Dred Scott Case: Its Significance in American Law and Politics* (New York: Oxford University Press, 1978), 305–334. I am indebted to Robert A. Burt for this reference.

55. Stowe v. Thomas, 23 Fed. Cas. 206–207.

56. Ibid. 208.

57. George R. Graham, "Black Letters," *Graham's Magazine* (February 1853), 209.

58. See Martial Epigram no. 52 (To Quinctianus); *Epigrams*, trans. Walter C. A. Ker (London: Heinemann, 1919) 1:63. I am indebted to Mario Biagioli for this reference.

59. William St. Clair notes that the late seventeenth century was the period in which the English slave trading companies were formed and that "arguments about the book industry of the time are full of slavery metaphors, knowledge being padlocked, authors slaves of the quill, enslaved to publishers, manumitted from one master only to be handed over to tyrannical corporations, and so on." See "Metaphors of Intellectual Property," in *Privilege and Property: Essays on the History of Copyright*, ed. Ronan Deazley, Martin Kretschmer, and Lionel Bently, 369–395 (Cambridge: Open Book Publishers, 2010), 389.

60. Lord Camden's speech in the House of Lords was reported in *Cobbett's Parliamentary History* and elsewhere; see Mark Rose, "Nine-Tenths of the Law: The English Copyright Debates and the Rhetoric of the Public Doman," in "The Public Domain," ed. James Boyle, *Law and Contemporary Problems* 66 (2003) 75–87, here 82.

61. See Michael Everton, *The Grand Chorus of Complaint: Authors and the Business Ethics of American Publishing* (New York: Oxford University Press, 2011), 104–105.

62. See Hedrick, *Stowe*, 234.

63. Homestead makes this point and also notes that the key sentences relating to Uncle Tom and Topsy were not included in the original report of the case, perhaps because Grier's venom was too obvious; see *American Women Authors*, 132n70.

64. I make this point in Rose, "Copyright and Its Metaphors," 13–14, where I also note that the terms of the copyright act were modeled on those of the Jacobean Statute of Monopolies (21 Jac. I, c. 3).

65. Stephen M. Best develops the analogy between slavery jurisprudence and intellectual property law in his suggestive but also slippery discussion in *The Fugitive's Properties: Law and the Poetics of Possession* (Chicago: University of Chicago Press, 2004). See also McGill's comments on Grier's use of the "figure of the freely circulating slave body" in the context of the polarization of the 1850s and the approach of the Civil War; McGill, *American Literature and the Culture of Reprinting*, 74.

66. Bracha, "Commentary on *Stowe v. Thomas*."

67. Copyright Act, 16 Stat. 198 (1870).

68. Eaton S. Drone, *A Treatise of the Law of Property in Intellectual Productions in Great Britain and the United States* (Boston: Little, Brown and Co., 1879), 455n4.

69. Ibid., 451.

70. Ibid.

71. *Folsom v. Marsh*, 9 F. Cas. 344.

72. Bracha, "Ideology of Authorship," 238.

73. Harriet Beecher Stowe, *A Key to Uncle Tom's Cabin* (Boston: John P. Jewett & Co, 1853), 4.

4. CREATING OSCAR WILDE

1. *Burrow-Giles v. Sarony*, 111 U.S. 53 (1884). For an important treatment of *Burrow-Giles*, see Jane M. Gaines, "Photography 'Surprises' the Law," in *Contested Culture: The Image, the Voice, and the Law* (Chapel Hill: University of North Carolina Press, 1991), 42–83. Gaines's discussion of the case is influenced by Bernard Edelman's stimulating discussion of photography in French law in *Le Droit saisi par la photographie* (1973), translated by Elizabeth Kingdom as *Ownership of the Image: Elements for a Marxist Theory of Law* (London: Routledge and Kegan Paul, 1979).

2. "Some Broadway Types," *New York Herald*, September 29, 1895. An article published shortly after Sarony's death remarks that the colorful photographer "became such a well-known figure uptown that many people got to know him by sight, and 'There's Sarony' followed his progress from many lips," *New Haven Register*, November 13, 1896. The anecdote about Sarony crouching as he entered a room is told by William Henry Shelton, "Artist Life in New York in the Days of Oliver Horn," *Critic* 43 (1903): 31–41. Shelton notes that the character of Julius Bianchi in F. Hopkinson Smith's novel, *The Fortunes of Oliver Horn* (New York: Charles Scribner's Sons, 1902) is modeled on Sarony. The only monograph on Sarony to date is Ben L. Bassham, *The Theatrical Photographs of Napoleon Sarony* (Kent, OH: Kent State University Press, 1978). Bassham provides an account of Sarony's career and practice and reproduces with comments many of his photographs. Most of my information about Sarony and his studio can be found in Bassham. For a helpful Web site devoted to establishing a Sarony chronology, see http://www.classyarts.com/sarony/Sarony_Chronology.htm.

3. See Gilson Willets, "Photography's Most Famous Chair," *American Annual of Photography* (1899), 56. Various sources report that Sarony in his time photographed either thirty thousand or forty thousand celebrities. The substantial *New York Times* obituary published on November 10, 1896, 9,

gives the figures as "30,000 actors and actresses, and 200,000 of the general public."

4. On Reynolds, see Martin Postle, ed., *Joshua Reynolds: The Creation of Celebrity* (London: Tate Publishing, 2005), esp. Postle's excellent essay, " 'The Modern Apelles': Joshua Reynolds and the Creation of Celebrity," 17–47. Barbara McCandless compares the strategies, careers, and reputations of Brady and Sarony, noting that by 1896, the year in which both died, Sarony was famous and Brady forgotten; see McCandless, "The Portrait Studio and the Celebrity," in *Photography in Nineteenth-Century America*, ed. Martha A. Sandweiss (New York: Harry N. Abrams, 1991), 49–73. Naomi Rosenblum provides a brief profile of Brady in her useful *World History of Photography* (New York: Abbeville Press, 1984), 190–191. During the Civil War, Brady shifted his efforts from portraiture to the battlefield images that, along with his pictures of Lincoln, are the source of his reputation today. In the postwar period, however, the public lost interest in images of war, and in the 1870s Brady lapsed into physical decline and ultimately bankruptcy. On Brady's portraits of illustrious Americans, see Alan Trachtenberg, *Reading American Photographs* (New York: Hill and Wang, 1989), esp. 45–52.

5. Shelton, "Artist Life in New York," 34. Bassham, *Theatrical Photographs*, gives the figure of $8,000 rent and describes Sarony's studio. Bassham also reprints an image of Sarony's reception room made in 1882, the year that Sarony photographed Wilde. Rosenblum, *World History of Photography*, 83, prints a photograph of Nadal's Paris studio showing his signature prominently affixed to the facade. This seems to have been the model for Sarony's New York studio. It is interesting to note that the crocodile hanging from the ceiling in Sarony's reception room is a feature that can also be found in Ferrante Imperato's famous *Dell'Historia Naturale* (Naples, 1599), the first pictorial representation of a Renaissance cabinet of natural curiosities. A partial inventory of items was printed in newspaper reports at the time of the sale of Sarony's collection in 1896; see esp. "Curios at Auction," *New-York Tribune*, April 2, 1896, 12.

6. "Sarony Is Very Ill," *Kansas City Times*, February 3, 1895, 12. Late nineteenth-century Parisians such as the academic painter Jean-Léon Gérôme displayed similar collections in their studios.

7. For Sarony's self-representation, see the profile in "High Lights in Photography, No. 4: Napoleon Sarony," *Photo-American*, V (September 1894), 323.

8. This anecdote is reported in various places including the *New York Times* obituary of Sarony published November 10, 1896.

9. Gilson Willets, "The Art of Not Posing: An Interview with Napoleon Sarony," *The American Annual of Photography and Photographic Times Almanac for 1896*, ed. Walter E. Woodbury, 188–194 (New York: Scoville and Adams Company, n.d.), 192, 190. Daniel A. Novak develops the point about the subject's submission to the photographer in his suggestive essay, "Sexuality in the Age of Technological Reproducibility: Oscar Wilde, Photography, and Identity," in *Oscar Wilde and Modern Culture: The Making of a Legend*, ed. Joseph Bristow (Athens: Ohio University Press, 2008), 63–95.

10. "High Lights in Photography," 323.

11. "Some Interviews with Mr. Sarony," *Wilson's Photographic Magazine* 30 (1893), 11.

12. An unpaginated bound collection of *Sarony's Living Pictures* (New York: A. E. Chasmar, ca. 1895) is on file in the Thomas J. Watson Library, Metropolitan Museum of Art (NH32.S27 A5L 1895). C. M. Fairbanks, the commentator, is unidentified but he appears to have been a writer on contemporary artistic subjects who also published on Frederic Remington. For Sarony's membership in multiple New York artists' clubs see Linda Henfield Skalet, "Bohemians and Businessmen: American Artists' Organizations of the Late Nineteenth Century," in Ronald G. Pisano, *The Tile Club and the Aesthetic Movement in America* (New York: Harry N. Abrams, 1999), 84–95, esp. 93.

13. Although the comment is often reported it has not been authenticated. For information about Wilde's 1892 American tour, see Richard Ellmann, *Oscar Wilde* (New York: Knopf, 1988), esp. 150–211. Wilde's tour is also treated by Lloyd Lewis and Henry Justin Smith, *Oscar Wilde Discovers America* (New York: Harcourt, Brace, 1936).

14. Ellmann, *Oscar Wilde*, 134–135, reports that Wilde, having been informed that the show alluded to him, wrote to George Grossmith, the actor playing Bunthorne, asking to reserve a box.

15. See "Bohemian Experiences of Oscar Wilde and Sir Samuel Baker," *San Francisco Chronicle*, October 2, 1897; on file at the W. A. Clark Library, Wildeiana, Box 10.

16. Oscar Wilde, "The English Renaissance of Art" in *Miscellanies*, 248–277, (London: Methuen, 1908), 257.

17. Ibid., 251.

18. Ibid., 258.

19. Ibid., 257.

20. Lewis and Smith, *Oscar Wilde Discovers America*, 39. The photographs are reproduced by Oscar Wilde's grandson, Merlin Holland, in *The Wilde Album* (New York: Henry Holt, 1997), 5–91.

21. The Straiton and Storm cigar advertisement is reproduced by Michael North, "The Picture of Oscar Wilde," *PMLA* 125 (2010): 185–191, here 186.

22. Given Sarony's claims as an artist, it is perhaps worth noting that Sackett was something of a poet as well as a lawyer; see Charles H. Weygant, *The Sacketts of America* (Newburgh, NY, 1907), 377.

23. The affidavits, along with other documents from *Burrow-Giles v. Sarony*, are on file with the National Archives and Records Administration.

24. See Rosenblum, *World History of Photography*, 208–243, who provides a useful overview of the early debates about the status of photography, quoting Baudelaire and Delacroix (210).

25. See R. N. Watson, "Art Photography and John Ruskin," *British Journal of Photography* 91 (1944), pt. 1: 82–83; pt. 2: 100–101; and pt. 3: 118–119.

26. See Rosenblum, *World History of Photography*, 210.

27. "Brief and Points for Plaintiff in Error," Supreme Court of the U.S., *Burrow-Giles v. Sarony*, 17. Burrow-Giles's answer to Sarony's complaint at the Circuit Court level did not develop the position but merely asserted that photographs were not protectable and that the statute under which Sarony

sued was unconstitutional and void; see the *Transcript of Record* filed on October 9, 1883, with the appeal to the Supreme Court, 9.

28. See, for example, Francis Hargrave, *An Argument in Defence of Literary Property* (London, 1774), 6–7.

29. Wilde, "The English Renaissance," 275.

30. *Transcript of Record*, 4. This crucial language was incorporated into Judge Coxe's findings of fact at the Circuit Court level and later cited verbatim in the Supreme Court decision.

31. "Brief and Points for Defendant in Error," Supreme Court of the U.S., *Burrow-Giles v. Sarony*, 6.

32. Ibid., 15.

33. See Leon Battista Alberti, *On Painting*, trans. John R. Spencer (New Haven, CT: Yale University Press, 1966), 66.

34. See D. J. Gordon, "Poet and Architect: The Intellectual Setting of the Quarrel between Ben Jonson and Inigo Jones," in *The Renaissance Imagination: Essays and Lectures by D. J. Gordon*, ed. Stephen Orgel, 77–101 (Berkeley: University of California Press, 1975), esp. 89–91. On *disegno*, see Robert Williams, "Vasari's Concept of *Disegno*," in *Art, Theory, and Culture in Sixteenth-Century Italy* (Cambridge: Cambridge University Press, 1997), 29–72.

35. See *The case of designers, engravers, etchers, etc.* (London: ca. 1735), sig. B1, cited in my discussion of the Engraver's Act of 1735. See Mark Rose, "Technology and Copyright in 1735," *Information Society* 21 (2005): 63–66.

36. Ann Bermingham, *Learning to Draw: Studies in the Cultural History of a Polite and Useful Art* (New Haven, CT: Yale University Press, 2000), 4–5.

37. "An Address to the National Photographic Association of the United States (1870)," *Philadelphia Photographer* VIII (October 1871), 321, cited by Alan Trachtenberg who makes this point about the photographic profession's strategy in *Reading American Photographs*, 27.

38. Thus when asked by an interviewer how he would handle an unwanted highlight on a sitter's cheek, Sarony responded, "I should use my charcoal on his cheek, and vamoose the high light." "Some Interviews with Mr. Sarony," 10. Sarony's "Living Pictures" series conspicuously combined photography with freehand charcoal work.

39. Christine Haight Farley makes the point about the difficulty of mediating between the validation of photography as art and documentary record in "The Lingering Effects of Copyright's Response to the Invention of Photography," *University of Pittsburgh Law Review* 65 (2004): 385–456.

40. 17 F. 591. Judge Coxe's findings of fact were reported in the Transcript of Record filed October 9, 1883, with the appeal to the U.S. Supreme Court.

41. 111 U.S. 53 (1884).

42. *J. E. Story v. J. H. Walker*, 79 Tenn. 515.

43. *City of New Orleans v. Louis Robira*, 42 La. Ann. 1098.

44. The New York context of Sarony's group portrait of the nine justices is identified by Mitch Tuchman, "Supremely Wilde," *Smithsonian Magazine* (May 2004).

45. *Burrow-Giles* was also important in the Supreme Court's 1991 decision in *Feist v. Rural Telephone*, which limited the reach of authorship by rejecting

the claim that the white pages of a telephone directory might be protected by copyright; see *Feist Publications, Inc. v. Rural Telephone Service, Co., Inc.*, 499 U.S. 340 (1991).

46. Wilde, "The English Renaissance," 256, 257.

47. *Bleistein v. Donaldson Lithographing Co.*, 188 U.S. 239 (1903).

48. See Farley, "Lingering Effects," 412–413.

49. See Postle, " 'The Modern Appelles,' " 17.

50. Bassham, *Theatrical Photographs of Napoleon Sarony*, 4.

51. Why some portions of the original complaint are printed and other portions entered by hand remains unclear. I note that Sarony's name as complainant is printed, but both his solicitor's name and the name of the court are entered by hand. As for the assertion that Sarony paid Wilde, I note that Sarony's revised complaint of May phrased the matter more vaguely, speaking about "good and valuable consideration paid and to be paid" to Wilde. Sarony's brief to the Supreme Court also referred to payment. Were these merely pro forma statements intended to establish Sarony's exclusive right?

52. Lewis and Smith, *Wilde Discovers America*, 39. I have not been able to confirm the Lewis and Smith assertion, but I note that it is accepted by Wilde's grandson Merlin Holland, though not perhaps on the basis of independent evidence. See Holland, *Wilde Album*, 64.

53. Ellmann, *Oscar Wilde*, 192.

54. Lewis and Smith, *Wilde Discovers America*, 53.

55. "The Aesthetic Apostle," *Boston Globe*, January 29, 1882, 5; reprinted in Matthew Hofer and Gary Scharnhorst, eds., *Oscar Wilde in America: The Interviews* (Urbana: University of Illinois Press, 2010), 49.

56. See Regenia Gagnier, *Idylls of the Marketplace: Oscar Wilde and the Victorian Public* (Stanford, CA: Stanford University Press, 1986), 51–99, for a suggestive discussion of the dandy in the late Victorian marketplace.

57. "The Creator of Oscar Wilde," *New York Tribune*, December 14, 1883, 1.

58. Ellmann, *Oscar Wilde*, 167–170. See also David M. Friedman, who speculates that the Whitman photograph was one taken at the Philadelphia studio of W. Curtis Taylor in 1877, in *Wilde in America: Oscar Wilde and the Invention of Modern Celebrity* (New York: Norton, 2014), 113–114.

59. See Daniel A. Novak, "Sexuality in the Age of Technological Reproducibility: Oscar Wilde, Photography, and Identity," in *Oscar Wilde and Modern Culture*, ed. Joseph Bristow, 63–95 (Athens: Ohio University Press, 2008), 92n31. In Wilde's tale, the photographer's name appears as "Saroni."

60. Warren and Brandeis's famous "Right to Privacy" essay arguing against the unauthorized circulation of portraits of private persons would not appear until 1890, but in any case Wilde had sanctioned Sarony's photographs. See Samuel D. Warren and Louis D. Brandeis, "The Right to Privacy," *Harvard Law Review* 4 (1890): 193–220.

61. For a sophisticated discussion of "authenticity" in commerce and art, see Laura A. Heymann, "Dialogues of Authenticity," *Studies in Law, Politics, and Society* 67 (2015): 25–57.

62. Susan Sontag, *On Photography* (New York: Farrar, Straus and Giroux, 1977), 154.

5. HOLLYWOOD STORY

1. *Nichols v. Universal Pictures Corporation et al.*, 34 F.2d 145 (1929); 45 F.2d 119 (2d Cir. 1930).
2. Alexander Lindey, *Plagiarism and Originality* (New York: Harper, 1952), 152.
3. *Gyles v. Wilcox*, 2 Atk 141, 3 Atk 269 (1740).
4. Moses L. Malevinsky, *The Science of Playwriting* (New York: Brentano's, 1925).
5. Anne Nichols, *Abie's Irish Rose: A Comedy in Three Acts* (New York: Samuel French, n.d.), 10. On "Cohen on the Phone," see Ted Merwin, "The Performance of Jewish Ethnicity in Anne Nichols' *Abie's Irish Rose*," *Journal of American Ethnic History* 20 (2001): 3–37, here 5. A version of the vaudeville monologue recorded by Joe Hayman in 1913 can be heard at www.youtube.com/watch?v=yvOONWjx5RU.
6. Nichols, *Abie's Irish Rose*, 56.
7. Edwin Schallert, "Abie's Irish Rose," *Los Angeles Times*, March 6, 1922, III:4.
8. For Hammond's quip and other early New York reviews, see "What the Critics Said About 'Abie," *Variety*, May 20, 1925, 7, and Lee Israel, "The Hit They Loved to Hate," *Theater Week*, August 5, 1991, 25–27.
9. *"Abie's Irish Rose* Number," *Variety* 79 (May 20, 1925).
10. "'Abie's Irish Rose' Ends Run Tonight," *New York Times*, October 22, 1927, 14.
11. "Nichols—and Dollars," *Wall Street Journal*, February 9, 1927, 3; "'Irish Rose' Film Sets Sales Record," *New York Times*, February 27, 1927, 30.
12. On Jews as the lowest group in the hierarchy of "whiteness" that formed after 1870 and on the restrictions placed on immigration in the postwar period, see generally Paul Spickard, *Almost All Aliens: Immigration, Race, and Colonialism in American History and Identity* (New York: Routledge, 2007).
13. Nichols, *Abie's Irish Rose*, 78–79. On applause that broke out after the priest and rabbi's exchange, see the unsigned review, "Anne Nichols's Little Human Comedy Heartily Received at Fulton," *New York Times*, May 24, 1922, 27.
14. See Nichols's uncompleted autobiography, *Anne Nichols Papers, 1873–1965*, New York Public Library for the Performing Arts: Billy Rose Theatre Collection (T-Mss 2001–012), Box 1, Folder 33. There are multiple drafts and fragments of this manuscript, some of which also appear in a box of uncataloged material in the *Nichols Papers*.
15. "The Whys of Anne Nichols," *Variety*, May 20, 1925, 7.
16. *Nichols Papers*, Box 1, Folder 33.
17. Ibid.
18. Ibid., uncataloged material.
19. See "Injunction on 'Abie's Irish Rose' Refused," *Variety*, May 26, 1922, 11; "Morosco Sues for $57,000," *New York Times*, June 20, 1922, 34; and "Settled, Says Morosco," *New York Times*, May 21, 1923, 6.
20. "Sues to Recover Scenery of Play," *Washington Post*, September 17, 1923, 9.
21. "Court Fight Today in Lively Mixup over 'Abie's Irish Rose,'" *Chicago Daily Tribune*, November 21, 1923, 21.

22. Aaron Hoffman, *Two Blocks Away: A Play in Three Acts* (New York: Samuel French, 1925).

23. For biographical information about Malevinsky see the substantial profile by Lorene Morrow, "Making the Grade in Gotham," *Dallas Morning News*, December 22, 1929, and the brief obituary in the *New York Times*, October 18, 1932.

24. Eaton S. Drone, *A Treatise on the Law of Property in Intellectual Productions* (Boston: Little, Brown and Company, 1879), 408.

25. Malevinsky, *Science of Playwriting*, 41. Malevinsky here is apparently referring to Matthews's testimony as an expert for the defense in *Simonton v. Gordon*, 12 F2d 116 (1925), a case in which Malevinsky represented the plaintiff. The case records for *Simonton v. Gordon*, including Matthews's testimony, are on file with the National Archives and Records Administration.

26. "Play Plagiarists," *New Yorker*, July 11, 1925, 3–4.

27. Malevinsky, *Science of Playwriting*, 42.

28. *Simonton v. Gordon*, 12 F2d 116 (1925). In this case Malevinsky invoked his special concepts—"basic emotion," "basic character," "personification," and "crucible"—both in his general argument and in cross-examining witnesses.

29. Malevinsky recounted having consulted Hughes in a letter to Mark Hellinger whose syndicated column appeared in the *New York Daily Mirror* and other papers; see Hellinger, "All in a Day," *San Mateo Times* and *Daily News Leader*, November 30, 1931, 16. The story of Malevinsky's consultation with Hughes was also briefly told in a report published at the time of Malevinsky's death; see "Law and Letters," *New Yorker*, October 29, 1932, 10–11.

30. Substantial reports of the day-by-day progress of the trial ran in the *New York Times* on December 22, 25, 27, 28, 29, and 31, 1928; January 3, 4, 5, 6, 9, 11, and 12, 1929.

31. Testimony of Anne Nichols, Cross Examination, *Record on Appeal* (*Nichols v. Universal*), 100–101. The Record on Appeal, along with other documents in *Nichols v. Universal*, is on file with the National Archives and Records Administration.

32. Ibid., 157.

33. Ibid., 103.

34. Testimony of Moses L. Malevinsky, *Record on Appeal* (*Nichols v. Universal*), 887.

35. Testimony of Harrison R. Steeves, *Record on Appeal* (*Nichols v. Universal*), 1339–1461.

36. Ibid., 1511–1512.

37. 34 F.2d 145 (1929), 147.

38. *Fisher v. Dillingham*, 298 F. 145 (S.D.N.Y.1924).

39. *Dymow v. Bolton*, 11 F. (2d) 690, 692.

40. For biographical information, see Gerald Gunther, *Learned Hand: The Man and the Judge* (New York: Knopf, 1994). Also valuable is Constance Jordan, ed., *Reason and Imagination: The Selected Correspondence of Learned Hand* (New York: Oxford University Press, 2013), which includes a very useful introduction.

41. Learned Hand, Pre-conference memorandum, *Nichols v. Universal*, Learned Hand Papers, 1840–1961, Harvard Law School Library, Box 188–18; cf. Gunther, *Learned Hand*, 324.

42. 45 F.2d 119 (2d Cir. 1930), 123.

43. Learned Hand, "Historical and Practical Considerations Regarding Expert Testimony," *Harvard Law Review* 15 (1901): 40–58. Hand's essay was reprinted from the *Albany Medical Annals*, November, 1900.

44. On the history of experts, see Tal Golan, *Laws of Men and Laws of Nature: The History of Scientific Expert Testimony in England and America* (Cambridge, MA: Harvard University Press, 2004). Golan quotes Judge William Foster, speaking to the New Hampshire Medical Society in 1897: "There are three kinds of liars: the common liar, the damned liar, and the scientific expert," 255.

45. I am indebted to Jessica Litman for the suggestion that the abstractness of Malevinsky's theory might have prompted Hand's approach to infringement analysis.

46. Hand, Pre-conference memorandum.

47. 45 F.2d 119 (2d Cir. 1930), 120.

48. Ibid., 121–122.

49. Ibid., 122.

50. Ibid.

51. Ibid., 121.

52. Ibid.

53. Ibid.

54. Ibid.

55. Ibid., 122.

56. Ibid.

57. Ibid.

58. Ibid.

59. Anne Nichols, *Abie's Irish Rose: A Novel* (New York: Grosset and Dunlap, 1927).

60. " 'Irish Rose' Film Sets Sales Record," *New York Times*, February 27, 1927, 30.

61. Arthur Gelb, "Author of 'Abie's Irish Rose' Reviews 40 Years," *New York Times*, May 21, 1962, 40.

62. "Radio: So Rich the Rose," *Time Magazine*, May 3, 1943, 72.

63. *Nichols Papers*, Box 1, Folder 8.

64. "Thumbs Down On 'Abie,' " *National Jewish Monthly*, January 1947, 165.

65. *Nichols Papers*, Box 1, Folder 14.

66. Ibid., uncataloged material.

67. Malevinsky, *Science of Playwriting*, 100.

68. In an important article on the idea/expression dichotomy, Robert H. Rotstein discusses the intellectual affinity between Hand's abstraction test and the concept of the literary work expounded by twentieth-century critics such as Cleanth Brooks; see Rotstein, "Beyond Metaphor: Copyright Infringement and the Fiction of the Work," *Chicago Kent Law Review* 68 (1993): 725–804. Interestingly, without knowing the actual history of the reaction against Nichols's play, Rotstein uses *Abie's Irish Rose* as a suggestive

example of how the reception of a text can change over time. Nichols's play, he remarks, traded in ethnic stereotypes that today would seem prejudiced.

6. PROHIBITED PARAPHRASE

1. Ian Hamilton, *In Search of J. D. Salinger* (New York: Random House, 1988), 4.
2. Salinger's letter, undated, is transcribed in full in the Joint Appendix filed with the Second Circuit Court of Appeals. This and other original documents from *Salinger v. Random House* are on file with the National Archives and Records Administration.
3. Hamilton, *In Search of J. D. Salinger*, 7.
4. Two biographies on which I have relied are Paul Alexander, *Salinger: A Biography* (New York: St. Martin's Press, 1999) and Kenneth Slawenski, *J. D. Salinger: A Life* (New York: Random House, 2010). David Shields and Shane Salerno's *Salinger* (New York: Simon and Schuster, 2013), published in conjunction with the documentary film *Salinger* (2013), is more a compilation than an analytical biography.
5. See Slawenski, *J. D. Salinger*, 252–253, for an account of the Blaney incident.
6. Quoted in Gerald Gunther, *Learned Hand: The Man and the Judge* (New York: Knopf, 1994), 643. Salinger's friendship with Hand is discussed by Slawenski, *J. D. Salinger*, 280–282.
7. See "Depositions Yield J. D. Salinger Details," *New York Times*, December 12, 1985, C-27.
8. See Slawenski, *J. D. Salinger*, 377.
9. Joyce Maynard, *At Home in the World* (New York: Picador, 1998), 159.
10. Lacey Fosburgh, "J. D. Salinger Speaks about His Silence," *New York Times*, November 3, 1974, 1. Slawenski, *J. D. Salinger*, 381–382, explains the circumstances under which Salinger contacted Fosburgh.
11. Betty Eppes, "What I Did Last Summer," *Paris Review*, July 24, 1981, 234.
12. Jack R. Sublette, *J. D. Salinger: An Annotated Bibliography, 1938–1981* (New York: Garland, 1984).
13. Hamilton, *In Search of J. D. Salinger*, 194.
14. *Salinger v. Random House*, 650 F. Supp. 413.
15. Hamilton Affidavit, October 3, 1986, in opposition to Plaintiff's Motion for a Preliminary Injunction.
16. U.S. Copyright Act of 1976, 17 U.S.C. § 102.
17. See Slawenski, *J. D. Salinger*, 326–327.
18. J. D. Salinger, *The Catcher in the Rye* (New York: Little, Brown, 1951), 1. Slawenski suggests that Holden's remark "was imported directly from the attitudes of Salinger's own mother and father" (*J. D. Salinger*, 5).
19. Salinger, *Catcher in the Rye*, 54–55.
20. Ibid., 213.
21. Maynard, *At Home in the World*, 190.
22. Ibid., 141.
23. J. D. Salinger, *Raise High the Roof Beam, Carpenters and Seymour: An Introduction* (New York: Little, Brown, 1963), 86.

24. Lionel Trilling, *Sincerity and Authenticity* (Cambridge, MA: Harvard University Press, 1971).

25. Daniel Pecchenino, "'If You Want to Know the Truth': Fair Use, Authenticity, and J. D. Salinger," *American Literature* 83 (2011): 597–619. See also Thomas Beller, *J. D. Salinger: The Escape Artist* (Boston: Houghton Mifflin Harcourt, 2014), who remarks on the frequency with which letters appear in Salinger's work: "It almost seems as if every other story involves someone fishing a letter out of his or her pocket" (9).

26. *Complaint, Salinger v. Random House*, October 3, 1986.

27. *Gyles v. Wilcox*, 2 Atk 131, 3 Atk 269. See William F. Patry, *The Fair Use Privilege in Copyright Law* (Washington, DC: BNA Books, 1995), esp. 6–7.

28. *Folsom v. Marsh*, 9 F. Cas. 342 (C.C.D. Mass. 1841), 348.

29. U.S. Copyright Act of 1976, 17 U.S.C.§ 107.

30. *Harper and Row v. Nation Enterprises*, 471 U.S. 539, 579.

31. Ibid., 555.

32. Transcript *of Appearance, Salinger v. Random House*, October 3, 1986, 17.

33. Ibid., 23.

34. Ibid., 47.

35. Ibid., 37.

36. Ibid., 48.

37. Ibid., 45.

38. Alexander, *Salinger: A Biography*, 283.

39. See Slawenski, *Salinger: A Life*, 391. Hamilton also provides an account of the deposition; see *In Search of J. D., Salinger*, 200–203.

40. Deposition of Ian Hamilton, *Salinger v. Random House*, October 16, 1986, 185–186. Some of Hamilton's deposition appears to be under seal.

41. These exchanges are quoted in the Circuit Court decision in *Salinger v. Random House*, 811 F.2d 90, 96. Judge Newman commented dryly, "But when dealing with copyrighted expression, a biographer (or any other copier) may frequently have to content himself with reporting only the fact of what his subject did, even if he thereby pens a 'pedestrian' sentence. The copier is not at liberty to avoid 'pedestrian' reportage by appropriating his subject's literary devices." By wrapping himself in the stylist's garb Hamilton clearly made a tactical error in his deposition.

42. *Salinger v. Random House*, 650 F. Supp. 413 (S.D.N.Y 1986), 423.

43. Ibid., 422.

44. Ibid., 426.

45. *Salinger v. Random House*, 811 F.2d 90 at 97.

46. *New Era Publications International v. Henry Holt and Company, Inc.*, 684 F. Supp. 1493 (S.D.N.Y. 1988), 1498.

47. Ibid., 1502.

48. Ibid., 1508.

49. Ibid., 1524.

50. Ibid.

51. Mark A. Fowler, "'The Quick in Pursuit of the Dead': Ian Hamilton and the Clash between Literary Biographers and Copyright Owners," in *Modernism and Copyright*, ed. Paul K. Saint-Amour, 217–242 (New York: Ox-

ford University Press, 2011), 224. I am indebted to Mark Fowler for providing access to case material in his firm's archives and making a number of valuable suggestions.

52. *New Era Publications v. Henry Holt*, 873 F.2d 576 (1989), 584.

53. Ibid., 582.

54. Ibid., 593.

55. Ibid., 585.

56. *New Era Publications v. Henry Holt*, 884 F.2d 659 (1989), 663.

57. David A. Kaplan, "The End of History?" *Newsweek*, December 25, 1989, 80.

58. John O. Newman, "Not the End of History: The Second Circuit Struggles with Fair Use," *Journal of the Copyright Society of the USA* 37 (1990): 12–18.

59. Public Law 102–492, approved October 24, 1992.

60. Jon O. Newman, "Copyright Law and the Protection of Privacy," Horace S. Manges Lecture, *Columbia-ULA Journal of Law and the Arts* 12 (1988): 459–479, here 460n2.

61. Ibid., 469.

62. Ibid., 473.

63. Pierre N. Leval, "Fair Use or Foul? The Nineteenth Donald C. Brace Memorial Lecture," *Journal of the Copyright Society of the USA* 36 (April 1989): 167–181, here 167.

64. Ibid., 168.

65. Ibid., 179.

66. Ibid., 171.

67. Newman, "Copyright Law and the Protection of Privacy," 463–464.

68. *The Question Concerning Literary Property Determined by the Court of King's Bench* (London: Strahan and Woodfall, 1773), 115.

69. Eaton S. Drone, *A Treatise of the Law of Property in Intellectual Productions in Great Britain and the United States* (Boston: Little, Brown, and Company, 1879), 51.

70. *Nichols v. Universal*, 45 F. (2d) 119, 121.

71. *Salinger v. Random House*, 811 F. (2d) 90, 98.

72. In considering Salinger's complaint, Judge Leval employed a chart prepared by Salinger's attorneys that juxtaposed the copyrighted letters and corresponding portions of Hamilton's biography. Leval underlined and color-coded each alleged infringement. He marked direct quotations in pink, impermissibly close paraphrases in yellow, materials excluded by exception to copyright in orange, and ideas and facts in blue and green. By an order dated February 18, 1987, Judge Leval added this document to the District Court record. Leval's color-coded chart apparently remains under seal.

73. *Salinger v. Random House*, 811 F. 2nd 90, 99, n. 5.

74. Ibid., 93n2.

75. *Salinger v. Random House*, 650 F. Supp. 413, 424.

76. *Salinger v. Random House*, 811 F. 2nd 90, 96.

77. Ibid., 93n2.

78. Jon O. Newman, "Word Words," *Verbatim* 23 (Autumn 1998): 13–17.

79. *Salinger v. Random House*, 811 F. 2d 90, 96.

80. Leval, "Fair Use or Foul?" 171.
81. *New Era Publications v. Henry Holt,* 884 F.2d 659 at 662.
82. Pierre N. Leval, "Toward a Fair Use Standard," *Harvard Law Review* 103 (1990): 1105–1136.
83. Ibid., 1114.
84. Ibid.,1111.
85. Ibid., 1116.
86. *New Era Publications v. Henry Holt,* 884 F.2d 659, 661.
87. Roger J. Miner, "Exploiting Stolen Text: Fair Use or Foul Play?" *Journal of the Copyright Society of the USA* 37 (1989): 1–11.
88. Ibid., 1.
89. Miner seems to have considered that letters written and sent would imply that the "authors had agreed to a dissemination of their correspondence to the public" (ibid., 11). Perhaps Miner was thinking primarily of the Hubbard case, but his statement seems to imply that Salinger's letters, which were indeed sent, would be subject to fair use analysis.
90. Ibid., 10.
91. *New Era Publications v. Henry Holt,* 695 F. Supp. 1493, 1506.

7. PURLOINED PUPPIES

1. Vilis R. Inde provides a helpful discussion of events in the case, including a description of the exchange of attorney's letters; see *Art in the Courtroom* (Westport, CT: Praeger, 1998), 1–47.
2. For important discussions of postmodern art, see Rosalind Krauss's classic, "The Originality of the Avant Garde: A Postmodernist Repetition," *October* 18 (1981): 47–66 and Martha Buskirk, *The Contingent Object of Contemporary Art* (Cambridge, MA: MIT Press, 2003).
3. Daniel McClean discusses the uneasy relationship between commercial photographers and artists, in "Piracy and Authorship in Contemporary Art and the Artistic Commonwealth," *Copyright and Piracy: An Interdisciplinary Critique,* ed. Lionel Bently, Jennifer Davis, and Jane C. Ginsburg (Cambridge: Cambridge University Press, 2010), 311–339.
4. Quoted by Gay Morris who surveys the mid-twentieth-century cases in which photographers sued artists, in "When Artists Use Photographs: Is It Fair Use, Legitimate Transformation or Rip-off?" *Artnews* 80 (January 1981): 102–106. See also the discussion of images based on other images in Buskirk, *The Contingent Object,* 81–86.
5. Quoted by Morris, "When Artists Use Photographs," 104.
6. "I have never felt that I was infringing on anyone's rights as I have consistently transformed these images . . . hopefully to give the work the possibility of being reconsidered and viewed in a totally new context," Rauschenberg wrote to Beebe in a letter that is interesting, among other things, for the way it appears to anticipate the language in Pierre N. Leval's "Toward a Fair Use Standard," *Harvard Law Review* 103 (1990): 1105–1136. Rauschenberg's letter, apparently written a decade before Leval's essay, is quoted by Morris, "When Artists Use Photographs," 104.
7. See Inde, *Art in the Courtroom,* 13.

8. See 751 F. Supp. 474 (1990); 960 F.2d 301 (1992); 506 U.S. 934 (1992).

9. *United Feature Syndicate v. Koons*, 817 F. Supp. 370 (1993).

10. *Campbell v. Koons*, No. 91 Civ. 6055 (S.D.N.Y. 1993).

11. Andrea Blanch, Complaint, August 18, 2004. This and other original documents from *Blanch v. Koons* are on file with the National Archives and Record Administration.

12. Quoted by John Powers, "I Was Jeff Koons' Studio Serf," *New York Times*, August 17, 2012, MM50.

13. See Ingrid Sischy, "Jeff Koons Is Back!" *Vanity Fair*, July 2014, 86.

14. Adam D. Weinberg, "Foreword," in Scott Rothkopf, *Jeff Koons: A Retrospective*, 7–9 (New York: Whitney Museum of American Art, 2014), 7.

15. Quoted by Calvin Tomkins, "The Turnaround Artist," *New Yorker*, April 23, 2007, 63.

16. Ibid.

17. Quoted by Ruth Lopez, "Conversation: Jeff Koons," *Chicago Magazine*, May 30, 2008. Available at http://www.chicagomag.com/Chicago-Magazine/June-2008/Conversation-Jeff-Koons/.

18. Quoted by Tompkins, "The Turnaround Artist," 63. Tompkins reports that sometimes, when an important personage was visiting the museum, Koons was asked to disappear for an hour or so.

19. Ibid., 64.

20. Richard Lacayo, "Artist Jeff Koons Makes, and Earns, Giant Figures," *People*, May 8, 1989. Available at http://www.people.com/people/archive/article/0,,20120233,00.html.

21. Quoted by Lacayo, "Artist Jeff Koons Makes, and Earns, Giant Figures."

22. Both these statements are made in Alison Chernik's 2004 documentary, *The Jeff Koons Show*, available from Voyeur Films.

23. Tomkins, "The Turnaround Artist," 65.

24. Katy Siegel, "Banality 1988," in *Jeff Koons*, ed. Hans Werner Holzwarth, 250–298 (Cologne: Taschen, 2009), 254.

25. Quoted in Jeff Koons, *The Jeff Koons Handbook* (New York: Rizzoli, 1992), 90.

26. Ibid., 114.

27. Michael Brenson, "Greed Plus Glitz, with a Dollop of Innocence," *New York Times*, December 18, 1988, 41.

28. Ibid.

29. On the rise of Koons's prices beginning in 1999, see Kelly Devine Thomas, "The Selling of Jeff Koons," *Art News*, May 2005. Available at http://www.artnews.com/2005/05/01/the-selling-of-jeff-koons/. Carol Vogel reports the $33.6 million sale of *Tulips*, in the *New York Times*, January 31, 2013, and the $58.4 million sale of *Balloon Dog (Orange)* at Christie's, New York, in the *New York Times*, November 12, 2013.

30. Paul Schimmel, former chief curator, Los Angeles Museum of Contemporary Art, quoted in Thomas, "The Selling of Jeff Koons." Thomas reports on the circle of collectors and others that have made Koons a phenomenal success.

31. *Rogers v. Koons*, 960 F.2d 301 (2nd Cir. 1992), at 304.

32. Scott Rothkopf, "No Limits," in Rothkopf, *Jeff Koons: A Retrospective*, 15–35, here 24. Rothkopf's excellent introductory essay is an important source of information about Koons.

33. Ibid., 25. Rothkopf, who has had access to Koons's personal archive, reports that photographs of the wedding appear in some six hundred separate print sources.

34. *Made in Heaven* was on display at Sonnabend in New York, November 23 through December 21, 1991. The show also appeared in Cologne and Brussels and several months later in Antwerp.

35. Michael Kimmelman, "Art in Review," *New York Times*, November 29, 1991, C28.

36. Paul Taylor, "The Art of P. R., and Vice Versa," *New York Times*, October 27, 1991, H1.

37. Andrew Renton, "Jeff Koons: I Have My Finger on the Eternal," *Flash Art* 23 (Summer 1990): 110–115.

38. *Rogers v. Koons*, 960 F.2d 301, 304.

39. Due to circumstances beyond my control, I am unable to print an image of Koons's sculpture. *String of Puppies* can be viewed at http://www.jeffkoons .com/artwork/banality/string-puppies.

40. Affidavit of Art Rogers, June 29, 1990, 10. This and other original documents from *Rogers v. Koons* are on file with the National Archives and Record Administration.

41. Affidavit of Cornell Capa, July 17, 1990, quoted by Inde, *Art in the Courtroom*, 2. Inde, 27, also reports on the Newman and Kinne affidavits. Inde mistakenly refers to Kinne as "Klein."

42. *Rogers v. Koons*, Reply Memorandum of Law, August 17, 1990.

43. Ibid., Affidavit of Brenda Richardson, August 14, 1990.

44. Ibid., Affidavit of Jan Groover, August 15, 1990.

45. Ibid., Affidavit of Ronald Feldman, August 14, 1990.

46. Meg Cox, "Feeling Victimized? Then Strike Back: Become an Artist," *Wall Street Journal*, February 13, 1989, A1, quoting Koons.

47. *Rogers v. Koons*, Jeff Koons, Deposition of February 14–15, 1990, 266.

48. Ibid., 290.

49. Ibid.

50. Ibid., 169.

51. Ibid., 170–173.

52. Ibid., 112.

53. Ibid., 201.

54. Ibid., Art Rogers, Deposition of March 22, 1990, 32–33.

55. Ibid., 113.

56. Ibid., 129.

57. Ibid., 108.

58. Ibid., 751 F. Supp. 474 (S.D.N.Y., 1990), 475.

59. John Koegel informs me that no copy of *String of Puppies* was available at the time for submission.

60. *Rogers v. Koons*, 751 F. Supp. 474, 477.

61. Ibid., 478.

62. Ibid., 479.
63. Ibid.
64. Ibid., 480.
65. Ibid.
66. Inde, *Art in the Courtroom*, 28–32, reports on further details of the judgment, describing the circumstances under which the judge adopted the plaintiff's draft order and the subsequent holding that Koons was in contempt of court for not delivering the fourth copy of his sculpture to Rogers.
67. *Rogers v. Koons*, Koons Appeal Brief, June 27, 1991, 33.
68. Ibid., 3.
69. Ibid., Rogers Appeal Brief, July 22, 1991, 27.
70. Ibid., 28.
71. Ibid., 30.
72. Ibid., 35–36.
73. Ibid., 25.
74. Ibid., 960 F.2d 301 (2nd Cir. 1992), 303.
75. Ibid., 303–304.
76. Ibid., 304–305.
77. Ibid., 311.
78. Ibid., 312.
79. Ibid., 313.
80. Quoted by Ronald Sullivan, "Appeals Court Rules Artist Pirated Picture of Puppies," *New York Times*, April 3, 1992, B3.
81. *Rogers v. Koons*, Petition for Rehearing, April 15, 1992, 6.
82. *United Feature Syndicate v. Koons*, 817 F. Supp. 370 (1993).
83. *Campbell v. Koons*, No. 91 Civ. 6055 (S.D.N.Y. 1993).
84. Buskirk, *Contingent Object*, 93.
85. *Blanch v. Koons*, Affidavit of Jeff Koons, June 10, 2005, 8. This and other original documents from *Blanch v. Koons* are on file with the National Archives and Record Administration.
86. Due to circumstances beyond my control, I am unable to print an image of Koons's painting. An image of *"Niagara"* can be viewed at http://www.jeffkoons.com/artwork/easyfun-ethereal/niagara.
87. Blanch's account of her decision to sue is reported on her blog: http://andreablanchblog.com/2011/03/10/blanch-v-koons.
88. *Blanch v. Koons*, First Amended Complaint, August 18, 2004, 8.
89. Ibid., Affidavit of Jeff Koons, June 10, 2005, 2.
90. Ibid., 5.
91. Ibid.
92. Ibid., 6.
93. Leval, "Toward a Fair Use Standard," 1111.
94. *Campbell v. Acuff-Rose Music*, 510 U.S. 569 at 579.
95. *Blanch v. Koons*, 396 F. Supp. 2d 476 (S.D.N.Y. 2005), at 483.
96. Ibid., 467 F.3d 244 (2d Cir. 2006), at 253.
97. Ibid., at 263.
98. See Blanch's blog entry, http://andreablanchblog.com/2011/03/10/blanch-v-koons.

99. Neil Weinstock Netanel examines the process through which the notion of "transformative use" gradually became accepted doctrine over the course of a decade; see "Making Sense of Fair Use," *Lewis and Clark Law Review* 15 (2011): 715–771.

100. *Salinger v. Random House*, Transcript of Appearance (*Salinger v. Random House*), October 3, 1986, 48.

8. AFTERWORD

1. "Some Interviews with Mr. Sarony," *Wilson's Photographic Magazine* 30 (1893), 11.

2. *Nichols v. Universal*, Testimony of Anne Nichols, *Record on* Appeal, 469.

3. William Blackstone, *Commentaries on the Laws of England*,4 vols. (Oxford: Clarendon Press, 1766), 2:406.

4. George Ticknor Curtis, *A Treatise on the Law of Copyright* (Boston: Charles C. Little and James Brown, 1847), 45.

5. Eaton S. Drone, *A Treatise of the Law of Property in Intellectual Productions in Great Britain and the United States* (Boston: Little, Brown, and Company, 1879), 451.

6. Peter Jaszi, "Toward a Theory of Copyright: The Metamorphoses of 'Authorship,'" *Duke Law Journal* (1991): 455–502.

Acknowledgments

I am indebted to the University of California (UC), Santa Barbara, for research assistance and for awarding me a Dickson Emeriti Professorship, which assisted me materially with my research, and to Oxford University, which granted me an Astor Lectureship that allowed me to try out and receive feedback on some of the material incorporated in this book. Other material was presented at various times at lectures or panels at the law schools at UC Davis, UC Irvine, and UC Los Angeles, and at lectures, colloquia, and panels at the California Institute of Technology, the George Washington University School of Law, Loyola Law School, the University of Pennsylvania, and the University of Toronto School of Law.

For research assistance, conversations, suggestions, and feedback of various kinds I am indebted to Ann Jensen Adams, Jay Barksdale of the New York Public Library, Lionel Bently, Giles Bergel, Mario Biagioli, Oren Bracha, James Brooke-Smith, Graeme Dinwoodie, Abraham Drassinower, Mark A. Fowler, Paul Geller, Chris Gushman of the National Archives, Sören Hammerschmidt, Constance Jordan, Dan Klerman, Barbara Knowles of the New York Public Library for the Performing Arts, John Koegel, David Marshall, Neil Netanel, David Nimmer, Donald Prutzman, Percy Ross, Jennifer Rothman, Robert Rotstein, Bonnie Sauer of the National Archives, David Tan, Brook Thomas, Gina Valentino, and Trina Yeckley of the National Archives. Lindsay Waters of Harvard University Press solicited and encouraged the project from the beginning. The anonymous referees for Harvard provided excellent feedback and suggestions. My research assistant, Chip Badley, was invaluable in preparing the final manuscript and securing permissions. Under a tight schedule, Emily Zinn labored nobly in preparing an excellent index. Besides providing general encouragement and support for years, Bo Burt intervened crucially in relation to the organization of the *Nichols* chapter. My greatest debt is to Ann Bermingham, who read every chapter multiple times, providing acute criticism as well as encouragement. This book is dedicated to her with love.

Index